SAMS Teach You

QUICKEN DELUXE 99

Sherry Kinkoph
Jennifer Fulton

in 10 Minutes

SAMS
A Division of Macmillan Computer Publishing
201 West 103rd St., Indianapolis, Indiana, 46290 USA

To my dear friends, and Quicken fans, Robin and Alan Oglesby—Sherry Kinkoph

To my daughter Katerina, whom I love very much—Jennifer Fulton

International Standard Book Number: 0-672-31359-6
Library of Congress Catalog Card Number: 98-85308

Printed in the United States of America

First Printing: October 1998

00 99 98 4 3 2 1

Executive Editor
Angie Wethington

Acquisitions Editor
Jamie Milazzo

Development Editor
Michael Beall

Managing Editor
Thomas F. Hayes

Project Editor
Tom Stevens

Copy Editors
Cheri Clark
Sydney Jones

Indexer
Angie Bess

Technical Editors
Michelle Hileman
Mark LaPlant

Proofreader
Megan Wade

Production
Steve Geiselman

Contents

Tell Us What You Think!

As the reader of this book, *you* are our most important critic and commentator. We value your opinion and want to know what we're doing right, what we could do better, what areas you'd like to see us publish in, and any other words of wisdom you're willing to pass our way.

As the Executive Editor for the General Desktop Applications team at Macmillan Computer Publishing, I welcome your comments. You can fax, email, or write me directly to let me know what you did or didn't like about this book—as well as what we can do to make our books stronger.

Please note that I cannot help you with technical problems related to the topic of this book, and that due to the high volume of mail I receive, I might not be able to reply to every message.

When you write, please be sure to include this book's title and authors as well as your name and phone or fax number. I will carefully review your comments and share them with the authors and editors who worked on the book.

Fax: [317-581-4663]

E-mail: `internet@mcp.com`

Mail: Angie Wethington
General Desktop Applications
Macmillan Computer Publishing
201 West 103rd Street
Indianapolis, IN 46290 USA

INTRODUCTION

Are you the proud new owner of a copy of Intuit's Quicken Deluxe 99 or Quicken Basic 99? Need to get up and running fast? Don't have a lot of time to spend wading through a manual or experimenting with the program yourself? If you answered yes to any of these questions, you're holding the right book for the job. Whether you're a brand-new Quicken user or just upgrading, this book can help you learn all you need to know to quickly utilize Quicken's basic features in the least amount of time.

WHAT IS QUICKEN?

Quicken is the number-one selling personal finance package. You can use Quicken to manage your checking and saving accounts, plan your taxes, balance your budget, track your investments, and do much, much more. In addition to using the program's basic financial tools, you can use Quicken to tap into the power of the Internet. Quicken Deluxe 99 comes bundled with Microsoft's Internet Explorer browser program (version 4.01) to help you connect to the Internet and pursue online banking and investing. Whether you're using Quicken at home or with a small business, you can easily take advantage of the program's numerous features to help you gain control of your finances.

HOW TO USE THIS BOOK

This book is designed to help you quickly learn Quicken's basic features (whether you're using Quicken Deluxe 99 or Quicken Basic 99) in straightforward, easy-to-understand lessons that can be completed in 10 minutes or less. Each lesson includes step-by-step instructions that show you how to use a specific feature or complete a particular task.

The *Sams Teach Yourself in 10 Minutes* approach helps you master the main features of the program without explaining every nuance or possible scenario you might encounter. If you're like most users, you don't need to know the intimate details of how the program works; you just need to know how to use the basic components to accomplish the work you need to do.

If you're an absolute beginner, you can start with the first lesson and progress from easier tasks to more complex features. If you're an experienced user, dive right into the tasks you want to learn more about.

Conventions Used in This Book

Several icons are used throughout the book that help save you time and point out important information. Be sure to read these tips to learn more about a feature or avoid a possible problem.

Tip These icons point out shortcuts and timesaving tips to help you use the program more effectively.

Plain English Look to these icons to learn new terms associated with the program.

Panic Button These tips warn you about potential problems or alert you to trouble you should avoid.

Along with the icons described previously, you also find specific conventions used in the book to help you recognize items you select onscreen and data you need to type:

- Menu items or other commands you select onscreen appear in colored type.
- Data you need to type in appears in **bold, colored** type.
- Command, Field, and Key names appear with the first letter capitalized.
- Onscreen messages appear in **bold**.

That's about all you need to know to use *Sams Teach Yourself Quicken Deluxe 99 in 10 Minutes*. The clock's ticking, so jump right in!

ABOUT THE AUTHORS

Sherry Kinkoph has authored over 25 computer books for Macmillan Publishing over the past five years, including books for both adults and children. Her recent publications include *How to Use Microsoft Office 97* and *Easy Office 97 Small Business Edition.* You can email Sherry at skinkoph@inetdirect.net.

Jennifer Fulton is a consultant, trainer, and best-selling author of over 50 books covering many areas of computing, including DOS, Windows 3.1, Windows 95, and Windows 98. Jennifer is a self-taught veteran of computing which means, of course, that if something can happen to a computer user, it has happened to her at one time or another. So, as a computer veteran, Jennifer brings what's left of her sense of humor to her many books, including *Ten Minute Guide to Windows 98*, *Windows 98 6 in 1*, and *Office 97 Cheat Sheet.*

ACKNOWLEDGMENTS

Special thanks to Jamie Milazzo, Michael Beall, Mark LaPlant, Tom Stevens, Cheri Clark, and Sydney Jones for assisting in the production of this book.

TRADEMARKS

LESSON 1

STARTING AND EXITING QUICKEN DELUXE 99

In this lesson, you learn how to start and exit the Quicken 99 program and use New User Setup to establish an account.

STARTING QUICKEN

There are several ways to start Quicken. One way is to use the familiar Start menu:

1. Click the Start button on the Windows taskbar.
2. Select Programs.
3. Select Quicken, and then select Quicken Deluxe 99 (see Figure 1.1).

When you install Quicken, a shortcut icon is added to your Windows desktop. To open Quicken using the shortcut icon, simply double-click the icon, as shown in Figure 1.2.

> **Did You Install Quicken?** If you can't locate the Quicken folder on the Programs menu or the Quicken shortcut icon on the desktop, you probably haven't installed the program yet. For help with installing Quicken, turn to Appendix A at the back of this book.

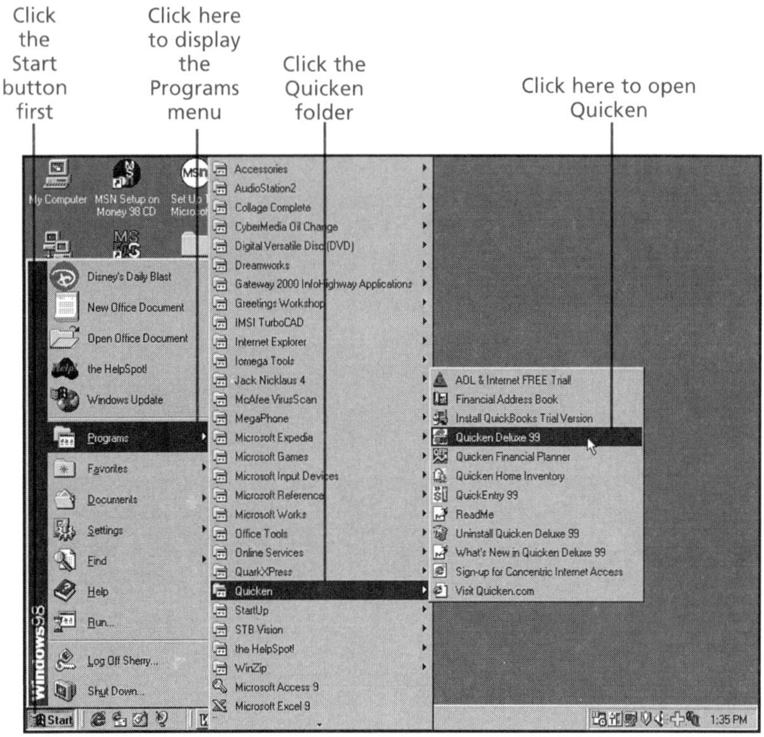

FIGURE 1.1 You can start Quicken through the Windows Program menu.

> **What About the Other Quicken Shortcut Icon?** The QuickEntry 99 shortcut icon that also appears on your desktop can be used to open your checking account's register and start recording transactions without opening all of Quicken. (Learn more about this feature in Lesson 5, "Recording Transactions.")

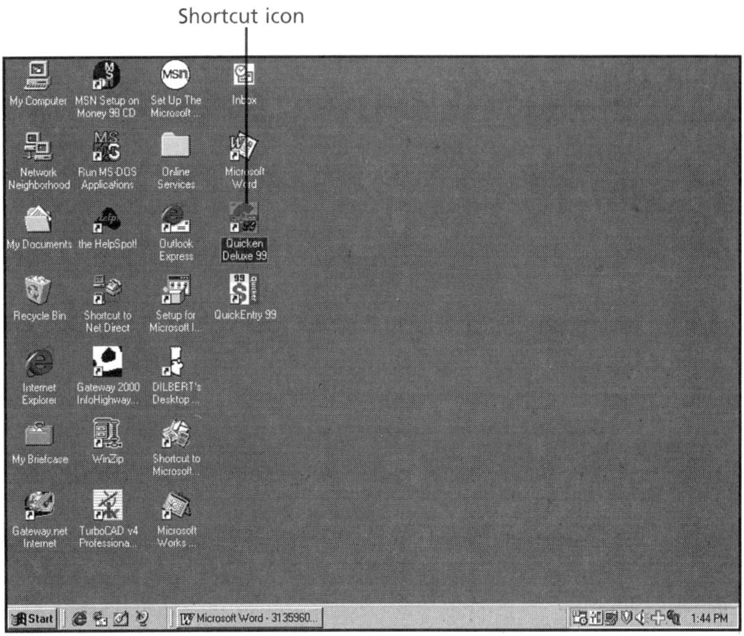

FIGURE 1.2 Another way to start Quicken is to use the shortcut icon.

> **Do I Have to Register?** When you open Quicken, you may see a Product Registration prompt box (this box pops up from time to time until you register the program). You can use this to log on to your Internet account and register your copy of Quicken online rather than filling out the paper form and mailing it in. To do this, click the Register button and follow the prompts. It may take a few minutes, but at least you'll have it over with.

WORKING WITH NEW USER SETUP

The very first time you use Quicken, the New User Setup automatically starts to help you set up new accounts. New User Setup walks you through the steps necessary to create an account, including filling in background information about yourself to determine the types of expenditures you incur and information about your bank balance so that you can record payments and deposits.

Before you begin, grab your last bank statement so that you can enter your ending date and balance to start your account.

> **What's Quicken Audio?** If you've got the Quicken CD-ROM in the CD-ROM drive, Quicken's Audio Help feature offers assistance during setup. Quicken Audio is a multimedia help system that offers you additional information when you perform new tasks. To turn the audio off, click the Quicken Audio window's Close (X) button. (Learn more about Audio Help in Lesson 3, "Finding Help.")

To start New User Setup, follow these steps:

1. Click **Next** to begin, as shown in Figure 1.3.

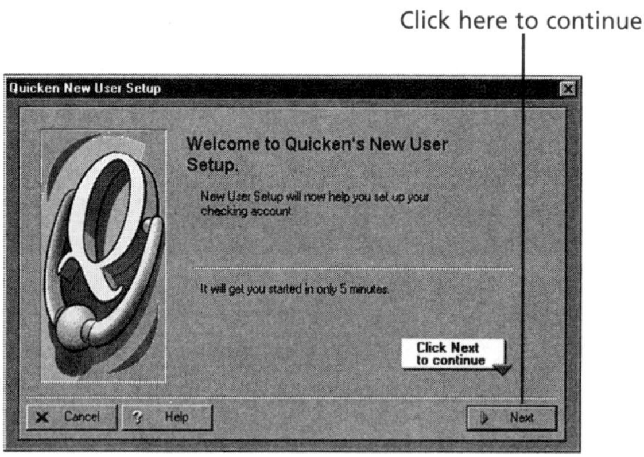

FIGURE 1.3 New User Setup walks you through the process of creating a new account.

2. Each Setup dialog box asks you questions and you can fill in the answers as needed. The dialog box shown in Figure 1.4 helps

Quicken establish categories for your account, such as childcare, housing expenses, and so on. Select the appropriate Yes or No answers and click **Next** to continue to the next box in the series.

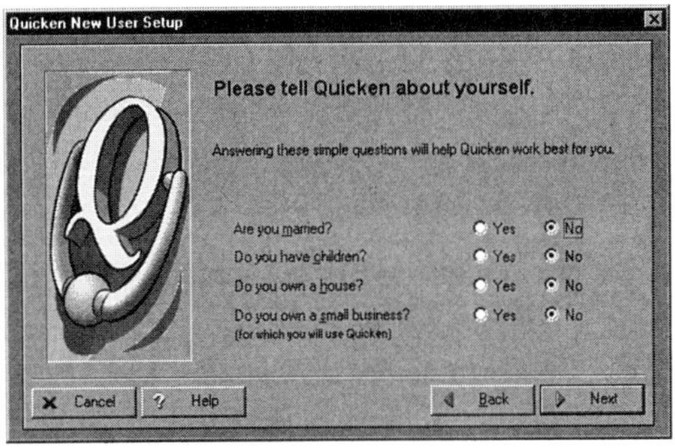

FIGURE 1.4 Each dialog box you encounter asks you to enter information about the type of account you want to create.

3. Use the next dialog box, shown in Figure 1.5, to enter a name for your account. If you plan to use more than one account in Quicken, give each a descriptive name that you can easily recognize. (In other words, avoid long, vague names.) Click **Next** to continue.

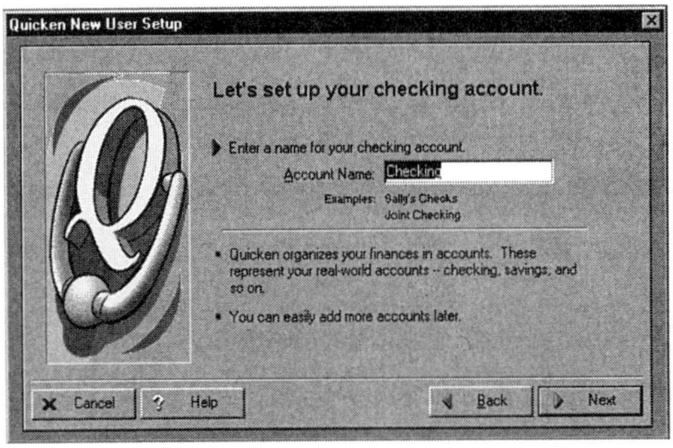

FIGURE 1.5 Assign a name to associate with the account.

4. In the next dialog box (see Figure 1.6), help Quicken to determine the date to begin tracking your account. Select Yes if you have your last bank statement available, and then click Next. If you don't have your statement handy, click No (you can update this information later) and skip to step 6.

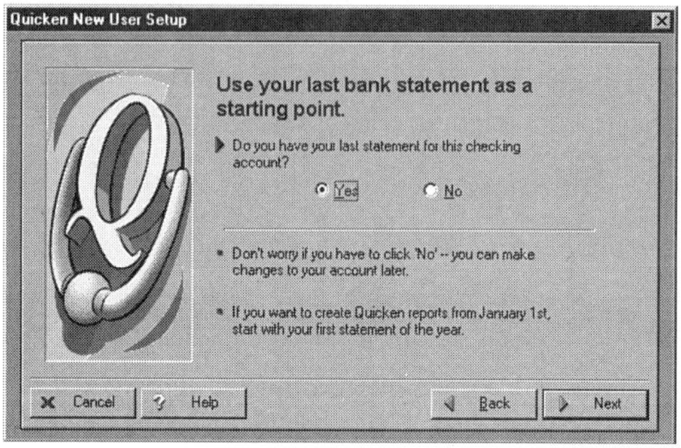

FIGURE 1.6 Have your last bank statement ready to start your account.

5. Enter your bank statement's ending date and ending balance in the appropriate boxes (see Figure 1.7). Click Next to continue.

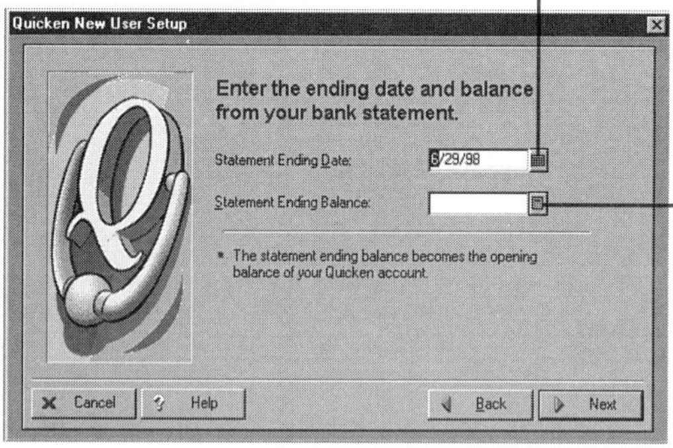

FIGURE 1.7 Enter an ending date and ending balance for your account.

> **Using the Calendar and Calculator Icons** You notice the Calendar and Calculator icons throughout Quicken; they appear in dialog boxes and in other areas, to the right of the Statement Ending Date and Statement Ending Balance text boxes (refer to Figure 1.7). Click the Calendar icon to display a miniature calendar from which you can select a date. Click the Calculator icon to display an onscreen calculator you can use to figure numbers or amounts.

6. At the final Setup dialog box, shown in Figure 1.8, check over the information you entered and click Done.

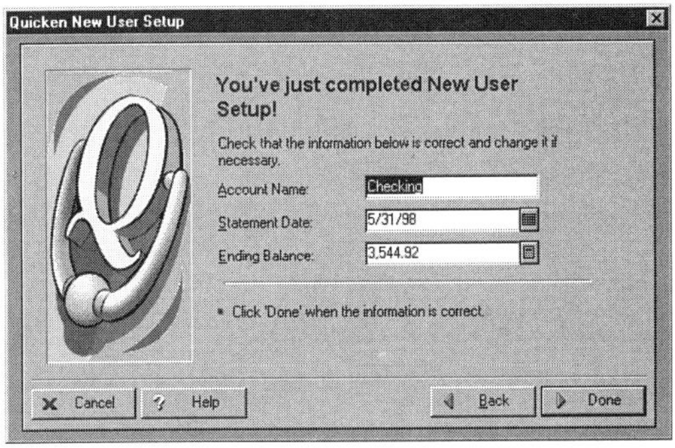

FIGURE 1.8 Click Done and the new account is created.

To make changes at any time during Setup, click the Back button to return to a previous Setup dialog box. (Learn more about creating new accounts in Lesson 4, "Creating Accounts.")

> **Do I Want an Overview?** When you finish creating the account, the Quicken Help window opens and offers a guided tour of the program. You can choose to see an overview of the program, or click the Help window's Close button to exit.

After you create the new account, Quicken opens the account register, shown in Figure 1.9, and you can begin entering transactions. (Learn all about the features you see in the Quicken program window in Lesson 2, "Navigating the Quicken Deluxe 99 Window.")

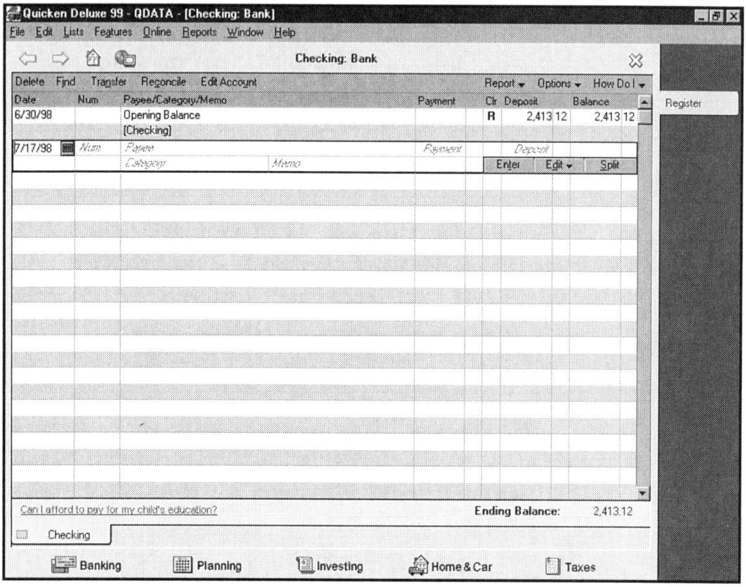

FIGURE 1.9 Quicken creates the account and opens the account register.

> **Editing Information** You can go back and make changes to your account information at any time. Select the account from the Account List. Click the Accounts QuickTab to display the list, and click the Edit Account button. This opens the Edit Bank Account dialog box where you can make changes to the information.

> **What If I Have a Previous Version?** If you used another version of Quicken before upgrading to Quicken 99, Quicken prompts you to upgrade your data. Click OK and Quicken converts the data to the new version. You can also import data, as explained in Lesson 10, "Backing Up and Restoring Data."

EXITING QUICKEN

When you finish working with Quicken, it's a good idea to close the program. Unlike other programs, you don't need to save your work. It's saved automatically every time you enter a transaction, update data, start a new budget, or use any of the other program features to enter or edit data.

You can exit Quicken in several ways:

- Open the File menu and choose Exit.
- Click the Close button in the upper-right corner of the program window.
- Press Alt+F4 on the keyboard.

When exiting Quicken, especially after making changes to the data or entering new data, you're prompted to back up your data. (To learn more about backing up data, see Lesson 10, "Backing Up and Restoring Data.") To bypass backing up the data right now, click Exit.

In this lesson, you learned how to open and close the Quicken program and set up an account. In the next lesson, you learn how to navigate the program window.

LESSON 2

NAVIGATING THE QUICKEN DELUXE 99 WINDOWS

In this lesson, you learn how to use the various onscreen elements and navigate the program window.

LOOKING AT THE QUICKEN WINDOW

If you just started Quicken for the first time and set up a new account, the checking account register appears onscreen ready for you to start recording transactions, as shown in Figure 2.1. If you are launching another session of Quicken, you are presented with the Quicken Home Page, which is covered later in this lesson.

> **What's New in Quicken 99?** The first time you start Quicken, you might be presented with a Quicken Help dialog box that lets you see a video about Quicken 99 and its new features. If your Quicken CD is inserted, you can click the Play button to view the video. To exit the Help box, click the Close button in the upper-right corner of the dialog box.

As with most Windows-based programs, the Quicken window opens to reveal the familiar title bar and menu bar, but everything else might look a bit different to you (unless you've used other versions of Quicken in the past). The following is a brief rundown of the onscreen elements found in the Quicken program window:

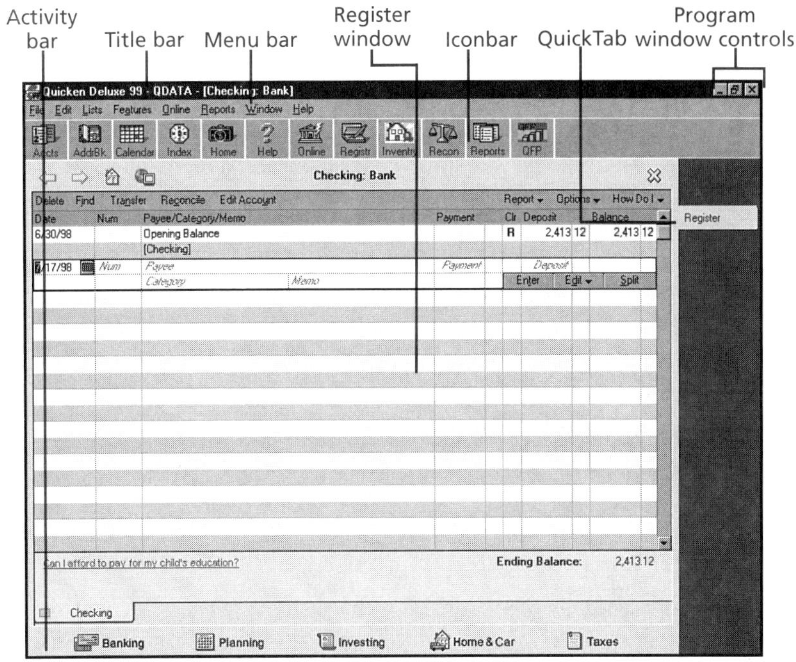

FIGURE 2.1 Immediately after setting up a new account, Quicken opens the account register.

Title bar. This area shows the program name and the name of the window that's currently displayed.

Menu bar. All Quicken's commands reside in the menu lists shown on the menu bar. To select a menu, click its name. To select a command from the menu list, click the command name.

Iconbar. The Iconbar comprises a collection of common Quicken tools or features you can quickly access with a click of a button.

Register window. Each feature you open in Quicken, whether it's your checking account register or the Banking Center (or any other feature), appears as a window inside the Quicken program window.

QuickTabs. Each open feature is represented by a QuickTab displayed on the right side of the screen. Use the QuickTabs to switch between open windows. Simply click the tab to display its window. As you open more features, more QuickTabs appear.

Activity bar. Located at the bottom of the Quicken window, the Activity bar offers pop-up menus to common Quicken features and topics, such as Taxes and Investing. To display a menu, click the icon.

No Iconbar? If the Iconbar isn't visible in your Quicken window, you can display it by selecting the Window menu and choosing Show Top Iconbar. Follow the same procedure to turn off the Iconbar display.

Repetition Is Rampant Many of Quicken's commands and features are duplicated. For example, buttons on the Iconbar activate commands also found on the menu bar. If you're not too keen on alternative paths to the same commands or features, consider turning off the Iconbar or Activity bar to free up more onscreen workspace.

If you exit the program and reopen it later, the Quicken Home Page appears, as shown in Figure 2.2. Each item you open in Quicken, whether it's an account register or another feature, appears as a window with a QuickTab. To close a window, click its QuickTab to activate the window (if it's not already displayed), and then click its Close (X) button (see Figure 2.2). Depending on the windows you open, you might see different controls at the top of each window pane. Some windows have additional menu buttons that differ from those found on the top menu bar. Regardless of the window type, all open windows have navigation buttons located on the feature window's title bar. Learn more about these controls later in this lesson.

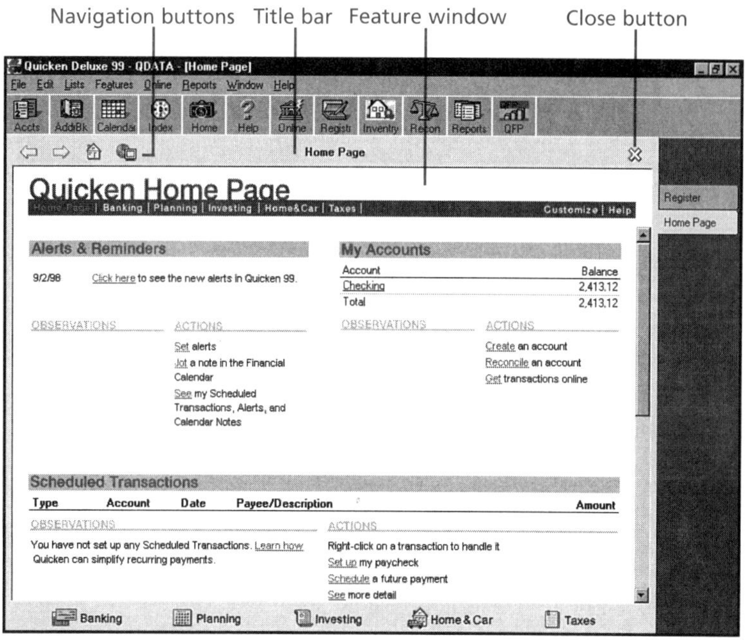

FIGURE 2.2 When you reopen Quicken, the Quicken Home Page appears.

> **Maximizing the Program Window** Use Quicken's program window controls (located at the far-right end of the title bar) to minimize, maximize, or close the program window. To take full advantage of the onscreen workspace, click the Maximize button to enlarge the program window.

Quicken's Home Page (see Figure 2.2) is sort of like home base, a starting point for all your Quicken activities. You can customize the Home Page window to help you get an overview of your financial status. The Home Page works like a Web page, with links to various other features in the program as well as online features found on Quicken's Internet site. Learn more about using the Home Page later in this lesson.

Is It a Window or Is It a Pane? It's both. The terms *window*, *pane*, and *page* are all used interchangeably to describe Quicken's opened features. As you can see in Figure 2.2, opened features appear as windows within the Quicken program window, much like tabbed pages in a notebook. Each opened window presents a new workspace, or view, you can use.

WORKING WITH THE MENU BAR

Every Windows program has a menu bar—it's used to access the program's many commands. Quicken's menu bar has eight distinct menus:

File. This menu lists commands pertaining to your Quicken files, such as printing, assigning passwords, and backing up data.

Edit. This menu groups commands for editing your data, such as the standard Cut, Copy, and Paste commands, Quicken's Find and Replace feature, and the Options command for customizing Quicken.

Lists. Use this menu to find any one of Quicken's many list features, including accounts, categories, transactions, and more.

Features. All Quicken's major features appear on this menu. Access the planning, banking, taxes, and investing features, as well as many other functions.

Online. If you plan to use Quicken's online features to perform electronic bill paying and check writing, access this menu for the full range of online functions.

Reports. Use this menu to quickly generate reports and graphs based on your Quicken data.

Window. Use this menu to toggle onscreen elements (such as the Iconbar) on or off, or to switch between open feature windows.

Help. Look to this menu when you need help with using any aspect of Quicken (learn more about Quicken's help features in Lesson 3, "Finding Help").

Mouse users can display menu lists and activate commands with a quick click. But if you're an avid keyboard user and you don't like your hands to leave the keyboard at any time, you can easily avoid using the mouse with Quick Keys (keyboard shortcuts for selecting and activating commands).

As with other Windows programs, Quicken's Quick Keys are scattered throughout the menu lists. You'll notice them to the right of menu commands, as shown in Figure 2.3—for example, to activate the Account List, press Ctrl+A. Of course, you'll have to memorize these key combinations to take full advantage of them.

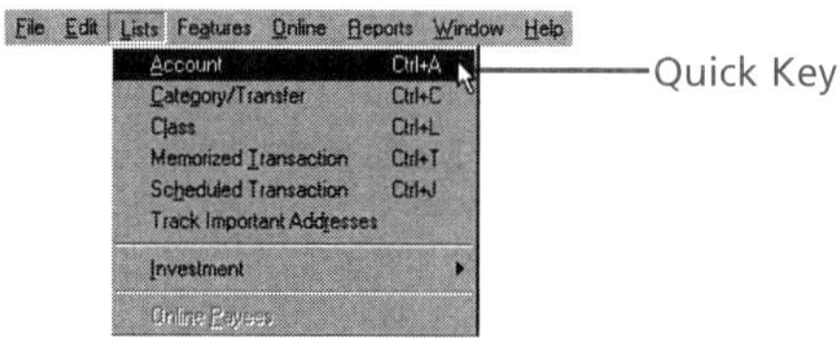

FIGURE 2.3 Use Quick Keys to activate Quicken commands from the keyboard.

> **Warning!** Don't attempt to use the old Cut, Copy, and Paste keyboard shortcut commands in Quicken. They don't work the same way. Pressing Ctrl+X, for example, doesn't cut the data—it activates the Go to Matching Transfer command. If you prefer using the standard keyboard shortcuts for cutting, copying, and pasting, you can change the setting in Quicken. Open the Edit menu, choose Options, Quicken Program, click the Settings tab, and select the Undo/Cut/Copy/Paste option. Click OK and the old Cut, Copy, and Paste shortcuts are back in action.

USING THE ICONBAR

You might be accustomed to using toolbars in other Windows programs. Quicken has a toolbar too, called the Iconbar, and it works the same way as other toolbars. The buttons on the Iconbar are shortcuts to Quicken's most commonly used features, such as the Account List, the checkbook register, and Financial Calendar. Simply click a button to access the associated feature. Table 2.1 lists the default Iconbar buttons.

TABLE 2.1 ICONBAR BUTTONS

ICON	ICON TEXT	FUNCTION
	Accts	Opens the Account List
	AddrBk	Opens the Financial Address Book
	Calendar	Opens the Financial Calendar
	Index	Opens Quicken's Help index
	Home	Opens the Quicken Home Page
	Help	Opens the Help window
	Online	Opens the Online Center
	Registr	Opens the current account register
	Inventry	Opens Quicken Home Inventory
	Recon	Opens the reconciliation feature
	Reports	Opens the Create Report window
	QFP	Opens Quicken's Financial Planner

Learn more about using these buttons in lessons to come.

Customize the Iconbar To customize the appearance of the Iconbar, open the Edit menu and select Options, Iconbar. This opens the Customize Iconbar dialog box. You can change which buttons appear on the bar, remove buttons you don't use, or add new ones for other features you use more regularly. Use the Show Icons and Show Text check boxes to turn the Iconbar on or off (or turn on just the text or just the icons). Click OK to exit the dialog box after making any changes.

USING QUICKTABS

Use QuickTabs to quickly switch among open windows. Every open window has a QuickTab; click the QuickTab to display the window you want to view (see Figure 2.4). To close a window, click its Close (X) button. You can also reorder a set of opened windows by dragging their QuickTabs to new positions in the list.

Other Routes to Closing You can also press Esc to close a feature window, or right-click the window's QuickTab and select the Close command from the pop-up menu.

When you exit the program, Quicken remembers which windows you had open, and those same windows appear open the next time you use the program. If you prefer a specific set of windows to open each time you use the program, you can designate a default set:

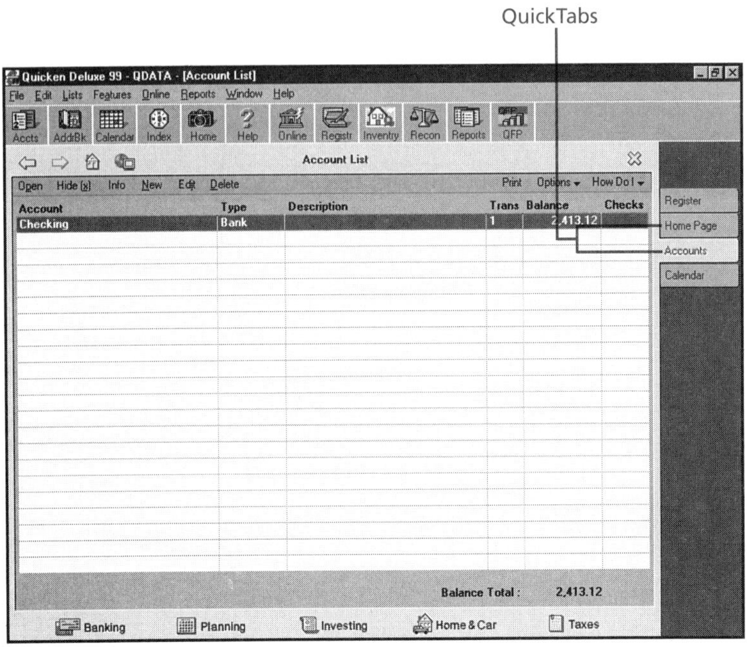

FIGURE 2.4 Use QuickTabs to switch among open windows.

1. Arrange the windows just the way you want them, and then open the Edit menu and choose Options, Desktop.
2. From the Save Desktop dialog box, select Save Current Desktop and click OK.
3. Open the Edit menu again and select Options, Quicken Program.
4. Display the Startup tab and select the None option.
5. Click OK to exit the dialog box. The next time you start Quicken, the windows will display as you arranged them.

USING THE ACTIVITY BAR

Quicken's Activity bar, located at the bottom of the Quicken screen, offers quick access to specific financial tasks. Hover your mouse pointer over an icon and a pop-up menu appears displaying a list of tasks associated with the topic. For example, Figure 2.5 shows the Banking menu displayed.

Don't Like QuickTabs? If you'd like some more onscreen space for working with windows, such as the checkbook register, turn off QuickTabs. Right-click over the QuickTabs and deselect the Show QuickTabs command in the pop-up menu. To turn QuickTabs on again, right-click over a feature window's title bar area and select the appropriate command.

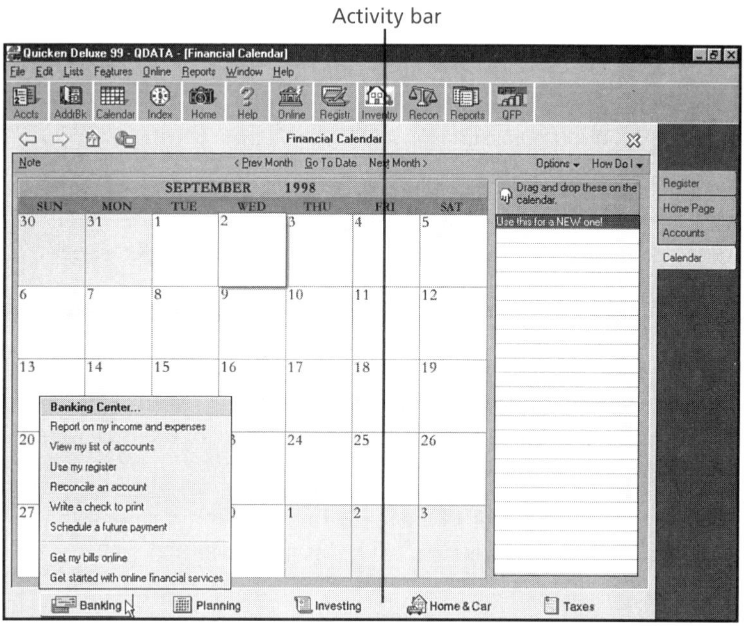

FIGURE 2.5 The Activity bar lists typical financial tasks you can perform with Quicken.

To select a task from the menu list, simply click the task name.

> **Turn It Off** You can turn off the Activity bar to free up more working space in the Quicken window. Right-click over the bar and deselect the Show Activity Bar command. To turn it on again, right-click anywhere in the QuickTabs area or at the top of the open feature window and select the command again.

USING THE HOME PAGE

As mentioned earlier, when you open Quicken, the Home Page is the first thing you see (unless you're using the program for the very first time). The Home Page gives you a quick glimpse of your financial status, and offers jumping-off points to many of Quicken's most popular features.

As you begin entering transactions and performing various Quicken tasks, the Home Page changes to show your current financial picture. Scroll down to the bottom of the Home Page window to see a graph of your income and expenses, as shown in Figure 2.6.

The underlined terms on the Home Page are links to other Quicken features. These links work the same way Web page links do; you click a link to follow it to related information. In the case of Quicken, clicking a link might open a Quicken feature, open another window, or even connect you to the Internet.

The icon buttons at the top of the Home Page window pane can help you navigate between open windows, as explained in Table 2.2.

TABLE 2.2 NAVIGATING OPEN WINDOWS

ICON BUTTON	FUNCTION
	Moves back a window
	Moves forward to the next open window
	Returns to the Home Page window

ICON BUTTON	FUNCTION
	Acts as a one-step Update feature, for downloading stock quotes and news from the Internet

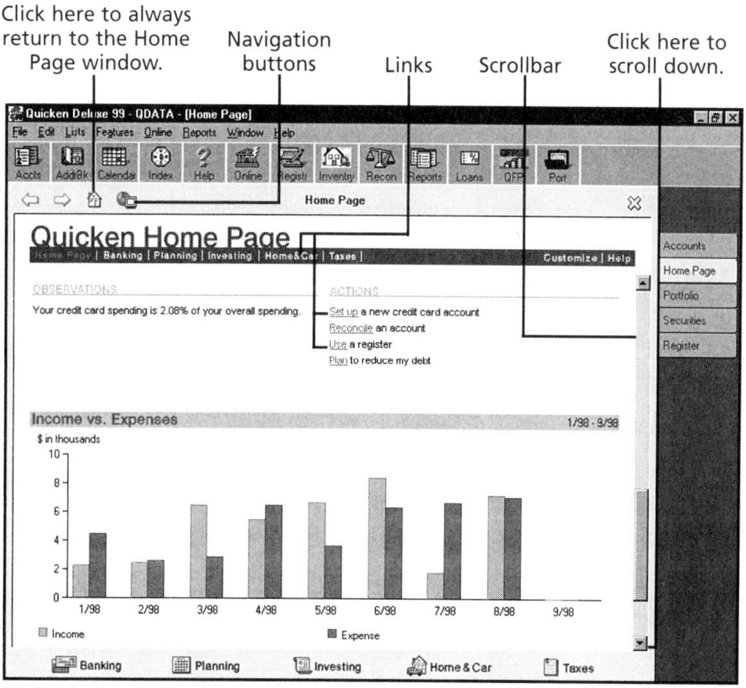

FIGURE 2.6 The Home Page shows your current financial standings.

To customize the items displayed on the Home Page, follow these steps:

1. Click the Customize link on the Home Page window (look for the word Customize in the upper-right corner of the page) and select Customize this view from the pop-up menu. This action opens the Customize View dialog box, shown in Figure 2.7.

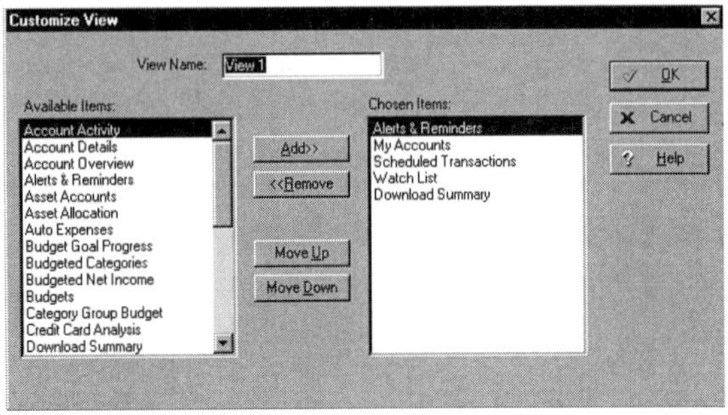

FIGURE 2.7 You can customize the items that appear on the Home Page window pane.

2. The Chosen Items list on the right shows you the current selections. To add to the list, select a feature from the Available Items list box, and then click the Add button.
3. To remove an item from the Chosen Items list box, select it and click the Remove button.
4. To reorganize how features are displayed on the Home Page, select an item in the Chosen Items list box, and then click the Move Up or Move Down button to move its position in the list.
5. When the list shows all the features you want included on the Home Page, click OK.

In this lesson, you learned how to work with the various onscreen elements to navigate the Quicken window and use the Home Page. In the next lesson, you learn how to find help when you need it.

LESSON 3

FINDING HELP

In this lesson, you learn how to use Quicken's many help features and how to set up Quicken to connect to the Internet for more helpful resources.

HOW HELPFUL IS HELP?

Quicken's help features are found all over the program—in dialog boxes, in the form of multimedia help, in menus, on the Internet, and more. Whenever you get into a jam, help is available, whether you need just a hint or complex information about a Quicken task. The following are just a few ways you can find help with Quicken:

- The always-reliable Help menu offers numerous help choices and groups them in one menu list. To display the menu, click the menu name.
- The Help and Index buttons on the Iconbar open Quicken's Help window, where you can look up help on specific topics in Quicken's help files.
- Each feature window has a How Do I? button (with the exception of the Quicken Home Page) you can use to find specific help topics related to the feature.
- If you're using the Quicken CD-ROM, pop it into your CD-ROM drive for multimedia help that includes overviews of Quicken's main features.
- Connect to Quicken's Web site and find more help in the form of Frequently Asked Questions (or FAQs), product support, and technical support.

You learn how to use each of these help features in this lesson.

USING HOW DO I? HELP

Many of Quicken's feature windows have a How Do I? button at the top of the window, as shown in Figure 3.1. When you click this button, it displays a list of help topics related to the window. For example, if you're viewing the Account List window, a click on the How Do I? button reveals topics such as how to create a new account, how to set up a loan, and how to track your assets.

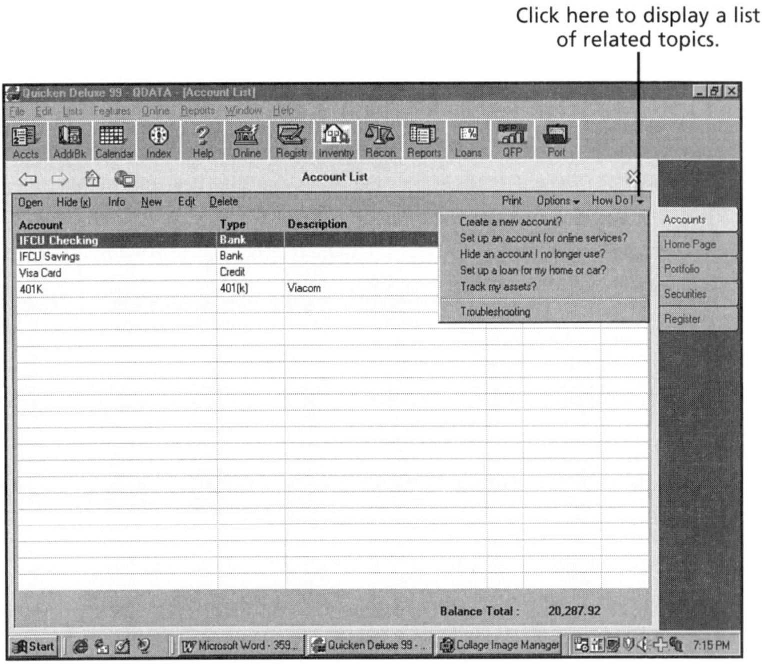

FIGURE 3.1 Use the How Do I? button to find help for tasks related to the window you're viewing.

To select a topic you want help with, click the topic on the list. This opens the Quicken Help window where you can read about the topic.

If the topic you want to know about isn't listed, click the Troubleshooting button. This also opens a Quicken Help window where you can look up the topic. You learn how to use the Help window in the next section.

I Changed My Mind! If, after displaying the How Do I? menu list, you choose not to select a topic, press Esc. If you've already opened a Help window associated with the topic, click the window's Close (X) button to exit.

USING THE HELP MENU

If you're at all familiar with other Windows programs, you've probably used help files before. Just about every program has a Help menu you can use to access a collection of help files related to the program. Quicken's Help menu works the same way. As shown in Figure 3.2, the Help menu groups several help features, including the help files.

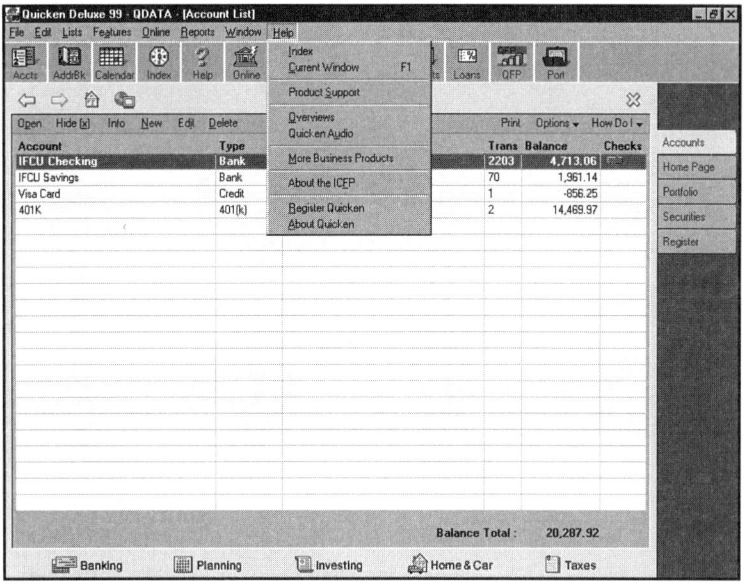

FIGURE 3.2 Click the Help menu to display a list of help features.

One way to tap into Quicken's help files is to open the Help Topics Index (shown in Figure 3.3). You can take one of several routes to this dialog box:

- Open the Help menu and select Index.
- Click the Index button on the Iconbar.
- Click the Index button from any Help window.

The Quicken Help Topics dialog box opens with the Index tab displayed. To look up a topic, type the word (or words) you're looking for into the text box; the list immediately scrolls to any matches (see Figure 3.3).

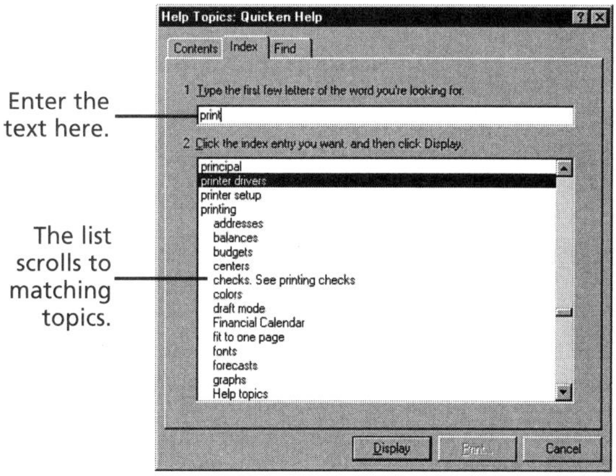

FIGURE 3.3 Use the Index tab to look up specific topics.

> **Using Help Contents** If you prefer to look up your own topics, click the Contents tab in the Quicken Help Topics dialog box and look through the available help topics until you find the one you want.

When you find a topic you want to know more about, double-click the topic. This opens a Help window (shown in Figure 3.4) with information you can read or with links you can click to find related information. Depending on the topic, some Help windows might contain more information than others and offer additional options.

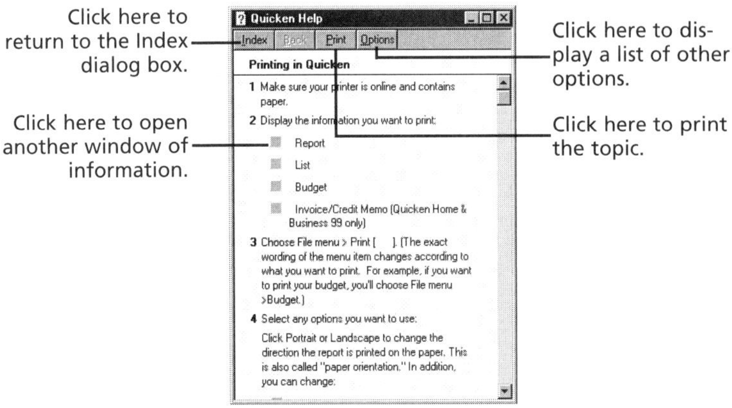

FIGURE 3.4 Use the Help window to read more about a Quicken topic.

> **The Trusty F1 Key** For context-sensitive help, it's hard to beat the F1 key. Pressing this key in just about every Windows program summons a Help window related to the current screen or activity. Press F1 in Quicken to do the same.

To close a Help window, click the window's Close (X) button.

USING QUICKEN AUDIO

Multimedia help can be a real bonus for brand-new Quicken users. If you have the Quicken CD-ROM, insert it into your computer's CD-ROM drive; then open Quicken's Help menu and make sure that the Quicken Audio option is selected (has a check mark next to it).

The Quicken Audio help feature appears as a floating box on the Quicken screen, as shown in Figure 3.5. You can move the box by dragging its title bar (click over the Quicken Audio title, hold the mouse button down, and drag the box to a new location onscreen).

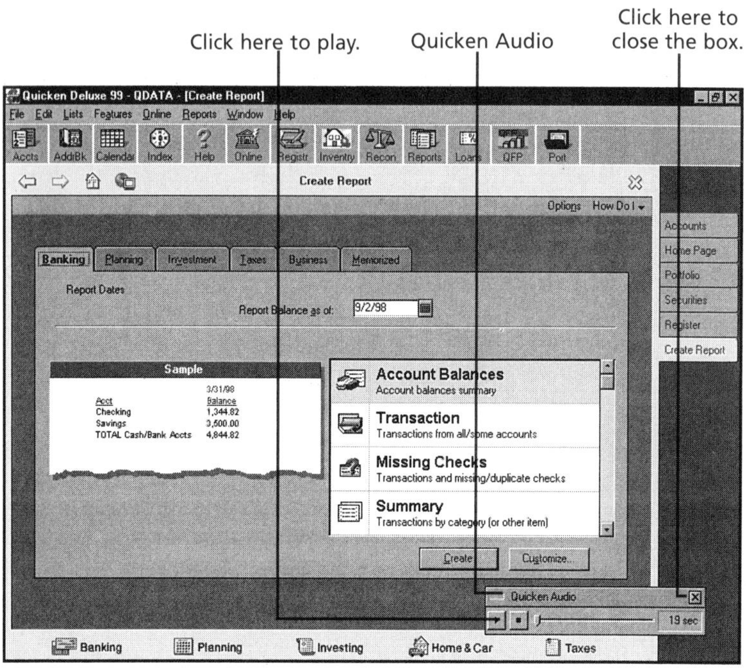

FIGURE 3.5 Use Quicken Audio to learn about a feature or to talk you through a procedure.

To start the audio, click the Play button. With some windows, Quicken Audio starts playing automatically when you select an onscreen item. Depending on the feature window you're viewing, the audio help explains how to perform a certain task related to the feature.

Stop the Music! To stop Quicken Audio during play, click the Stop button. If you prefer to turn off all Quicken's other sound effects, open the Edit menu and select Options, Quicken Program. Click the General tab and deselect the Turn On All Quicken Sounds check box. Click OK.

OTHER HELP OPTIONS

As if you didn't have enough help options to choose from, you can find additional Quicken help online, via the Internet. If your computer has a modem (most computers do these days), a Web browser (Microsoft Internet Explorer comes with Quicken Deluxe 99), and an account with an Internet service provider, you can visit Intuit's Web site and find help for using Quicken. You can find links to Quicken's Web site on the Quicken Home Page pane, as well as on the Help menu and the Online menu.

> **Internet Service Provider** A company that allows you to access the Internet and the World Wide Web through the company's computers, for a small fee.

Before you can use Quicken on the Internet, you first must set up everything with the Internet Connection Setup Wizard. When you select an Internet feature for the first time, Quicken presents the dialog box shown in Figure 3.6. Click Continue and the wizard walks you through the steps necessary to set up Quicken to access the Internet.

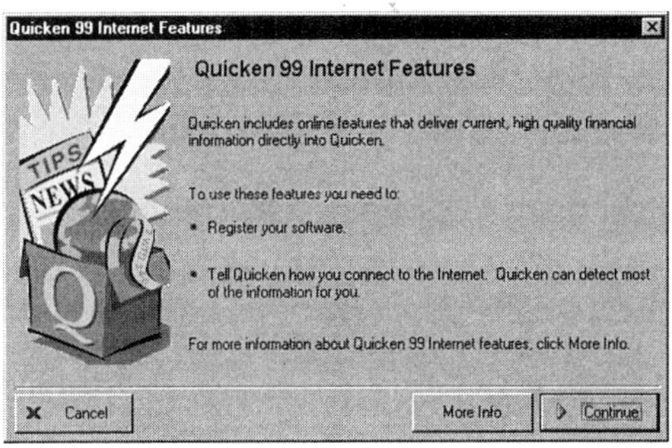

FIGURE 3.6 Before going online with Quicken, you must first set up the program to access the Internet.

You can activate Internet Connection Setup in the following ways:

- Select a Quicken Internet feature.
- Click an Internet link on the Quicken Home Page pane.

- Open the Online menu, choose Quicken on the Web, and select an Internet option. If you've not previously set up Quicken to work online, the Internet Connection Setup Wizard appears.
- Open the Online menu and select Internet Connection, Setup.

Follow these steps to use the Internet Connection Setup Wizard:

1. The first wizard dialog box asks whether you're connected to the Internet. Select the appropriate answer for your situation. For example, if you already have an Internet service provider and an online account, select the I have an existing dial-up Internet connection option. Click Next to continue.

Don't Have an Internet Account? If you currently don't have an Internet service provider, select the Tell me how to sign up for an Internet account option; then click Next and click the Help button. This opens a Help window explaining how to sign up for an account.

2. In the next dialog box (shown in Figure 3.7) choose which Internet connection to use (if you have more than one) and click Next.

FIGURE 3.7 Choose your Internet service provider account and click Next.

3. Internet Connection Setup Wizard instructs you to use Internet Explorer as your browser (click Next) and then asks you to select a browser from those found on your computer. Make your selection from the list, and then click Next to continue.

4. Setup asks whether you want to send diagnostic data to Intuit. This doesn't include financial or personal data, but rather data about your modem and service provider to help Intuit maintain the best connection with you. Click Yes, I want to send diagnostic data, and then click Next. (If you do not want to send this data, select the No option.)

5. Setup then summarizes your answers, as shown in Figure 3.8. Click Finish.

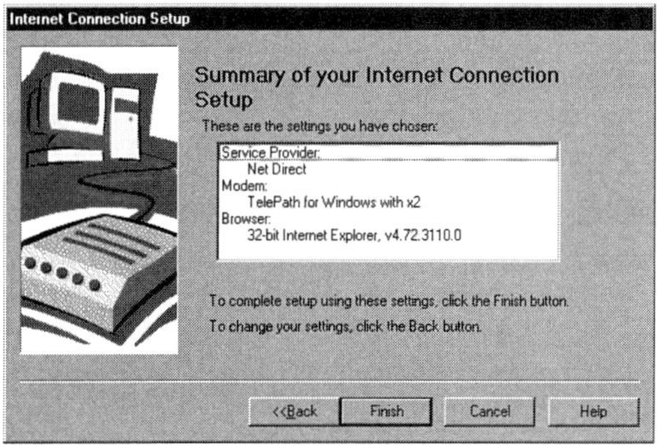

FIGURE 3.8 Check over the summary. If you need to change anything, click the Back button and edit your input.

6. The Internet Connections Options dialog box opens, as shown in Figure 3.9, listing additional options you can set. Make any necessary changes to the options, and then click OK.

7. Quicken attempts to connect you to the Internet, as shown in Figure 3.10.

When connected, you see a Web page displayed in the Internet window (depending on the Internet feature you selected, the page might vary). Like the other Quicken features, the Internet feature opens the Web page in its own window within the Quicken program window (see Figure 3.11).

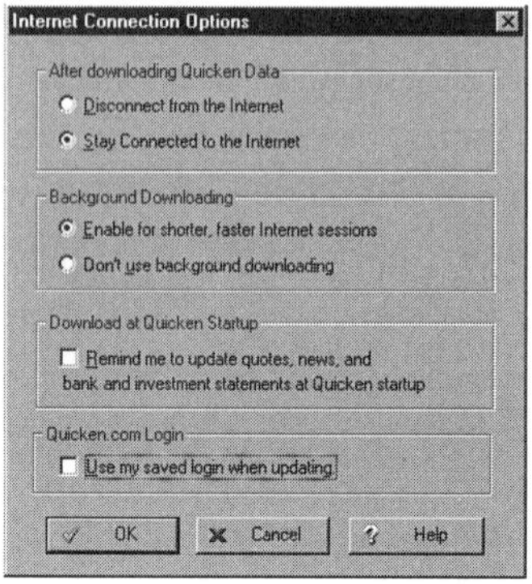

FIGURE 3.9 Check over the connection options in this dialog box, making any changes as needed.

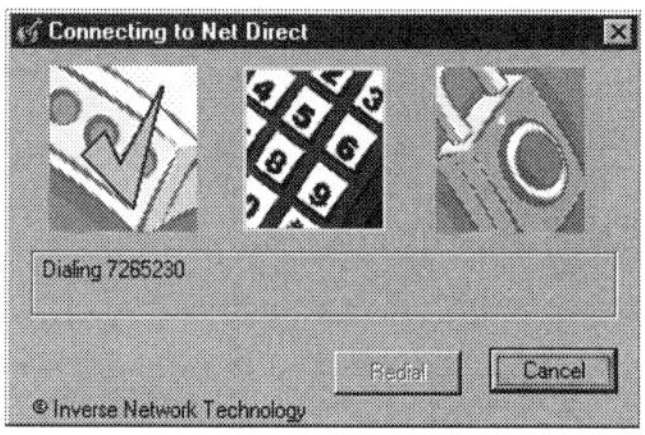

FIGURE 3.10 Quicken attempts to use your Internet connection to connect to Quicken's Web site.

You can find plenty of help on the Web site, including product support, frequently asked questions (called FAQs), technical support, and more. Be sure to explore all Quicken's Web features (open the Online menu and select Quicken on the Web, and then select the option you want to view). One of the best places to start is with Quicken's frequently asked questions page (open the Online menu and select Quicken on the Web, Quicken FAQs). Here you can find common questions about Quicken and their answers.

The next time you want to use Quicken's Internet features, you won't have to use the Internet Connection Setup Wizard. You'll use a regular Dial-up Connection dialog box to dial into your Internet service provider. Learn more about using Quicken's other online features in Lessons 23–27.

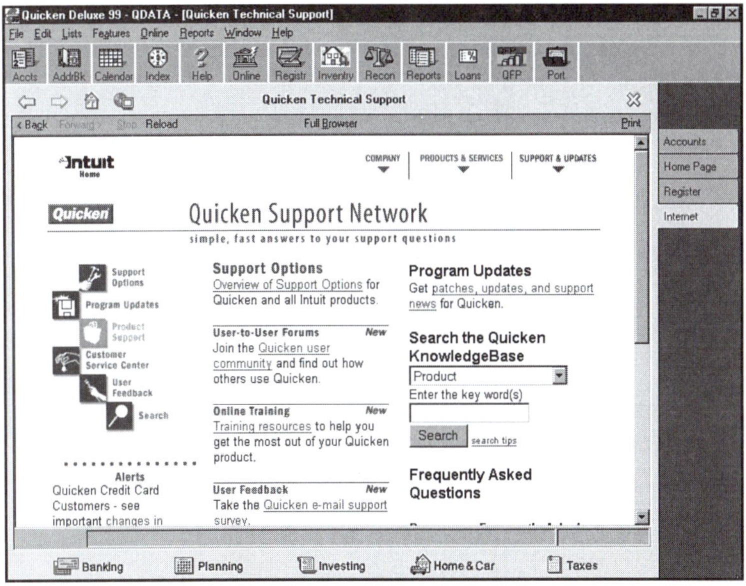

FIGURE 3.11 Quicken can connect you to all kinds of help on the Internet.

> **How Do I Exit?** Use the steps you normally do to end your Internet connection.

> **I Still Need More Help!** If Quicken's help features and Internet help still didn't answer your problem, turn to Quicken's technical support team. Open the Help menu, select Product Support, and then click the Call for Support button to find a phone number you can call. You can even fax in your questions using the Learn More by Fax option.

In this lesson, you learned how use Quicken's help features to learn more about the program or find help when you need it, and you learned how set up Quicken to use the Internet. In the next lesson, you learn how to create new accounts and assign passwords.

LESSON 4
CREATING ACCOUNTS

In this lesson, you learn how to create new accounts, assign passwords, and use the Account List.

UNDERSTANDING ACCOUNTS

When you install and open Quicken for the first time, New User Setup takes you through the necessary steps to create your first account—a checking account. Maintaining and balancing a checking account is one of Quicken's primary uses. But you might want Quicken to track other types of accounts as well:

- *Checking Account*. Quicken can help you track and write checks based on your checking account, and reconcile the account based on your bank statements with this type of account (considered an asset account). You can even use Quicken's Internet features to pay bills electronically from this account. For most users, a checking account is the primary reason for using Quicken.

> **What About Debit Cards?** If you use a debit card as part of your checking account, you need not set up a separate account for the card. Use your checking account and record debit-card transactions just as you would any other checking transaction.

- *Savings Account*. Quicken can help you keep track of transfers and deposits made to your savings account with this type of account (also an asset account).

- *Credit Card Account.* With this type of account (a liability account), Quicken can help you manage your credit card, complete with reminders for when you're approaching your limit, or letting you know how much credit you have left on the card.
- *Cash Account.* With this type of account (an asset account), Quicken can help you track spending and receiving, which is particularly useful in a small business setup. This type of account can help you manage petty cash, slush funds, or other emergency funds.
- *Money Market Account.* With this type of account (another asset account), Quicken can help you speculate on the money market, including certificates of deposit, Treasury bills, and other mutual fund investments.
- *Investment Account.* If you buy and sell securities and other investments, Quicken can help you track these as a group.
- *401(K) Account.* Quicken can help you track your retirement funds with this type of account (also considered an investment account), including all the tax-deferred items that go along with such accounts.
- *Asset Account.* Use this type of account to manage assets such as money you might have loaned to others and property equity.
- *Liability Account.* Use this type of account to track long- and short-term liabilities, such as personal loans and mortgages.

> **Defining Asset and Liability** An *asset* is something you own, such as cash, real estate, or a portfolio. Assets contribute positively to your overall balance. A *liability* is any financial obligation that involves debt or potential loss—things you owe. Liabilities contribute to the negative side of your overall financial balance.

When you're just starting out with Quicken, you might need only to manage your checking account, but if you use more than one bank account, do a lot of investing, or maintain a loan or credit card, Quicken can help you with these financial obligations too. Accounts are the best way to manage your various financial assets and liabilities. You can always add a new account when you need one by following the steps in the next section.

CREATING NEW ACCOUNTS

You can have as many accounts as you need in Quicken. Each one can help you track your finances. To create a new account, follow the steps given next (in the example, I'm creating a credit card account). Keep in mind that the steps might vary slightly depending on the type of account you're creating.

1. Open the Features menu and select Banking, Create New Account. This opens the Create New Account dialog box, shown in Figure 4.1.

> **Other Ways to Create New Accounts** If you're already viewing the Account List, click the New button at the top of the list window. You can also select the Edit menu from the menu bar and choose Account, New. Or if you're an avid keyboard user, just press Ctrl+N.

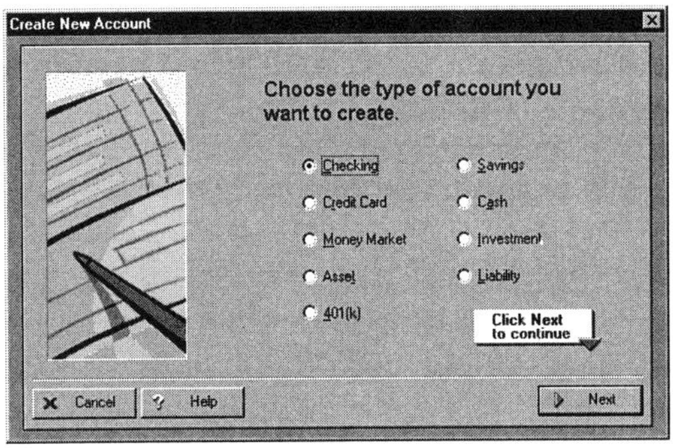

FIGURE 4.1 Use the Create New Account dialog box to start a new Quicken account.

2. Choose the type of account you want to create. You have nine types of accounts to choose from. After you make a selection, click Next to continue.

3. You can skip right through the question-and-answer dialog boxes for setting up an account and go right to the Summary tab to enter all the relevant information. Click the Summary tab (shown in Figure 4.2).

Not 401(K) Accounts! If you're setting up a 401(K) account, you can't take the shortcut described in step 3. You'll have to go through each question-and-answer dialog box to create the account, so follow the directions in each box.

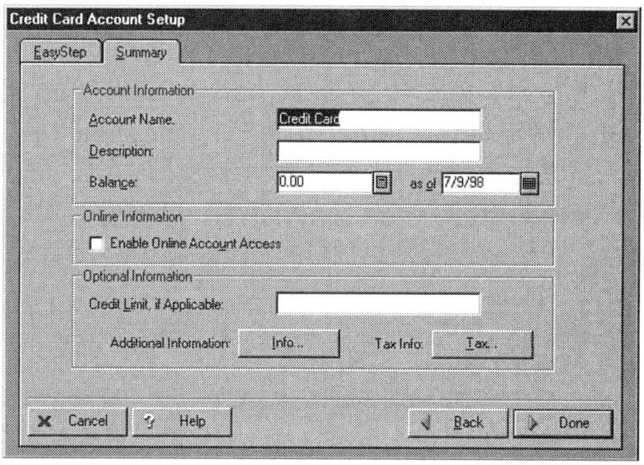

FIGURE 4.2 Jump to the end of the account setup procedure by clicking the Summary tab and entering all the relevant information about the account.

4. Click inside the Account Name text box and enter a name for the account. The account name appears on the QuickTab.

5. Click inside the Description text box and enter a description for the account.

6. If you receive statements for this account (credit card statements, for example), click inside the Balance text box and enter

the ending balance shown in the last statement you received. Then in the box to the right, enter the statement date.

If you don't receive statements, you can record the date you purchased the asset or incurred the liability in the Balance text box and a date in the as of date box.

7. If the account can be set up for online transactions, set the Online Information options in the Summary tab. For example, if the account is set up with a financial institution that's registered with Quicken's online services, click the Enable Online Account Access check box and you can download statements and transfer funds.
8. Under the Optional Information, enter any additional information pertinent to your account. For example, if you're creating a credit card account, you would enter a credit limit (or set one for yourself).
9. Use the Info button to enter more information. Use the Tax button to set up a tax-deferred account.
10. Click Done and the account is created.

Can I Change the Account Information? Yes, you can go back and edit the information you entered to set up the account. From the Account List window, select the account, and then click the Edit button. You can also right-click over the account and choose Edit. Make the necessary changes and then click Done. You can also use the Info button in the Account List window to add more details, such as the account number or phone number of the financial institution.

USING THE ACCOUNT LIST

You can view all your accounts from the Account List window, as shown in Figure 4.3. To display the list, do one of the following:

- Click the Accts button on the Iconbar.
- Open the Lists menu and select Accounts.
- Select the Banking icon on the Activity bar and choose View my list of accounts.

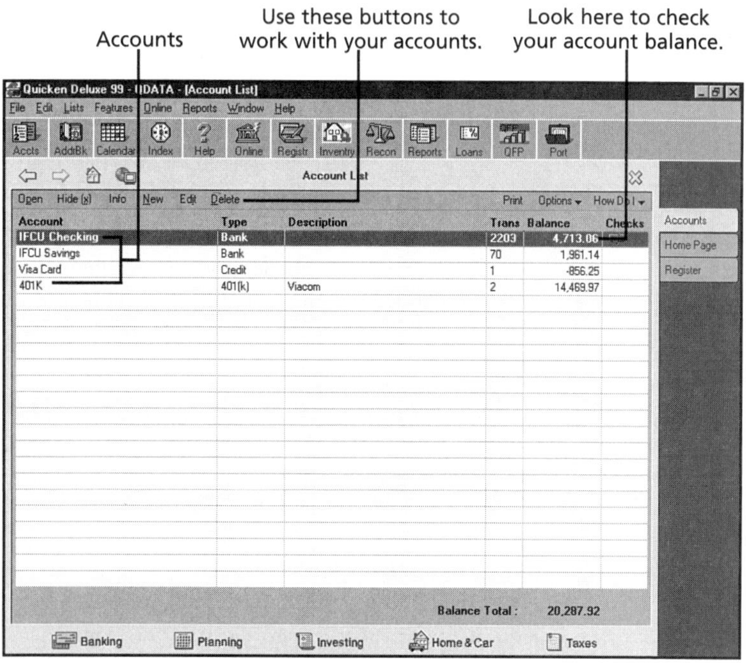

FIGURE 4.3 Use the Account List to view your accounts.

> **Automate Transactions?** After completing a new account, you might see a prompt box that offers to automate your transactions. It might say something such as *Would you like to learn how to save time when entering credit-card transactions?* If your Quicken CD is loaded and you select Yes in the prompt box, Quicken Audio instructs you how to automate your transactions via the Internet, and a series of dialog boxes shows you how. Click No to skip this procedure and return to the Account List view.

To open the register for any account and record transactions, double-click the account name (learn all about recording transactions in Lesson 5, "Recording Transactions"). You can also select the account and click the Open button to open the register. Use the Options button at the top of the Account List window to change which accounts are displayed in the list.

> **I Want to Delete the Account** When you delete an account, all its data is permanently removed. Be very careful about doing this (if you prefer not to see the account but want to keep it, use the Hide button). If you're absolutely sure you want to delete the account, select it and click the Delete button at the top of the Account List window. You'll be asked to confirm the deletion. Type **Yes** and click OK.

ASSIGNING PASSWORDS

If you consider your financial data sensitive and want to protect it from unauthorized access or changes, you can assign a password to the file, or assign a transaction password to protect transactions.

File passwords can keep others from viewing your financial data; the file can't be opened without the proper password. A password can't, however, protect your data from being deleted, moved, copied, or renamed.

Transaction passwords can be set to protect transactions you entered before a particular date. For example, if you just finished closing an account period, assign a password to the transactions so that no accidental changes can be made to the entries.

Follow these steps to assign a file password:

1. Open the File menu and select Passwords, File. This action opens the Set Up Password dialog box (shown in Figure 4.4).
2. Enter a password for your file in the Password text box. You can use up to 16 characters, including spaces. (Don't worry about upper- or lowercase letters; Quicken doesn't distinguish these in passwords.)

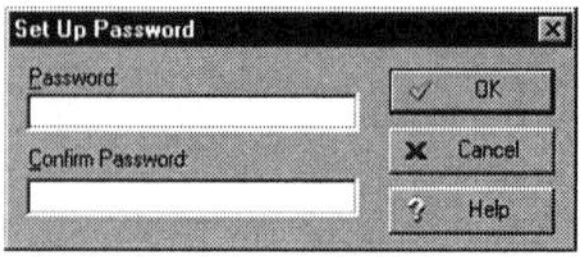

FIGURE 4.4 Set up a file password with this dialog box.

3. Enter the password again, exactly the same, in the Confirm Password text box.
4. Click OK.

The next time you open Quicken, you must enter the password.

> **Remember It!** Be sure to write down the password and keep it in a safe place. It's very important that you reenter the password exactly as you assigned it in the Password dialog box.

To assign a transaction password, take these steps:

1. Open the File menu and select Password, Transaction. This selection opens the Password to Modify Existing Transactions dialog box (shown in Figure 4.5).

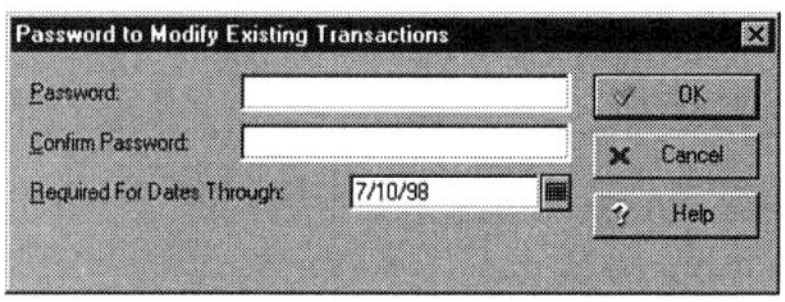

FIGURE 4.5 Use the Password to Modify Existing Transactions dialog box to set a transaction password.

2. Enter the password to use in the Password text box.
3. Enter it again in the Confirm Password text box.

4. Set the date for the transactions by using the Required For Dates Through box. You can use the Calendar tool to set a date, or you can type one directly into the text box.
5. Click OK.

Now if you try to change a transaction dated before the date you specified in step 4, you must first enter a password.

> **Can I Change My Filename?** Sure, you can rename your Quicken file at any time. Open the File menu and select File Operations, Rename. This action opens the Rename Quicken File dialog box. Enter a new filename and click OK.

In this lesson, you learned how to work with Quicken accounts, set up new accounts, and assign passwords. In the next lesson, you learn how to record transactions.

LESSON 5
RECORDING TRANSACTIONS

In this lesson, you learn how to record transactions for your accounts, transfer funds between accounts, and create split transactions.

WHAT ARE TRANSACTIONS?

For each account you create in Quicken, you record transactions to move money in and out of your accounts. You can perform three types of transactions in Quicken:

- *Inflows*. Amounts you record that increase the funds in an account.
- *Outflows*. Amounts you record that decrease the funds in an account.
- *Transfers*. Amounts you record that move funds from one account to another.

For example, when you write a check to pay a bill and record the transaction in Quicken, the transaction type is an *outflow*. When you get a paycheck and deposit it into your checking account, the transaction is an *inflow*. If you transfer money from your savings account to your checking account, the transaction is a *transfer*. Transactions include checks you've written, cash withdrawals, deposits, ATM transactions, debit card transactions, and so on. By recording every transaction you make to an account, you can use Quicken to keep track of the bottom line—your financial status.

RECORDING A TRANSACTION

One way to record a transaction is to do so directly in Quicken, as explained in the following steps. These steps are applicable to every type of Quicken account except 401(K) accounts, Investment accounts, or Invoices/Receivables accounts. (Another way is to use Quicken's Write Checks features, as explained in Lesson 7, "Writing and Printing Checks.") Figure 5.1 shows an example of a checking account register.

> **More About 401(K) or Investment Accounts** If you set up an investment account or a 401(K) account in Quicken, the transaction register works a little differently than one for a checking account. The register looks very similar, but obviously the fields are applicable to the buying and trading of shares rather than payments and deposits. If you need help entering transactions in 401(K) or investment accounts, pop in your Quicken CD-ROM and let Quicken Audio talk you through the procedure.

To move from field to field in the register, press the Tab key. You can also click inside the field you want to use. When you finish entering a transaction, press Enter.

> **Using Quicken Sounds** If your Quicken sounds are turned on, you hear a "ka-ching" sound (like a cash register) every time you record a transaction, which is a bit depressing after awhile because it reminds you of all the money that's leaving your account. To turn off the sounds, open the Edit menu and choose Options, Quicken Program. Click the General tab and deselect the Turn On All Quicken Sounds check box, and click OK.

To record a transaction, follow these steps:

1. Select the account you want to use. To display the Account List, click the Accts button on the Iconbar, or open the List menu and choose Account.

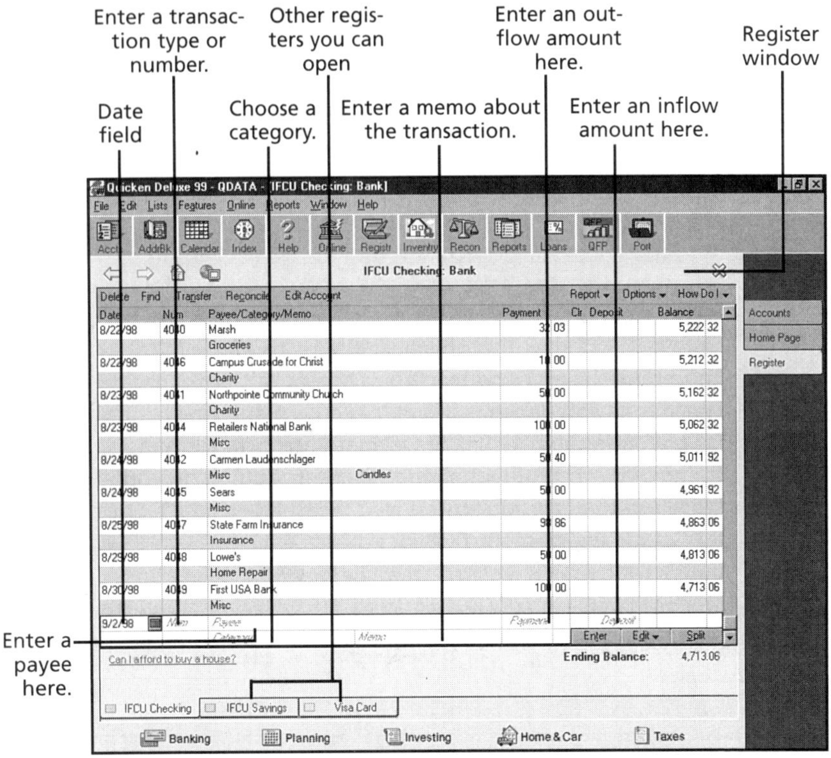

FIGURE 5.1 Use the Register window to record transactions.

2. Select the account you want to use from the Account List and open the register; double-click the account and the register opens, as shown in Figure 5.1.

> **Other Routes to the Register** You can also access your checking account register by opening the Features menu and selecting Banking, Use Register. This action immediately opens the last register you used. Or you can hover your mouse pointer over the Banking icon on the Activity bar and choose Use my register from the pop-up menu.

3. To record a new transaction, start by recording the date of the transaction. By default, Quicken awaits your first entry with the insertion point in the Date field of a new transaction line. Type a date, or click the Calendar icon to choose a date from a pop-up monthly calendar, as shown in Figure 5.2.

   To choose a date from the calendar, use the arrows at the top of the calendar to change the month, and then click the date you want to use for the transaction. Press Tab to move to the next field.

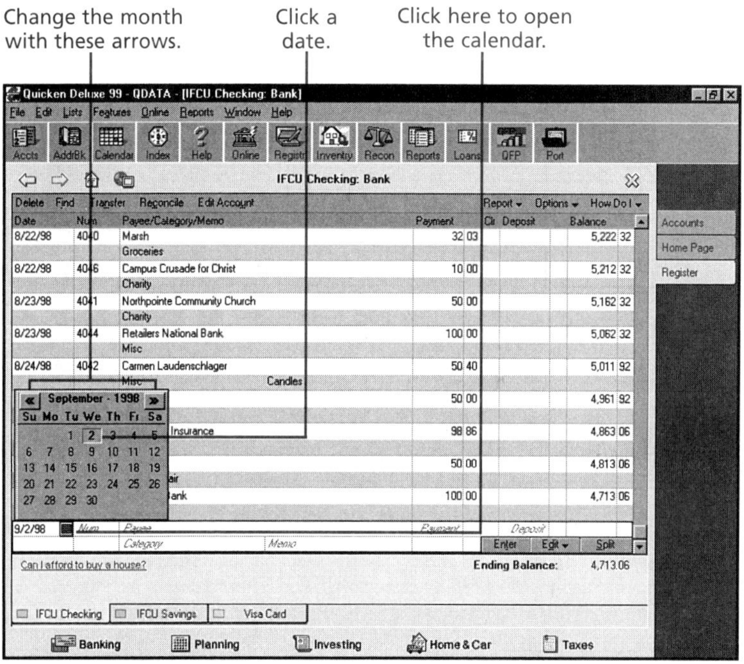

FIGURE 5.2 Use the Calendar tool to select transaction dates.

4. Click the down arrow, as shown in Figure 5.3, to display a list of transaction types, and choose the type you want to record. If you're recording a check you've written, enter the check number directly. Press Tab to continue.

Click here to display the list.

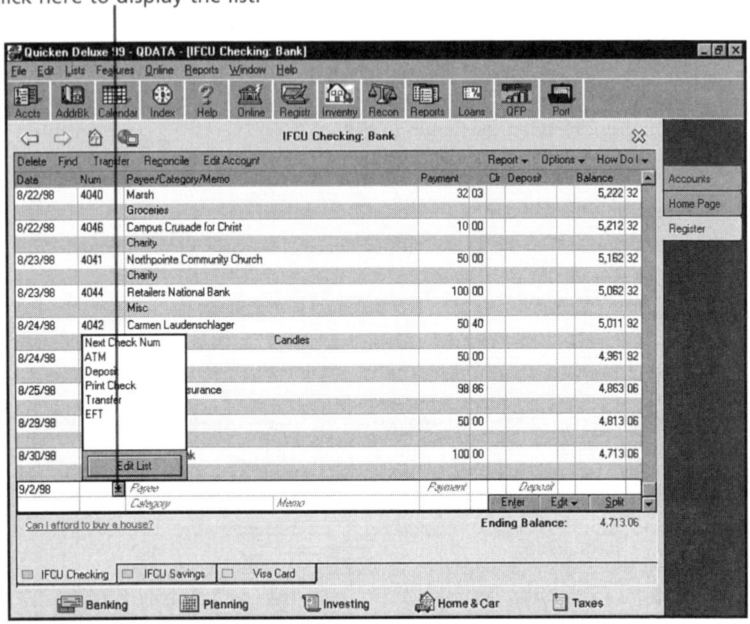

FIGURE 5.3 Choose a transaction type or enter a check number.

Choosing a Transaction Type Use the list shown in Figure 5.3 to specify the type of transaction you're recording. You can choose from ATM, Deposit, or even EFT (electronic funds transfer). If the choices in the list don't cover all the types of transactions you make, use the Edit List button to change the options.

What About Check Numbers? If you're recording checks you've written, select the Next Check Num option in the transaction type list (see Figure 5.3), and the next subsequent check number appears in the field. If you record another check transaction after this one, simply enter the first number of the check number and Quicken fills in the rest of the number for you.

5. Enter a payee. Quicken memorizes every payee you record and keeps the names in an alphabetical list. When you start typing in the Payee field, the list displays (or you can click the arrow to display the list). Figure 5.4 shows an example of a payee list. Choose a payee from the list, or enter a new payee and press Tab to continue.

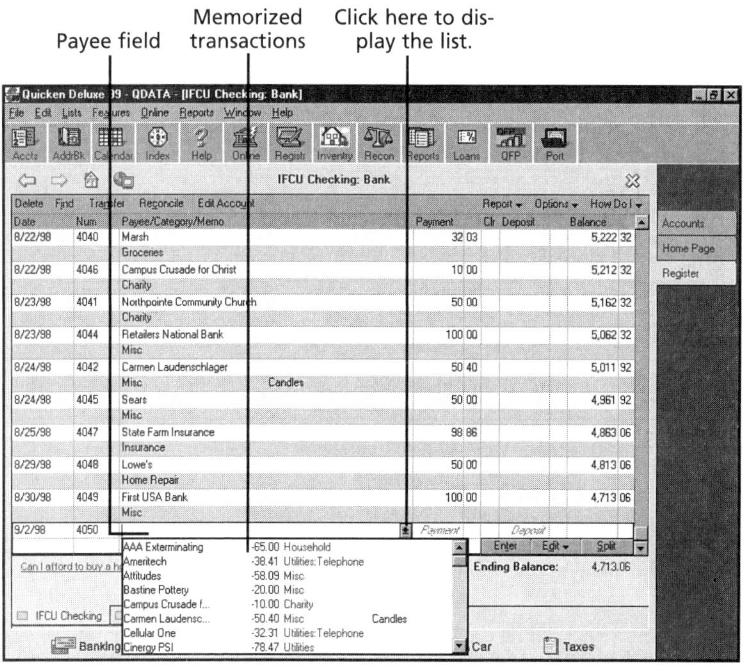

FIGURE 5.4 Quicken keeps a list of memorized transactions, making it easy to record frequent transactions to the same payee.

6. Enter the amount of payment in the Payment field or a deposit amount in the Deposit field. Depending on the type of register you're using, these fields might have different names (such as Payment, Decrease, Spend or Charge). After entering an amount, press Tab to continue. Figure 5.5 shows an amount entered in the Payment field in a checkbook register.

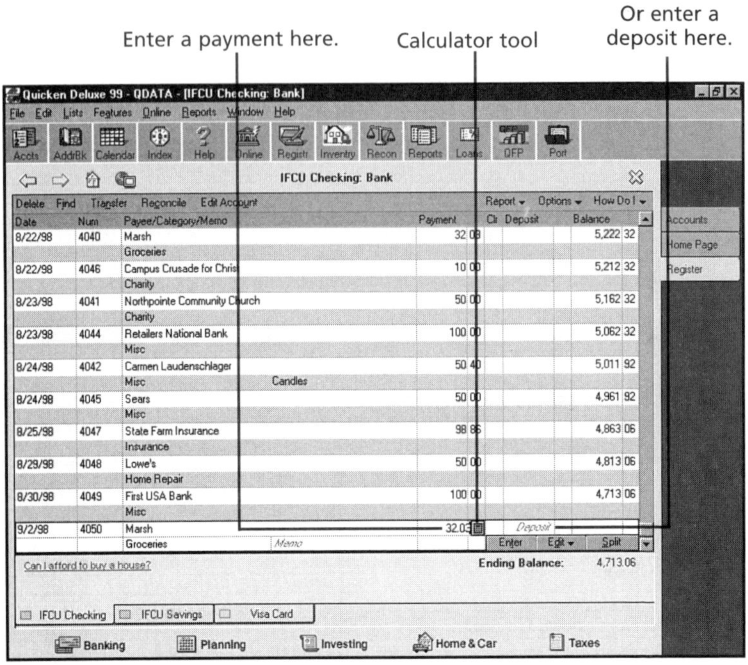

FIGURE 5.5 The next step is to enter the amount of the payment or deposit for the transaction.

> **Using the Calculator Tool** Click the Calculator icon in step 6 to display Quicken's built-in calculator. Use the calculator to perform quick calculations, pressing Enter when finished to place the amount in the current field.

7. Choose a category. Quicken uses categories to help you organize and track your transactions. You learn more about using categories in Lesson 6, "Working with Categories," but for now, click the arrow to display the category list, and choose a category for the transaction, as shown in Figure 5.6. Press Tab to continue.

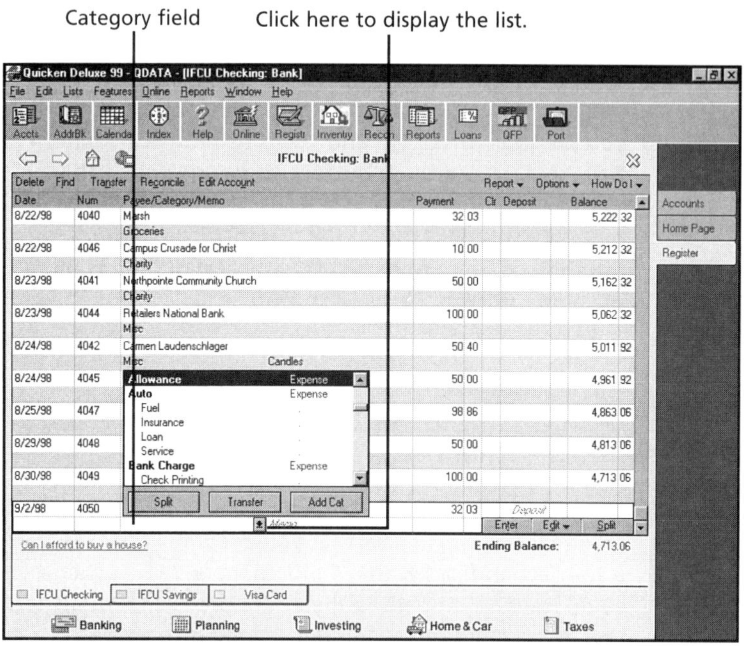

FIGURE 5.6 Select a category for the transaction.

> **I Don't Know What Category to Choose!** If you're not too sure about choosing a category, press Tab and select No to Quicken's prompt to choose a category. You can enter a category for the transaction later, after you learn more about categories in Lesson 6.

8. Use the Memo field to record a memo about the transaction (a note to yourself to help identify the transaction).
9. Press Enter to record the transaction, and Quicken adds it to the register list. Repeat steps 1–9 to record additional transactions.

> **Other Ways to Record Transactions** When you begin entering a transaction, several transaction buttons appear on the transaction line itself. For example, if you're entering a transaction in a checking account, you see the Enter, Edit, and Split buttons (see Figure 5.6). You can use these buttons to record or edit the transaction, or create a split transaction (you learn more about splits later in this lesson). Instead of pressing the Enter key to record the transaction, for example, you can click the Enter button.

To learn how to edit, delete, or void transactions, see Lesson 8, "Writing Transactions."

> **Using QuickEntry** Now that you know how to record a transaction from within Quicken, here's a fast way to do it without opening the entire program. When you install Quicken, a QuickEntry 99 shortcut icon is added to the desktop. Double-click this icon to quickly open your Quicken register and start recording new transactions. The next time you open your Quicken program window, an Accept Transactions dialog box lists the new transactions. Click Accept All to add them to the register.

TRANSFERRING FUNDS

Many of your Quicken accounts might require you to transfer funds from one account to another. For example, you might transfer money from your savings account into your checking account, or shift funds from a savings to an investment account. The account from which the funds originate is called the *source account.* The account to which you're moving the funds is called the *destination account.*

Transfers are recorded with brackets around the destination account name in the Category field of your register. For example, if you're moving money from a checking account to a savings account named IFCU Savings, the category would appear as [IFCU Savings]. As you complete the transaction in the source account, a duplicate of the transaction appears in the destination account.

To transfer funds directly, follow these steps:

1. Record the transaction as described in the preceding steps, but stop at the Category field.
2. Enter the destination account name enclosed in brackets, such as [IFCU Savings].
3. Press Tab to move to the Memo field, and enter a memo about the transfer.
4. Press Enter and the transfer transaction is recorded in both the source and the destination accounts.

To check the transfer in the destination account, open the destination account's register.

RECORDING SPLIT TRANSACTIONS

Use split transactions to siphon the amount to different Quicken categories. For example, you might enter your paycheck as a deposit transaction but split it to pay different bills or obligations (such as rent or mortgage, car payment, and utility bills). You can split a transaction up to 30 ways.

Record a split transaction using these steps:

1. Fill out the transaction as usual. If you stop at the Category field, click the arrow to display the Category list and click the Split button at the bottom of the list box, as shown in Figure 5.7. You can also click the Split button on the transaction line (also pointed out in Figure 5.7).
2. The Split Transaction window opens, as shown in Figure 5.8. Now choose a category as you normally would, press Tab, and enter a memo.

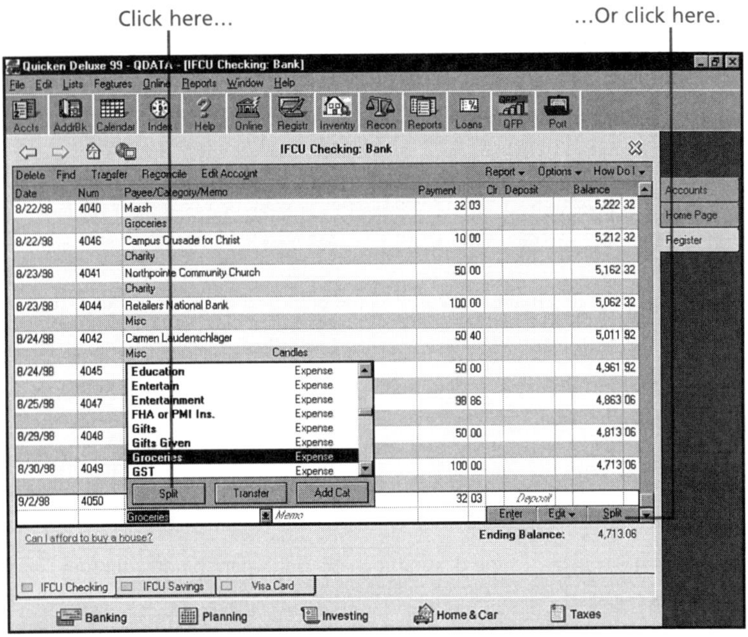

FIGURE 5.7 Click the Split button to turn the transaction into a split transaction.

3. Press Tab again and enter an amount.
4. Press Enter (or click the Next button) to move to the next line of the split.
5. Continue entering additional lines for splitting the transaction; for each line of the split, choose another category, enter a memo, and enter an amount. The Remainder total at the bottom of the window lets you know how much is left to allocate.
6. When you finish entering the split transactions categories and amounts, click the OK button to record the splits and return to the register.
7. Type a memo and press Enter to record the split transaction.

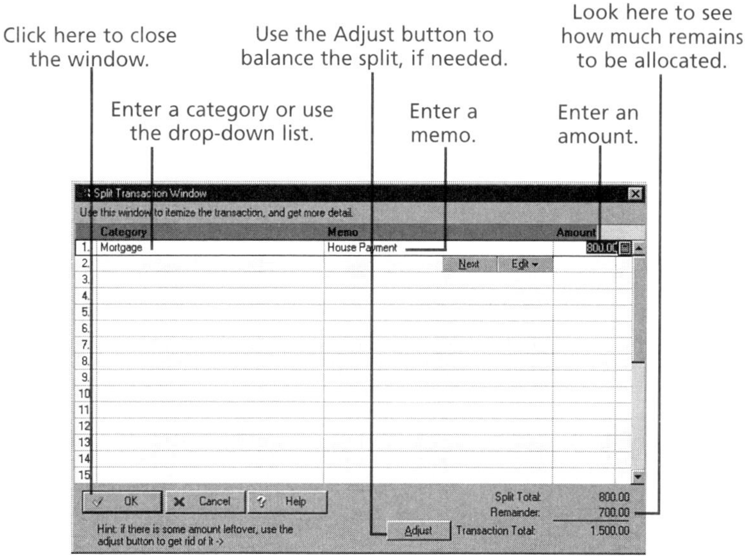

FIGURE 5.8 Use the Split Transaction window to split your transaction to several different categories.

> **What About Transfers?** You can mix transfers and categories when recording split transactions. Just remember to enclose with brackets the account name to which you want to transfer when entering it into the Category field.

To recognize a split recorded in Quicken, look for the word Split in the category field of the transaction. To see details about the split, click the small green check mark icon in the Category field.

To learn how to edit, delete, or void transactions, see Lesson 8.

In this lesson, you learned how to record various transactions into your accounts. In the next lesson, you learn how to work with Quicken's many categories.

LESSON 6

WORKING WITH CATEGORIES

In this lesson, you learn how to use Quicken's categories to help organize and track your financial data.

HOW TO USE CATEGORIES

Quicken's categories are the backbone for organizing your financial data. By detailing transactions with categories, you can track where your income and expenses go, specify tax-related items to help at tax-preparation time, and plan and maintain budgets and future financial goals.

For example, let's say you're recording a transaction that pays your rent or mortgage. By assigning the transaction to a Rent or Mortgage category, you can easily generate a report that shows how much you pay each month, every six months, or each year. If you don't assign a category, Quicken can't help you track your spending as easily.

Categories can be broken down into subcategories. For example, you can have a parent category called Utilities with individual subcategories for each type of utility payment you make each month. When you write a check for the electric bill, you can assign the subcategory Electric. When you write a check for your telephone bill, you can assign the subcategory Telephone. Both transactions are part of your spending on utilities, so you can group them under the Utility category.

> **Parent category** Like many computer elements, categories are arranged in a hierarchical manner, much like file folders. The parent category has subcategories, just as folders have subfolders. Related parent categories can be grouped into Category Groups (such as Income or Expense), or supercategories.

Quicken comes with several prebuilt category lists. When you created a checking account with New User Setup (see Lesson 1), Quicken asked you several questions—such as whether you're married, have children, or own your home—that related to the types of categories you might need. Based on the answers you provided, Quicken created a default category list customized to your situation. For example, if you said yes to the question about children, your default category list reflects a childcare category. If you said yes to married status, your list includes a category for your spouse's salary.

Quicken's default list does a good job of covering all types of income and expense categories you might need, but you can also tailor the list to your own needs. You can edit existing categories, add new categories, and delete categories that don't apply to you. As your circumstances change, you can adjust the categories as needed.

> **Using Classes** As if group categories, categories, and subcategories aren't enough, Quicken also lets you group transactions into classes. A class is not a category, but rather a "tag" to assign to transaction items. For example, if you own two homes — one you live in and the other you rent out — you use the same set of categories for each house (such as utilities). Rather than create duplicate categories, use one set but tag the transactions to different classes, one for each house. Classes are beyond the scope of this book, but you can consult Quicken's help system for additional details on working with classes.

LOOKING AT THE CATEGORY & TRANSFER LIST

To check out the prebuilt category list, open the Lists menu and choose Category/Transfer. This opens the Category & Transfer list shown in Figure 6.1. You'll find income categories at the start of the list and expense categories in the remainder of the list. Use the scrollbar to scroll through the list and examine the categories.

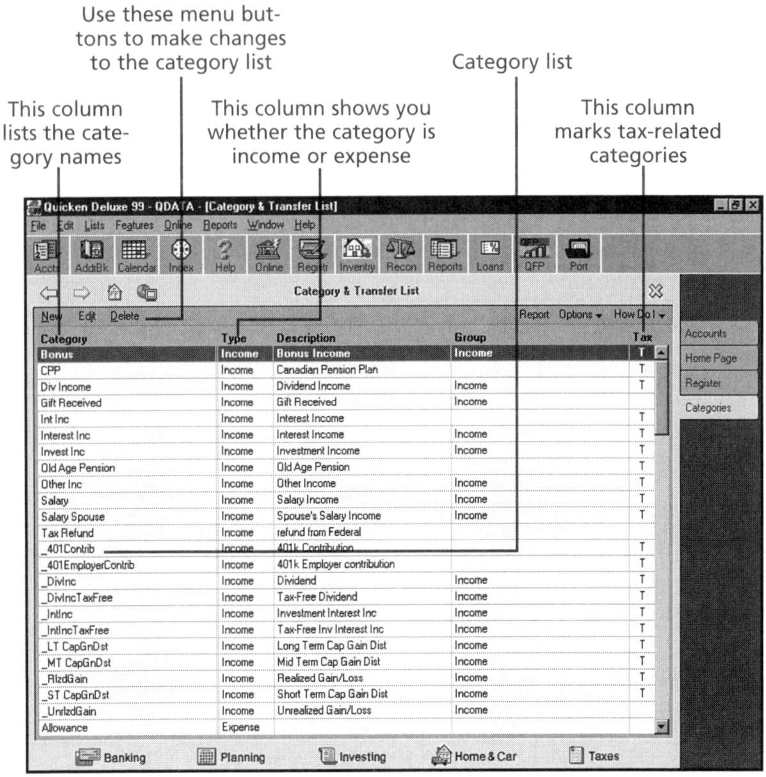

FIGURE 6.1 The Category & Transfer List shows all the categories and subcategories you can use.

Use the Options menu, shown in Figure 6.2, to change how categories are displayed in the window. For example, you can choose to show only income categories, or only tax-related categories. Click the Options drop-down arrow to display the list, and then make your selection from the menu. Notice the default is to display all the categories, along with their descriptions.

EDITING CATEGORIES

If you need to modify a Quicken category, you can do so from the Category & Transfer List window. Use these steps:

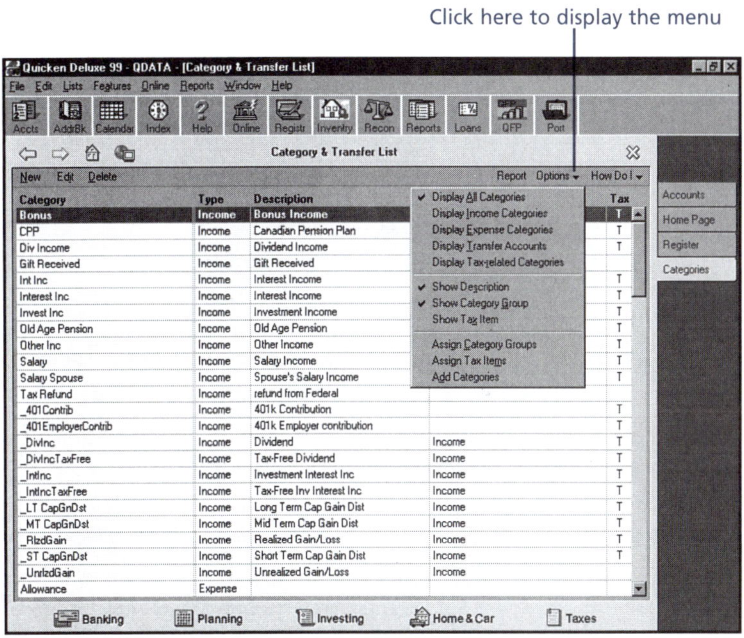

FIGURE 6.2 Use the Options menu to change the category display.

1. Select the category you want to modify from the list.
2. Click the Edit button to open the Edit Category dialog box, shown in Figure 6.3. (You can also right-click over the category and choose Edit from the pop-up menu.)

Close It Up To exit the Category & Transfer List window, click the window's Close (X) button at any time. You can also leave the window open and view another open window by clicking the appropriate QuickTab or using the navigation buttons at the top of the window.

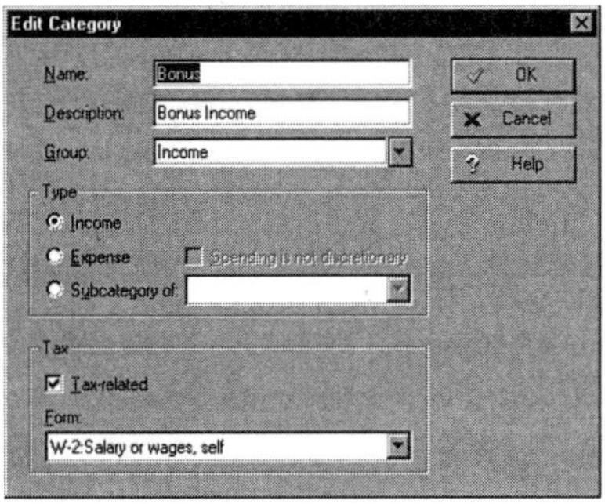

FIGURE 6.3 You can modify an existing category using the Edit Category dialog box.

3. To make changes to the name of the category, click inside the Name text box and enter a new name or modify the existing name.
4. To change the category description, click inside the Description text box and edit the description.
5. To assign the category to another group, click the Group drop-down arrow and choose another.
6. Use the Type area of the dialog box to change the category type, or assign it as a subcategory to another category. If it is a nondiscretionary expense type item, click the Spending is not discretionary check box.
7. If the category is tax-related, select the Tax-related check box.
8. Click OK to exit the Edit Category dialog box and apply the changes.

> **Merging Categories** You can also merge categories. If you have two similar categories, use the Edit Category dialog box described earlier and assign the category to another parent category.

ADDING TO THE PREBUILT CATEGORY LIST

If your circumstances have changed since you used New User Setup to create your account, you can add categories from Quicken's built-in category lists. Perhaps, for example, you've just had a baby and need to add child-related categories to your list. Quicken comes with six prebuilt lists. The lists assigned to your account depend on your answers to Quicken's questions during the New User Setup steps. The lists include the following options:

- Standard
- Married
- Homeowner
- Business
- Children
- Investment

To add categories to your default list, follow these steps:

1. Open the Options menu from the Category & Transfer List window and select Add Categories. This opens the Add Categories dialog box (see Figure 6.4).

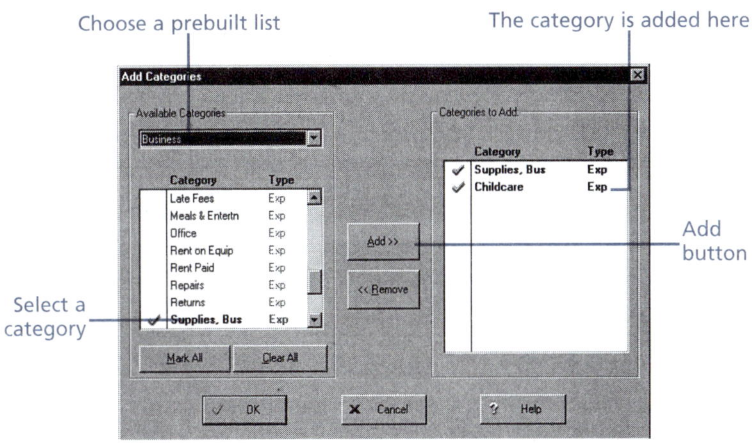

FIGURE 6.4 You can add prebuilt categories to your default category list.

2. From the Available Categories drop-down list, select the built-in category list you want to add categories from. (Some lists have only one category; others have numerous categories from which to choose.) You can pick and choose categories to add from each prebuilt list.

3. Select the category you want to add in the list box and click the Add button to place the category in the Categories to Add list box on the right. (If you want to add all the categories shown, click the Mark All button before clicking the Add button.)

> **Oops, I Don't Want That Category!** If you change your mind about adding a category in the Add Categories dialog box, select the category from the Categories to Add list box and click the Remove button.

4. After you list all the categories you want to add, click OK. The Category & Transfer List window now reflects your additions.

DELETING CATEGORIES

To tailor your Quicken categories to reflect your own situation, consider removing categories you don't need from your category list. To delete a category, select it from the list and click the Delete button at the top of the Category & Transfer List window.

> **Deleting Subcategories** If you delete a subcategory, you are asked whether all transactions that were assigned to that subcategory should be reassigned to the parent category. Click Yes to reassign transactions, No to leave them unassigned, or Cancel to cancel the delete.

CREATING NEW CATEGORIES

If Quicken's many prebuilt categories still don't meet your needs, you can add new categories to the list. You have two ways to add new categories. You can create a new category as you're recording a transaction, or you can add new categories from the Category & Transfer List window.

To create a new category from the Category & Transfer List window, follow these steps:

1. Click the New button. This opens the Set Up Category dialog box, shown in Figure 6.5.

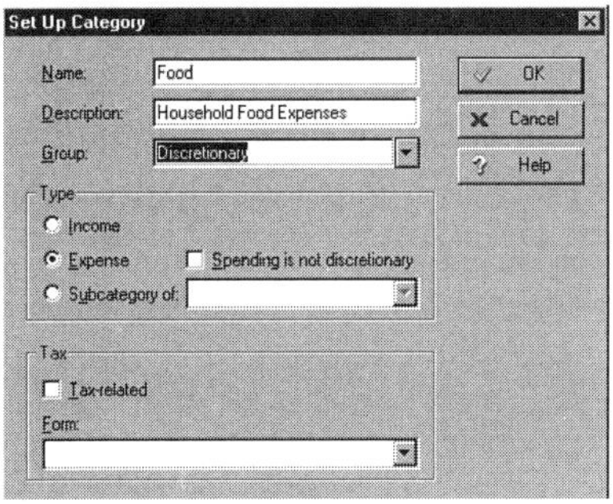

FIGURE 6.5 Use the Set Up Category dialog box to add details about the new category you're creating.

2. Click inside the Name text box and enter a new name for the category. You can use up to 32 characters, including spaces.
3. Click inside the Description text box and enter a description.
4. To assign the category to a particular group, click the Group drop-down arrow and choose the group.
5. Use the Type area of the dialog box to designate the category type, or assign it as a subcategory to another category. If it is a nondiscretionary expense type item, click the Spending is not discretionary check box. If the category is tax-related, select the Tax-related check box.
6. Click OK to exit the dialog box, and the new category is created.

> **Creating Subcategories** Follow the steps for creating new categories to create subcategories. In the Type area of the Set Up Category dialog box, click the Subcategory of option and choose a parent category to assign the new subcategory to.

To create a new category on-the-fly while entering transaction information in a register window, click inside the Category field and start typing a new category name. Quicken's QuickFill feature attempts to complete the entry for you with the closest match available. Keep typing to enter a new name; then press Tab. A prompt box appears asking if you want to create a new category; click Yes. Quicken then opens the Set Up Category dialog box (refer to Figure 6.5). Fill out this dialog box as explained in the previous steps, and then continue with recording your transaction.

USING CATEGORY GROUPS

As mentioned at the beginning of this lesson, you can also group categories into larger groups (often called *supercategories*). Use category groups to organize categories into broader areas. Category groups help simplify how you view your financial data and are perfect for reports and budgets.

For example, to get a quick look at your discretionary spending as a whole, you can generate a report that looks at the total spending that falls under this category group.

Quicken uses four default category groups:

- *Discretionary*. Includes nonessential expense categories, such as entertainment.
- *Nondiscretionary*. Includes all essential expense categories, such as mortgage, rent, utilities, and taxes.
- *Other Income*. Includes investment and interest income categories.
- *Salary Income*. Includes salary, wages, tips, and bonus categories.

Follow these steps to reassign a category group:

1. Open the Options menu.
2. Select Assign Category Groups. This opens the Assign Category Groups dialog box (see Figure 6.6).
3. Select the category you want to reassign from the list box on the left. (To select multiple categories, hold down the Ctrl key while clicking categories.)
4. Select a group from the list on the right.
5. Click the button at the bottom of the dialog box.

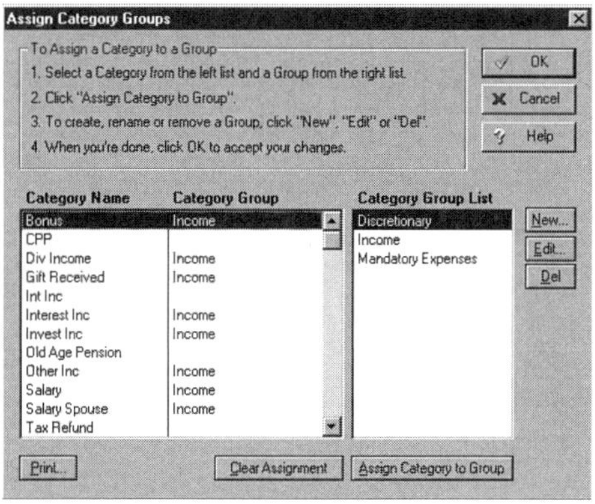

FIGURE 6.6 You can reassign the default category groups, if needed.

6. To remove a group assignment, select the category (or categories), and then click the Clear Assignment button.
7. To add a new group name to the list, click the New button, enter a new group name, and click OK.
8. When you finish making your changes to the Assign Category Groups dialog box, click OK to exit.

> **Can I Assign Category Groups While Recording Transactions?** Transactions are assigned to categories, which in turn are assigned to category groups. The transaction might appear under a particular category group in a report, but the transaction is never directly linked to the category group. When entering the transaction, however, you can click the drop-down arrow and choose Add Cat. This action enables you to add a new category and assign or create a new group.

In this lesson, you learned how use Quicken's categories to help you organize and track your data. In the next lesson, you learn how to write and print checks.

LESSON 7

WRITING AND PRINTING CHECKS

In this lesson, you learn how to order, write, and print checks using Quicken and your printer.

ORDERING CHECKS

Not only is Quicken the perfect tool for recording transactions for your various accounts, but you also can use it to write and print checks to pay your bills. Of course, there's nothing wrong with the old-fashioned method of bill paying—you can continue to write checks using your bank's checkbooks and record each transaction using the Quicken register. But you can really speed things up if you go the electronic route to check writing—load your printer with the checks and print just one or a complete batch at once.

The first step in using Quicken to write checks is to order some checks to write on. You can order blank checks through Quicken's Web site, called Intuit Market, to fit your printer setup. Before you can do this, however, you must have a modem and an Internet account with an Internet service provider.

> **Ready for the Internet?** If you haven't yet signed up with an Internet service provider, revisit Lesson 3, "Finding Help," to learn more about going online with Quicken. You also find steps for setting up Quicken to work with your existing Internet account.

You have three check styles to choose from with Quicken:

- **Standard Checks** Select this check style if you're looking for the typical business check, without a stub. Each sheet has three checks, and you can print them all at once.
- **Voucher Checks** This check style includes a single check at the top of the page and two tear-off stubs for maintaining records for both you and the payee. This style is ideal for accounts payable and payroll accounts.
- **Wallet Checks** This style of check includes a tear-off stub at the far-left side of the page and three checks per page. The stub gives you a record of the check, which is helpful for bill paying.

To order checks from the Intuit Market, follow these steps:

1. From the Quicken window, open the Features menu and select Bills, Order Checks. Quicken connects you to your Internet account and opens the Internet window onscreen, as shown in Figure 7.1.
2. Locate the Shopping or On-line Store link and click it; the Web pages you see might vary because Intuit updates the site occasionally.
3. Click the Checks link if you want to order checks, as shown in Figure 7.2. (Notice the other supplies you can order for use with Quicken.)

> **See the Whole Page** To open the full browser window to view the Intuit Market Web site, click the Full Browser button at the top of the Internet window. This opens Internet Explorer to view the Web pages.

4. The next page you view instructs you to register with the Web site before you can purchase checks (see Figure 7.3). Click the appropriate response listed.

FIGURE 7.1 Log on to to your Internet account to visit Intuit's Web site.

5. The Web site displays a registration form, similar to that shown in Figure 7.4. Fill out the form, assign yourself a password, and click the Submit Info link.
6. The next Web page displays the registration information you entered. Click the Continue Shopping link.
7. A page displays with various types of checks you can order (see Figure 7.5). Click the type of checks you want to buy.

> **More Designs** Click the Design Choices link to open a page displaying the various custom check designs you can select.

Click here.

FIGURE 7.2 Intuit's Market page lists the various types of supplies you can order.

8. On the next page that appears, enter the printer type, design choice, quantity, and so on, and click the Next link.

9. The next page displays the cost of the checks. Use the Make Changes link button to revisit your selections and make any changes to the order. Click Next to continue ordering your checks.

10. The remaining pages ask you to fill in imprint information, including bank name, account number, and so on. Click Next to continue each time. Eventually, you'll have to enter information about how you're going to pay for the checks. Then all you have to do is wait for the checks to arrive at your doorstep.

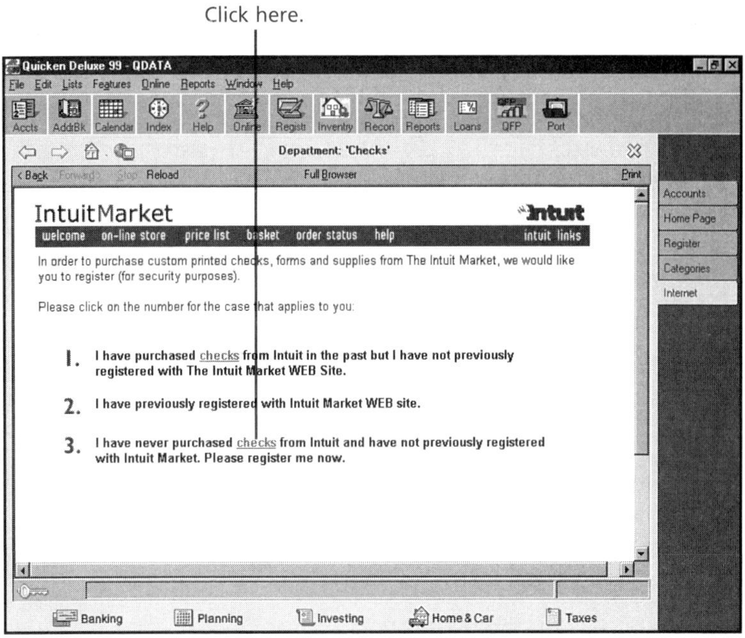

FIGURE 7.3 You must first register with the Web site.

WRITING CHECKS

Use these steps to open Quicken's Check Writing feature:

1. Open the Features menu and choose Bills, Write Checks. (You can also hover the mouse pointer over the Banking icon on the Activity bar and select Write a check to print from the pop-up menu.) The Write Checks window opens, as shown in Figure 7.6.

2. The tabs at the bottom of the window show all the accounts that support Quicken's check-writing features. Choose which account you want to write checks from by clicking the appropriate tab.

3. The upper portion of the window is for filling out the check itself. The insertion point awaits you in the Date field; type a date for the check or use the Calendar tool to select a date. Press Tab to move to the next field.

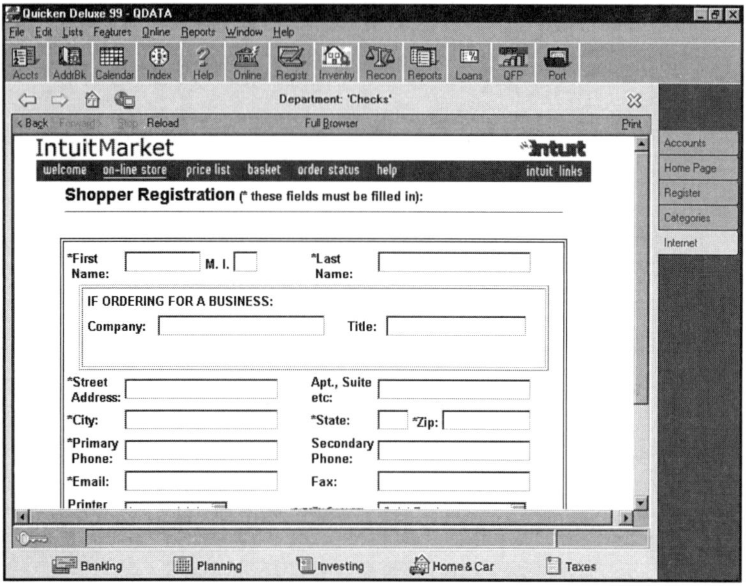

FIGURE 7.4 Fill out the registration form as needed.

4. In the Pay to the Order of field, enter a payee. The drop-down list is Quicken's standard payee list from your account register. Choose a payee from the list or type a new payee, and press Tab.

5. Enter a numeric dollar amount for the check. The written amount automatically appears filled in when you enter the dollar amount. Press Tab to move to the next field.

6. In the Address field, enter a payee address to be printed on the check, if applicable, and press Tab. This field is useful if you're using Quicken's windowed envelopes to mail checks.

7. Type a memo for the check, if needed, in the Memo field. Press Tab.

8. Use the Category field to assign a category for the check. Click the drop-down arrow and choose a category.

Select a check type.

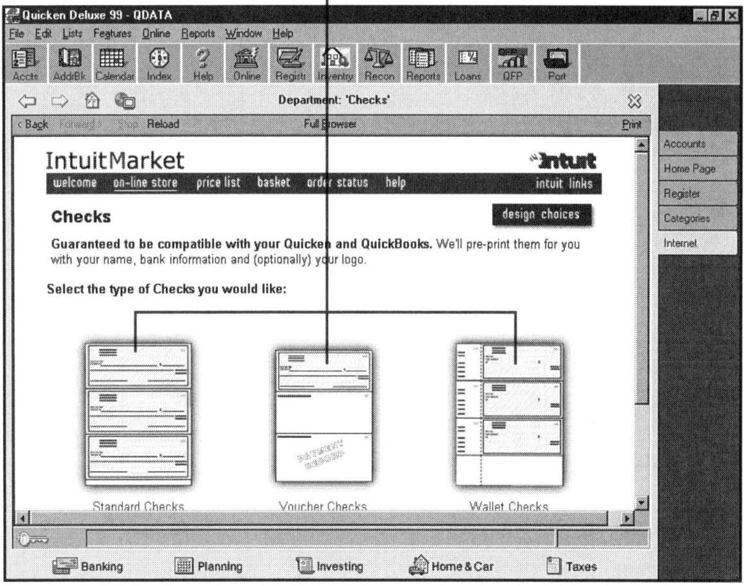

FIGURE 7.5 Choose the type of checks you want.

9. Click the Record Check button to store the transaction and open a new blank check window(see Figure 7.7). The check you just wrote appears in the Checks to Print list in the lower portion of the Write Checks window.

PRINTING CHECKS

You can choose to print your checks one at a time, as you write them, or as a batch. The very first time you print checks, you need to set up your printer to handle the checks.

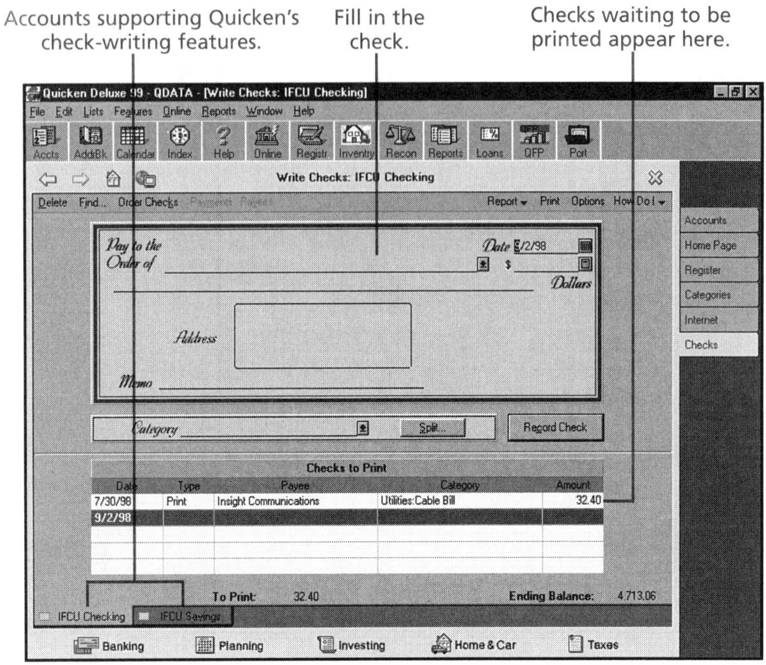

FIGURE 7.6 Use the Write Checks window to write and print Quicken checks.

PREPARING TO PRINT

Follow these steps to tell the printer how to handle the checks:

1. Open the File menu and select Printer Setup, For Printing Checks. This opens the Check Printer Setup dialog box, shown in Figure 7.8.
2. If needed, click the Printer drop-down arrow and choose your printer from the list.
3. Select the Page-oriented option (common for laser printers) or the Continuous option (common for dot-matrix printers).
4. Use the Check Style drop-down list to select the type of checks to print on (the style you ordered from Intuit).

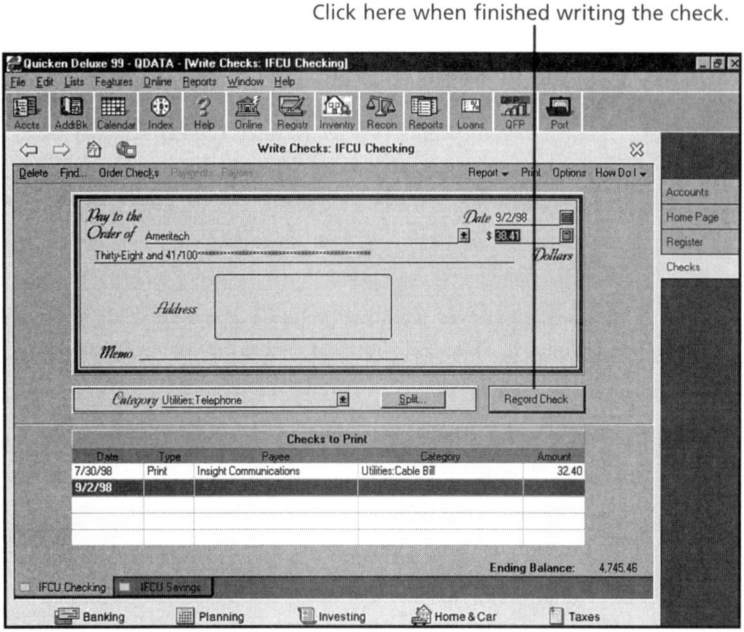

FIGURE 7.7 After filling out the check, you're ready to record it and print.

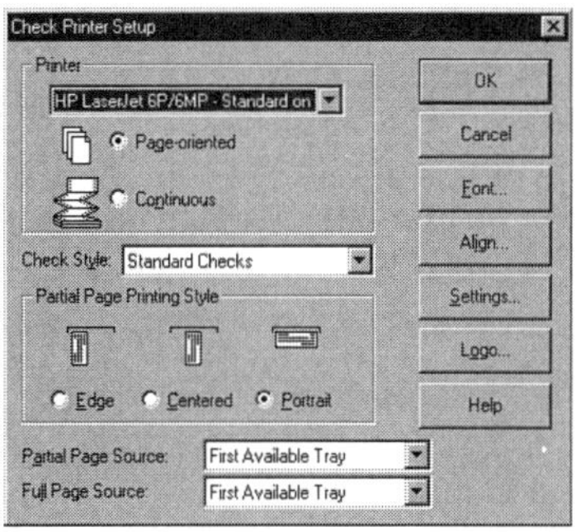

FIGURE 7.8 Use the Check Printer Setup dialog box to prepare your printer to print checks.

5. The remaining options in the dialog box are optional:

   - Use Partial Page Printing Style area to control how the check is printed to the edge or center of the paper. Select Edge if your printer prints envelopes (and checks) to the left edge of the paper. Choose Centered if your printer centers envelopes. Choose Portrait if your printer prints the long edge of the envelope (or check).
   - If you need to hand-feed the checks into the printer, set the Partial Page Source option to Manual Feed. If your printer handles full sheets of checks, set the Full Page Source option to the appropriate tray.
   - To change the font used, click the Font button and choose another font style.
   - To change alignment, click the Align button and adjust the alignment settings.
   - To adjust any printer settings, click the Settings button.
   - If you're printing a logo on your checks, click the Logo button and choose the logo file.

6. Click OK to exit the dialog box. Now you're ready to print.

PRINTING

To print your checks from the Write Checks window, click the Print button at the top of the window. You can also open the File menu and select Print Checks. The Select Checks to Print dialog box opens, similar to the one shown in Figure 7.9.

> **Don't Print Yet!** Before committing a sheet of expensive check paper to printing the first time, try a test run with a regular sheet of paper. You can always check the results against the actual check paper (hold both sheets up to the light) to see how everything lines up.

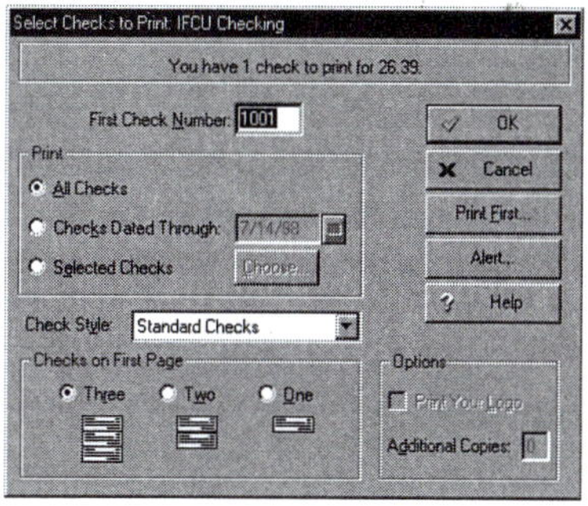

FIGURE 7.9 When you're ready to print, open the Select Checks to Print dialog box.

Follow these steps to print:

1. In the First Check Number text box, enter the first number of the check on the top sheet of checks loaded in the printer. (Don't rely on the default number that appears.)
2. Under the Print area, select which checks you want to print. If you select the All option, every check you recorded in the Write Checks window is printed.
3. Use the Check Style drop-down list to choose the check style.
4. Under the Checks on First Page area, designate how many checks should appear on the first page to be printed.
5. To print the first check in the list, click Print First. To print the entire batch (if you selected the All option), click OK.

> **Other Printing Options** You have a couple of other ways to print from the Select Checks to Print dialog box. Select the Checks Dated Through option to print checks recorded on a certain date. Choose the Selected Checks option if you want to print particular checks in the list, and then click the Choose button and select the checks.

When printing is complete, Quicken opens a dialog box similar to the one shown in Figure 7.10. Before you click OK, look over the checks and make sure that everything is correct. If not, enter the number of the first check containing a mistake, and give it another go. If everything printed okay the first time, click OK.

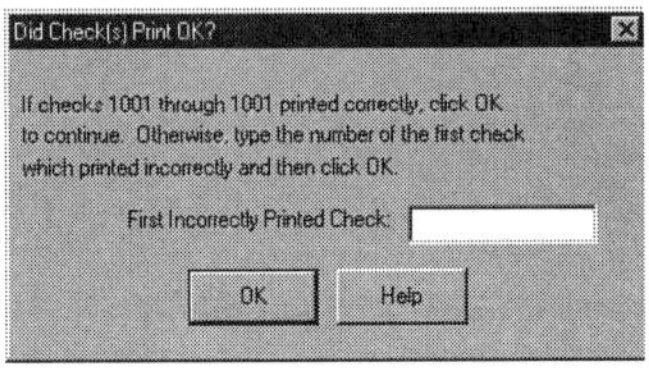

FIGURE 7.10 Quicken asks you to make sure that the checks printed accurately.

In this lesson, you learned how to order, write, and print checks using Quicken. In the next lesson, you learn how to edit transactions.

LESSON 8

WRITING TRANSACTIONS

In this lesson, you learn how to edit, delete, and void transactions that you record in your account registers and work with memorized transactions.

USING MEMORIZED TRANSACTIONS

Quicken memorizes transactions you record and keeps a list of them organized alphabetically by payee. For example, let's say you record a payment to the utility company in October for $76.15. When November rolls around, you enter another payment to the same utility company. As you begin typing the first few letters of the payee, Quicken looks through its list of memorized transactions and displays the previous matching payee, including the amount, category, and memo written for the October transaction. If the transaction is exactly the same as before, press Enter to record the new transaction with the new date and check number. If the transaction amount has changed, press Tab and enter a new amount.

This ingenious feature saves you some time entering the same transactions repeatedly. Quicken can memorize up to 2,000 entries. To view your list of memorized transactions, open the Lists menu and select Memorized Transaction. This opens the Memorized Transaction List window, shown in Figure 8.1.

You can easily edit the list as needed. You can delete entries that were one-time payees and won't be used again. To do this, select the transaction in the list, and then click the Delete button at the top of the window. You can edit the fields for existing transactions, such as changing the category. Or you can add new payees to the list (although you can also do this when recording the transaction for the very first time in the register window).

FIGURE 8.1 The Memorized Transaction List keeps a record of every payee you've written a check for, including the most recent amount of the check.

If you find the Memorized Transaction List getting too large, you can set up Quicken to automatically remove transactions you haven't used for a while. To do this, follow these steps:

1. From the Quicken menu bar, open the Edit menu and select Options, Quicken Program. This selection opens the General Options dialog box.
2. Click the General tab, shown in Figure 8.2, and select the Remove Memorized Transactions Not Used in Last … Months, and enter a number of months (from 1 to 999) in the text box. Entering 3 or 4 should keep the list manageable.
3. Click OK to exit the dialog box and apply the new setting.

To close the Memorized Transaction List window, click the window's Close (X) button. You can also click the left-arrow Navigation button to return to the previous window, or simply click the QuickTab representing the window you want to view. For the next section, return to the register window for the account you're working on.

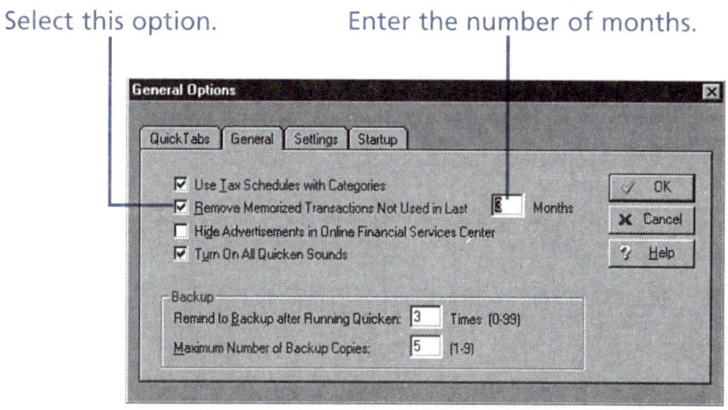

FIGURE 8.2 You can tell Quicken how long to keep transactions in the Memorized Transaction List.

> **Locking Transactions** Click in the Lck column in the Memorized Transaction List to lock a transaction to protect it from any changes. When you record a new transaction in the register window for the same payee and make any changes to its memorized fields, those changes won't affect the memorized transaction if it's locked. This helps keep you from accidentally changing the transaction while recording new entries, and it allows you to "memorize" regular transactions but occasionally use a different amount with the same payee.

> **Marking Calendar Transactions** Click the Cal column to mark transactions that should appear in the Financial Calendar. Learn more about using the Financial Calendar in Lesson 11, "Using the Financial Calendar."

EDITING TRANSACTIONS

You can return to a transaction after you've already recorded it and make changes to the various fields. For example, if you notice you entered the wrong amount for a payment, you can go back and edit the amount.

Open the account register you want to edit, and then select the transaction in the register window (see Figure 8.3). Three buttons appear at the far-right end of the transaction line.

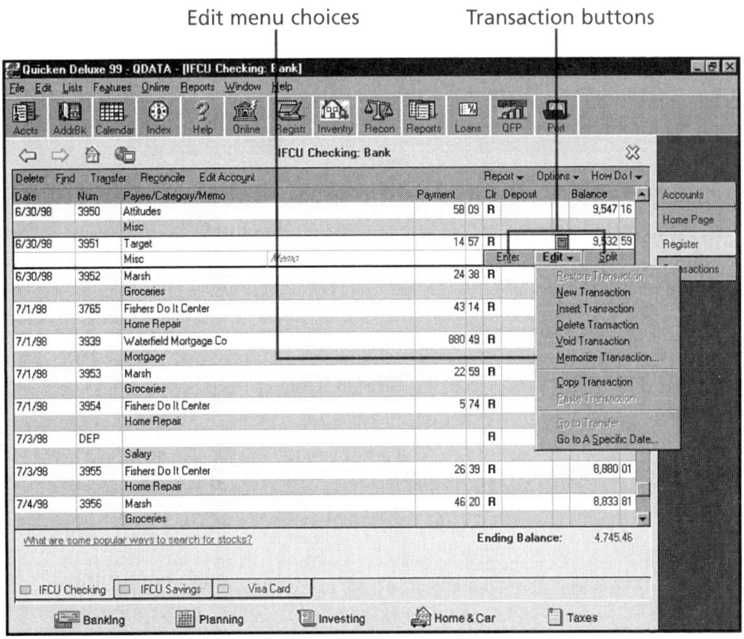

FIGURE 8.3 Use the transaction buttons to make any changes to the transaction.

Make your changes to the transaction as needed, and then click the Enter button or press Enter to record the changes. Use the Edit button to display a menu of editing functions you can choose from. Here's what you can do using the Edit menu list:

- To remove the transaction completely, select Delete Transaction from the Edit menu list.

- If you make changes to the transaction fields but decide not to keep them, select Restore Transactions.
- To mark the transaction as void, select Void Transaction.
- If you need to enter another transaction into the register, choose the Insert Transaction command. This places a new transaction before the selected transaction, using the same date as the selected transaction.
- To add your changes to Quicken's Memorized Transaction List, select the Memorize Transaction command. Any changes you make to an existing transaction aren't memorized unless you select this command.
- If you're a seasoned Windows user, you're probably very familiar with the Copy and Paste commands used to duplicate data and place it in other areas of a file or into another program. Quicken also lets you copy and paste transactions. To do so, select the Copy Transaction command on the Edit drop-down list and then paste it into another transaction record using the Paste Transaction command.

Using Go To At the bottom of the Edit drop-down list on the transaction line, you find two Go To commands: Go to Transfer and Go to A Specific Date. Use these to look for a specific transfer or transaction in your register window. When selected, each command opens a Go To dialog box with which you can locate a specific entry.

What About the Split Button? Use the Split button to create a split transaction (a transaction that is assigned to more than one account category). Learn more about this type of transaction in Lesson 5, "Recording Transactions."

DELETING AND VOIDING TRANSACTIONS

When you delete a transaction from the register window, it's removed from Quicken permanently—there's no way to get it back. When you attempt to delete a transaction, a prompt box appears, asking you to confirm the deletion. Click Yes and the item is deleted.

To delete a transaction, select it in the register window and do one of the following:

- Click the Edit button on the transaction line (refer to Figure 8.3) and select Delete Transaction.
- Open the Edit menu on the Quicken menu bar and choose Transaction, Delete.
- Click the Delete button at the top of the register window.
- Press Ctrl+D on the keyboard.

When you void a transaction, the transaction isn't deleted; it stays in the register and is marked with the word **VOID** in front of the payee name. The transaction amount remains empty. Figure 8.4 shows an example of a voided transaction.

> **Cleared Transactions** When you reconcile an account, as you learn to do in Lesson 9, "Reconciling Accounts," transactions are marked as cleared in the register window. When you void a transaction, it's automatically marked as reconciled.

To void a transaction, select the transaction from the register and use one of the following methods:

- Click the Edit button on the transaction line and choose Void Transaction.
- Open Quicken's Edit menu and select Transaction, Void Transaction.

- Right-click over the transaction and select Void Transaction.
- Press Ctrl+V on the keyboard.

This transaction is marked as void.

A voided transaction is automatically marked as reconciled.

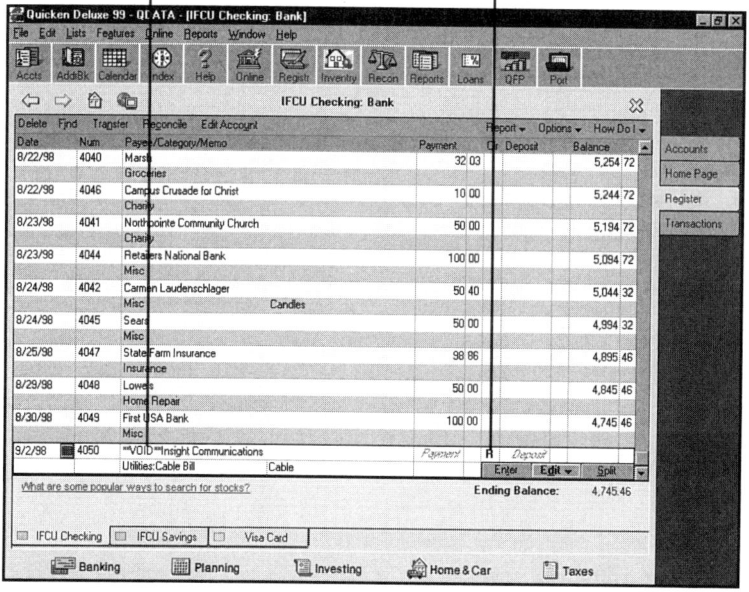

FIGURE 8.4 Voided transactions stay in the register but are marked as void.

FINDING TRANSACTIONS

The more you use Quicken and record transactions, the longer your register-window list is. When you need to search through the list to make changes to fields, scrolling and reading each transaction line can prove time-consuming and difficult. An easy way to find transactions you're looking for is to use Quicken's Find feature.

To open the Quicken Find dialog box, click the Find button located at the top of the register window, as shown in Figure 8.5.

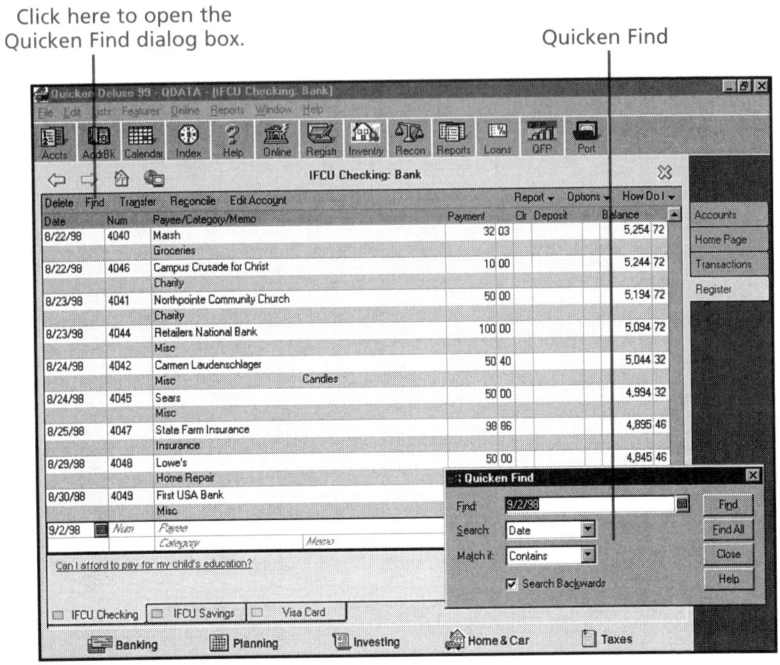

FIGURE 8.5 Use Quicken Find to search for transactions.

Enter the data you want to find in the Find text box, and then use the Search drop-down list to tell Quicken which field to look in. For example, if you're looking for a particular check number, enter the number in the text box, and then select Check Number from the Search drop-down list, as shown in Figure 8.6. (To search all the fields, choose All Fields from the list.)

> **Matching Criteria** Use the Match if drop-down list in the Quicken Find dialog box to narrow your search criteria. By default, Contains is selected, and Quicken searches your transactions for records containing the text you entered in the Find text box. You can choose from several other options, such as Less, Greater, or Starts With.

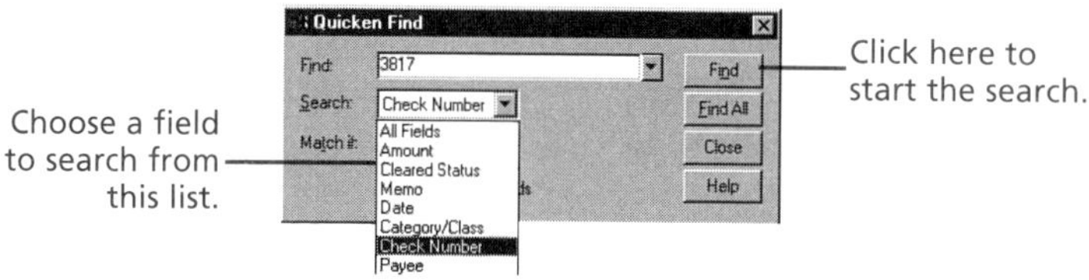

FIGURE 8.6 Enter the data you want to find, and then choose which field to search.

To search from the current transaction backward in the register list, click the Search Backwards check box. To search from the current transaction onward, deselect the check box.

Click the Find button and Quicken searches for any matches and selects them in the register window. After you find a match, you can make changes as necessary, or search for the next match (if needed). To close the Quicken Find dialog box, click Close.

Click the Find All button in the Quicken Find dialog box to display all the found matches in the Quicken Find window, as shown in Figure 8.7. To go to a particular transaction in the register window, double-click the transaction in the Quicken Find window.

FINDING AND REPLACING DATA

Use Quicken's Find and Replace feature to search your transactions and replace data. For example, if you misspelled a payee name, you can search for each record and correct the mistake. To use this feature, follow these steps:

1. Open the Quicken Edit menu and select Find & Replace, Find/Replace. This opens the Find and Replace dialog box (shown in Figure 8.8).
2. Enter the data you want to search for in the Find text box, and use the Search drop-down list to select a particular field to search.
3. Click the Find All button. Quicken lists the found transactions, as shown in Figure 8.9.

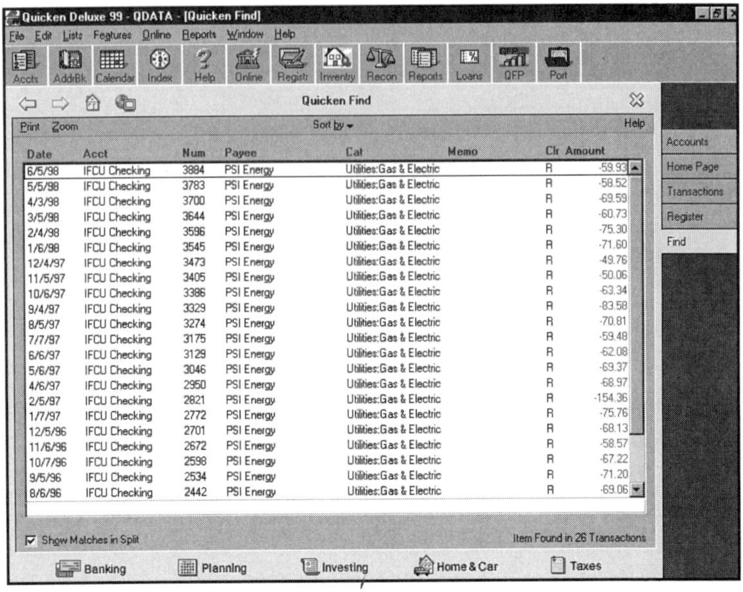

FIGURE 8.7 The Quicken Find window lists all the matches found in your register.

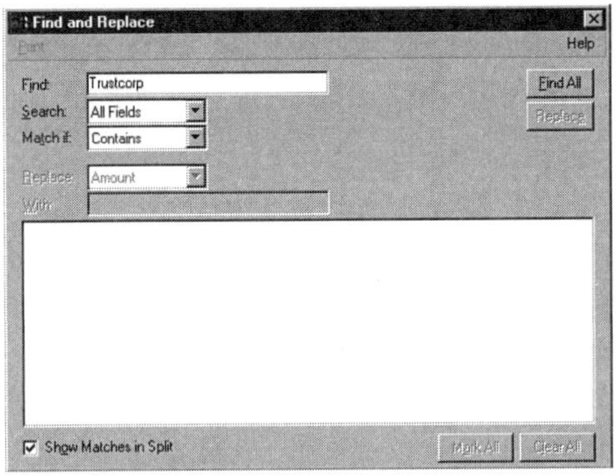

FIGURE 8.8 Use the Find and Replace dialog box to find and replace transaction data.

4. Select the transaction containing the data you want to replace, and then use the Replace drop-down list to select which field to replace.

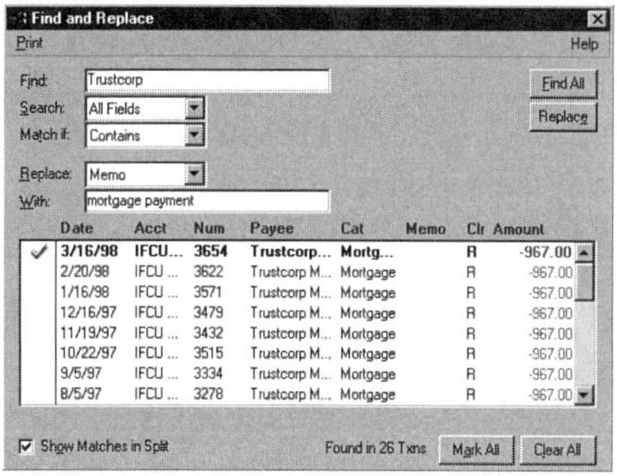

FIGURE 8.9 After looking up the data you want to find, enter the replacement data.

5. Use the With text box to enter the replacement data.
6. To replace all the occurrences, click the Mark All button at the bottom of the dialog box.
7. When you're ready to replace the data, click the Replace button.

> **Password Required** If you've assigned a password to your Quicken transactions to protect them from accidental changes (see Lesson 4, "Creating Accounts"), you must enter the password before Quicken replaces the data.

8. When Quicken finishes replacing the data, a prompt box appears, indicating how many items were replaced. Click OK.
9. To exit the Find and Replace dialog box, click its Close (X) button in the upper-right corner.

You can also sweep through your transactions list and reassign categories using Quicken's Recategorize tool. Follow these steps to find and replace categories in the transactions list:

1. Open the Edit menu and select Find & Replace, Recategorize. This opens the Recategorize dialog box.
2. Select the category you want to replace using the Search Category drop-down list.
3. Click the Find All button. Quicken lists all the transactions using the category, as shown in Figure 8.10.

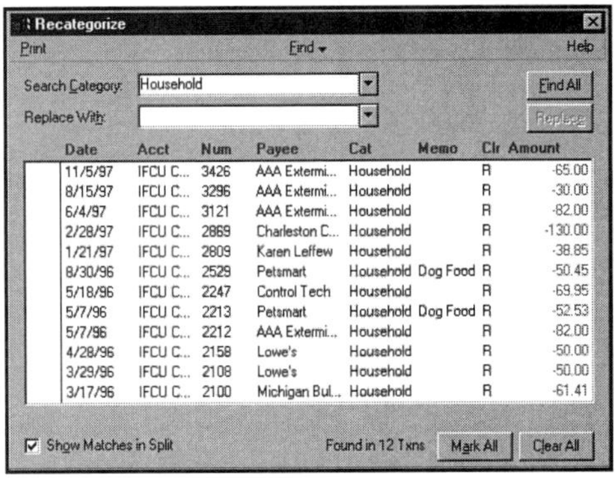

FIGURE 8.10 Use the Recategorize dialog box to search and replace categories you assigned to your transactions.

4. Select a transaction to replace, and then specify a new category to assign using the Replace With drop-down list.
5. Click the Replace button.

Transaction Password? A prompt box appears before you can replace the data if you assigned a transaction password back in Lesson 4. Remember, transaction passwords are assigned to prevent any accidental data deletions. To remedy this situation, you must enter the transaction password before Quicken replaces the data.

6. When Quicken finishes replacing the data, a prompt box appears, indicating how many items were replaced. Click OK.
7. To exit the Find and Replace dialog box, click its Close (X) button in the upper-right corner.

In this lesson, you learned how to work with memorized transactions, edit transactions, and search for transactions. In the next lesson, you learn how to reconcile your accounts.

Lesson 9

Reconciling Accounts

In this lesson, you learn how to balance and reconcile your Quicken accounts.

Understanding Reconciliations

Reconciling an account means to compare Quicken's records with those from your bank or financial institution. The easiest way to reconcile accounts is to do so each month when you receive a bank statement. Reconciling keeps your Quicken data up-to-date and accurate, lets you know which checks are outstanding and whether you or the bank made any errors.

To make the reconciliation a smooth process, the best strategy is to keep your recorded transactions up-to-date. If you record transactions on a weekly basis, for example, you won't have to spend a lot of time recording everything before attempting to reconcile the account. Of course, if you don't have time each week to enter your transactions, you can always do so before performing a reconciliation.

Performing a Reconciliation

When you first set up an account, you might have entered an opening balance based on your most recent bank statement at the time. When you reconcile an account, you use the ending balance of your latest statement to compare against the opening balance and check every transaction amount, both income and expenses (payments and deposits), in between the dates of the opening balance and ending balance.

> **No Balance?** If you didn't enter an opening balance when starting the account (see Lesson 1), scroll up to the top of the register window and enter the correct opening balance now, based on your statement, before performing the reconciliation. You can also enter the opening balance in the Reconcile Bank Statement dialog box (see Figure 9.1).

Follow these steps to perform a reconciliation (the accompanying figures show a checking account reconciliation):

1. Open the register you want to reconcile.
2. Click the Recon button on the Iconbar or click Reconcile on the button bar at the top of the register window. The Reconcile Bank Statement dialog box opens (see Figure 9.1).

> **Another Way to the Reconcile Window** You can also open Quicken's Features menu and select Banking, Reconcile.

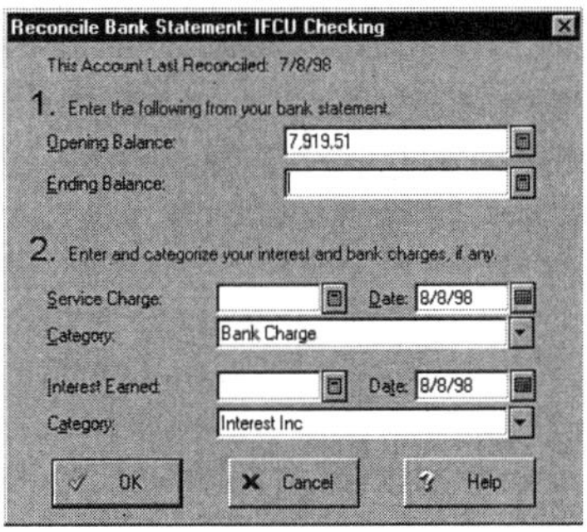

FIGURE 9.1 To begin reconciling an account, start by entering the ending balance.

3. Click inside the Ending Balance text box and enter the ending balance shown on the bank statement.

4. Check your bank statement for any service charges and enter those in the Service Charge text box. Use the Date text box to assign a date to the charge and use the Category drop-down list to assign a category.
5. If the account accrued any interest, enter the amount into the Interest Earned text box, the date it was recorded into your account, and assign a category.
6. When you finish entering data into the Reconcile Bank Statement dialog box, click OK to open the Reconcile Bank Statement window (see Figure 9.2).

> **Back to the Reconcile Bank Statement Dialog Box** To return to the Reconcile Bank Statement dialog box from within the reconciliation window, click the Statement button at the top of the window.

7. Mark off each transaction (payments and withdrawals) in the Payments and Checks list box that appears on the bank statement. Click an item in the list to mark it with a check mark. (Click again to deselect if you make a mistake.) Figure 9.3 shows marked items in the list boxes.

> **Need to Make Some Edits?** You can stop and edit your existing transactions while in the middle of reconciling your account. Use the buttons (New, Edit, Delete) at the top of the window to make changes, delete, or enter new transactions you might have forgotten previously. After making the necessary changes, click the Return to Reconcile button located on the transaction line or the Reconcile button at the top of the window to return to the Reconcile Bank Statement window.

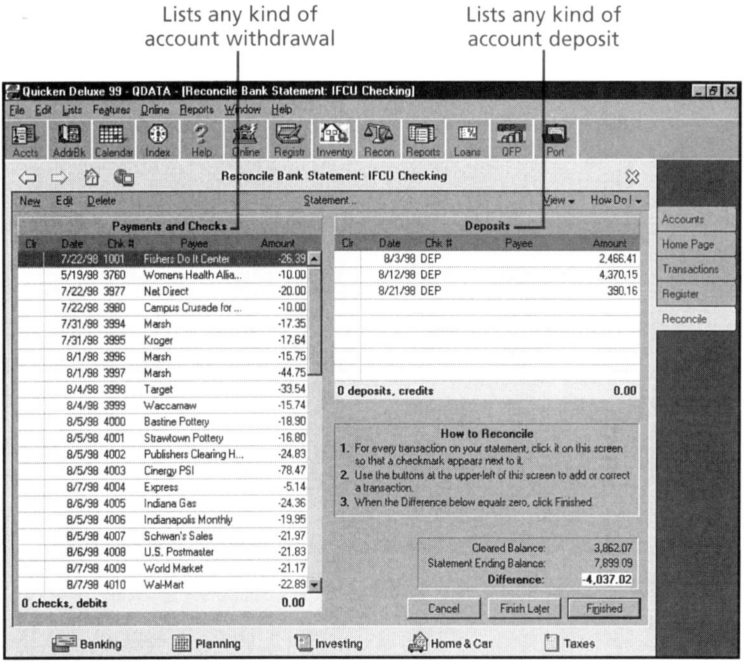

FIGURE 9.2 Use the Reconcile Bank Statement window to reconcile your account.

> **Different Orders** The transactions listed on your bank statement might not appear in the same order as your Quicken register transactions. Click the View button at the top of the window to change the order in which transactions are displayed.

8. Mark off each deposit transaction that appears in the Deposits list box (refer to Figure 9.3) and also on your bank statement.
9. After marking each transaction in your Quicken register that appears on your bank statement, look in the lower-right corner of the window to see if your Cleared Balance matches your Statement Ending Balance. If it does, congratulations! Click the

Finished button at the bottom of the window and Quicken prompts you to generate a report. Learn more about reports in Lesson 13, "Working with Reports and Graphs."

Cleared items appear marked with a check mark.

Look here when finished marking transactions.

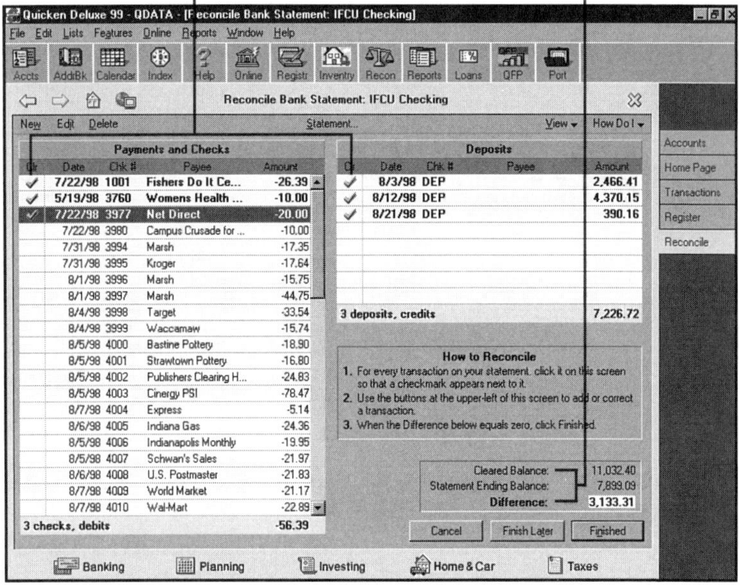

FIGURE 9.3 Check off each cleared transaction found on your bank statement.

10. If your account doesn't balance and there's a discrepancy in the Difference amount, you need to revisit the previous steps and make sure you checked off the correct transactions against your bank statement.

> **It Won't Balance!** If you're having difficulties balancing, first be sure to go over all your transactions and match them against the bank statement. Don't forget to check your deposit slips, checkbook register, and ATM receipts to make sure that everything's recorded correctly. If the difference is relatively minor, click Finished and Quicken creates an adjustment transaction for the amount of the difference and records it in your register. Simply type in the date and click Adjust.

> **Pause** You can stop a reconciliation and come back and finish it another time. To do so, click the Finish Later button at the bottom of the window. To return and complete the job, open the account register window and click the Reconcile button on the Iconbar or at the top of the register window. Click OK at the opening dialog box, and then start reconciling again.

In this lesson, you learned how to reconcile Quicken accounts. In the next lesson, you learn how to back up and restore your Quicken data.

LESSON 10

BACKING UP AND RESTORING DATA

In this lesson, you learn how to use Quicken's Backup features to save copies of your data and the Restore feature to restore the data.

USING QUICKEN'S BACKUP FEATURE

As you enter data into Quicken, it's automatically saved for you in a default file called *Qdata*. You don't ever have to save the file yourself. As soon as you enter a transaction, the data is automatically saved.

To keep your data safe, it's a good idea to back up your file frequently. That way, in case something happens to the original data (such as a computer crash), you always have a backup file to work with.

Backing up your data at least once a month is a good habit to start and keep. In fact, you should back up more than that if you use Quicken daily with several different accounts. Store your backups on floppy disks that you can then keep in a safe place.

> **Different Storage Media** You can back up to floppy disks, zip disks, or any compatible storage device—even your computer's hard disk drive (although this isn't as safe as the other choices).

By default, Quicken asks you if you want to back up the data every third time you exit the program. But you can also choose to do a backup at any time. Follow these steps to use Quicken's Backup feature:

1. If you're exiting Quicken, you can start a backup by selecting Backup in the exit prompt box (see Figure 10.1).

   To start a backup without exiting, open the File menu and choose Backup.

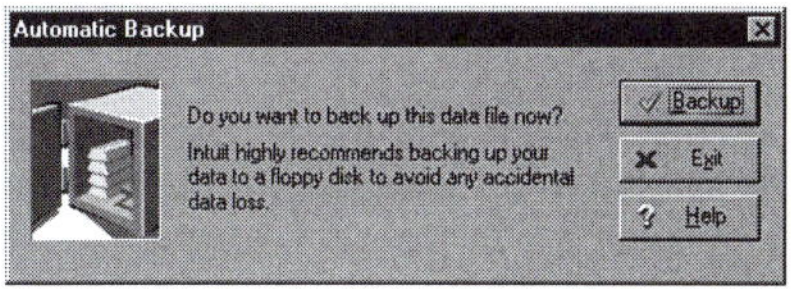

FIGURE 10.1 Quicken prompts you to back up your data before exiting the program.

2. The prompt box shown in Figure 10.2 appears and asks you to prepare a floppy disk for the backup. Put the appropriate storage disk into the drive and click Yes to continue.

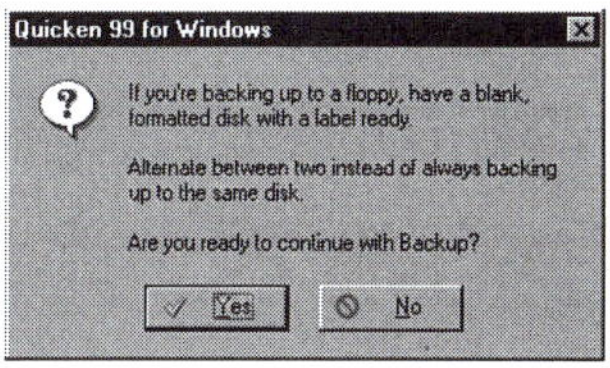

FIGURE 10.2 Quicken prompts you to prepare a floppy disk.

3. In the Select Backup Drive dialog box, shown in Figure 10.3, use the Backup Drive drop-down list to specify the floppy disk drive (or other drive) you're backing up to, and click OK. If you choose to back up to the hard disk, you are prompted for a folder name.

> **Can I Back Up Another Quicken File?** Choose the Select from List option in the Select Backup Drive dialog box if you want to back up a file other than the current Quicken file you're using.

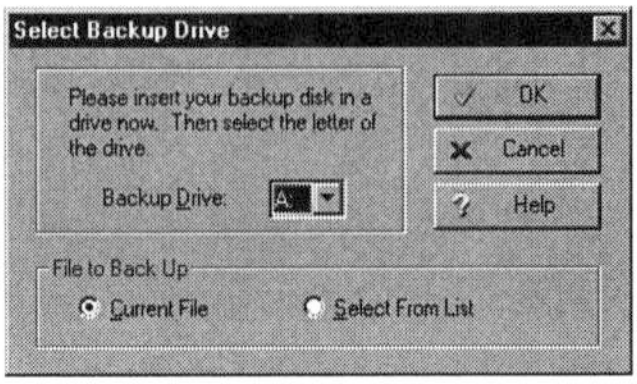

FIGURE 10.3 Choose your backup drive and click OK.

Quicken begins backing up your data in earnest. Depending on how much data you have, the procedure might take only a few seconds, or several minutes. If the backup requires more than one disk, Quicken prompts you.

4. When Quicken is finished, another prompt box appears to inform you that the backup was a success (see Figure 10.4). Click OK.

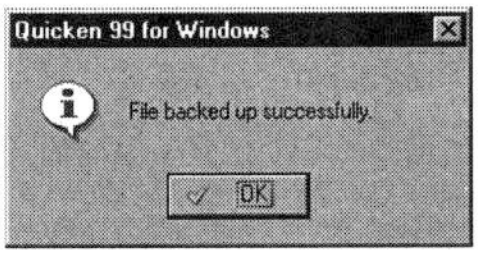

FIGURE 10.4 Quicken informs you the backup is finished.

RESTORING DATA

If something drastic does happen to your computer or Quicken data file, rest assured that restoring a backup file is simple. To reuse any backup file you created, follow these steps:

1. If you backed up your data onto a floppy disk or a zip disk, insert the disk into the appropriate drive.
2. From the Quicken program window, open the File menu and choose Restore Backup File. This opens the Select Restore Drive dialog box (see Figure 10.5).
3. Use the Restore files from Drive drop-down list to tell Quicken which drive you're restoring files from, and click OK to continue.

FIGURE 10.5 Use the Select Restore Drive dialog box to specify the disk drive.

4. Use the Restore Quicken File dialog box, shown in Figure 10.6, to specify which backup file to restore (see Figure 10.6). Click the file you want to restore and click OK.

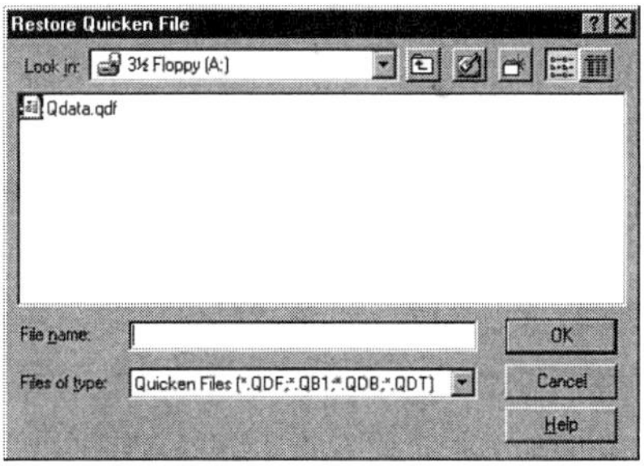

FIGURE 10.6 Select the backup file to restore.

5. Quicken restores the file to its original location. If the file is the same version as the one you're currently using, Quicken asks you if you want to overwrite the data. Select Yes to overwrite, or No to cancel.

6. After the file is restored, a prompt box appears telling you the file was successfully restored. Click OK.

In this lesson, you learned how to back up and restore your Quicken data file. In the next lesson, you learn how to work with Quicken's Financial Calendar.

LESSON 11

USING THE FINANCIAL CALENDAR

In this lesson, you learn how Quicken automatically handles transactions that occur periodically, such as monthly bills and semiannual dividend deposits.

LEARNING THE TRANSACTIONS

Generally, an account is a statement of transactions that have already occurred. In an ordinary checkbook's register, you normally would not list checks you have yet to write. What makes using Quicken different from using a checkbook is the fact that Quicken can automatically handle those bills, statements, and other events that happen regularly. You teach Quicken what those events are by way of its Financial Calendar.

Quicken maintains three types of *transactions* (see Lesson 5, "Recording Transactions") with which you need to be familiar:

- *Registered transactions.* Those posted to your Register and that have actually occurred—in other words, they are historical events.
- *Memorized transactions.* These are details of previously registered transactions, which Quicken can use automatically should the same type of transaction occur again.
- *Scheduled transactions.* These consist of transactions that Quicken posts automatically on a regular basis. (Scheduled transactions are the concern of this lesson.)

Periodic events to be recorded on your accounts are listed on the Scheduled Transaction List, shown in Figure 11.1. To open this list, select

Scheduled Transaction from the Lists menu. A tab marked Sched. Txns. shows up in the set of QuickTabs at the right. At first, the Transaction List is blank.

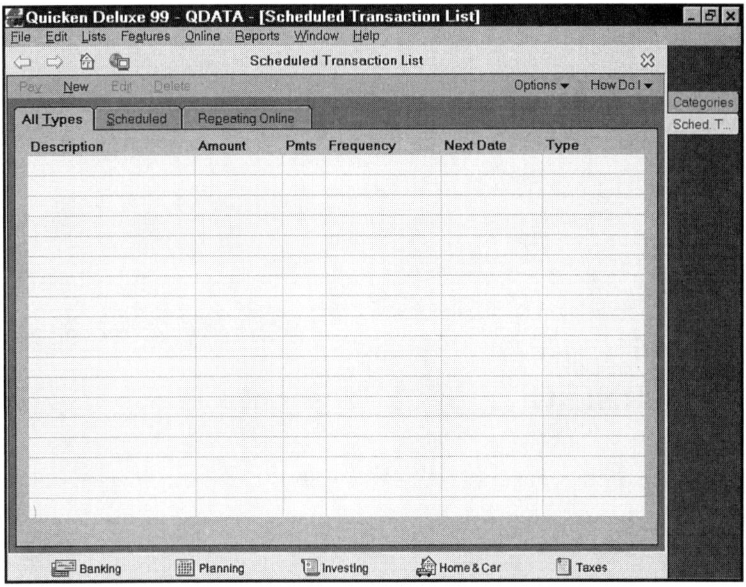

FIGURE 11.1 The Scheduled Transaction List.

SCHEDULING NEW PERIODIC TRANSACTIONS

Types of transactions you might want to schedule include any monthly bills, income payments, periodic deposits into your bank accounts, or automatic online utility payments. To schedule a new periodic transaction, do the following:

1. On the Scheduled Transaction List button bar, click New.
2. If you've set up Quicken to handle so-called *repeating online payments*, in which regular electronic transactions are handled for you automatically (see Lesson 26, "Managing Bills and Payments Online"), then the Scheduled Transaction Type dialog

box appears. Here, you have only two options: Single or Multiple Scheduled Payments (which are recorded by Quicken but that you mail yourself) or Repeating Online Payments. Choose one of these and click OK. After that, or if you don't see this dialog box, the Create Scheduled Transaction dialog box appears, as shown in Figure 11.2.

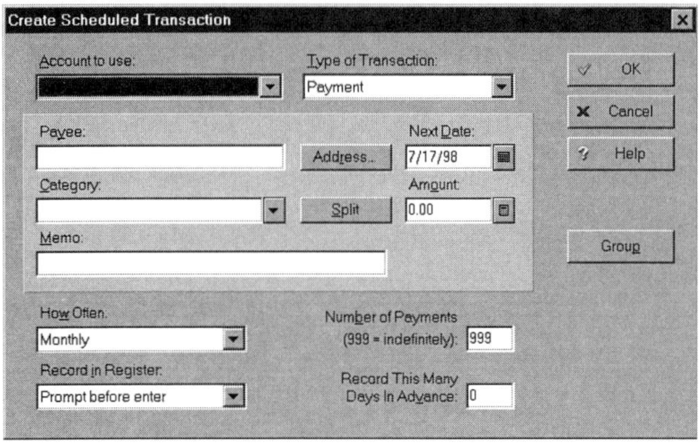

FIGURE 11.2 The Create Scheduled Transaction dialog box.

3. Choose the account to which the transaction applies, from the drop-down list box marked Account to Use.
4. Choose whether the transaction is a payment, deposit, printed check, or online payment, from the drop-down list box marked Type of Transaction.
5. Under Payee, type the recipient's name or select one from the drop-down list. Optionally, you can look up the recipient's address by clicking the Address button. If the payee you chose is the recipient for one of your loan accounts (see Lesson 16, "Managing Loans with Quicken Deluxe 99"), Quicken may bring up a dialog box asking you to confirm how much of your payment you want distributed to principal, and how much to interest. Click OK when that's done.
6. Optionally, so that Quicken can help you keep track of this type of transaction, choose a category from the Category list. This list

contains those categories that Quicken has created automatically, as well as any you might have added yourself (see Lesson 6, "Working with Categories").

7. Under Next Date, enter the next date on which this transaction is to take place. You can click the calendar button to the right of this field to bring up a monthly calendar, and choose the date from there.
8. Under Amount, enter the amount of the payment or deposit for each transaction.
9. Type a description of the transaction in the field marked Memo.
10. Choose the length of the period between these transactions from the list marked How Often. By default, Monthly is chosen.
11. By default, Quicken continues to record this transaction automatically, forever. To change this setting so that Quicken records only a finite number of transactions, type that number into the field marked Number of Payments.
12. Quicken warns you before it posts any transaction. If you don't want Quicken to tell you when it records this transaction, choose Automatically enter from the list marked Record in Register.
13. If you want this transaction entered in advance of the time it is actually to take place, enter the number of days in the field marked Record This Many Days in Advance.
14. Click OK to enter this new periodic transaction into the list. You are prompted that the periodic transaction was entered and when the first recording will start. Click OK.

Encountering a Deficit Situation If you enter a scheduled transaction — or any kind of transaction that forces you to exceed the budget Quicken helped generate for you (see Lesson 12, "Creating and Maintaining a Budget"), Quicken warns you of this excess at this point and allows you to cancel the transaction before your budget truly is blown.

To change information about a transaction already scheduled, double-click that transaction in the Scheduled Transaction List. Quicken displays the Record Scheduled Transaction dialog box, shown in Figure 11.3, which works much the same way as does the dialog box for creating new scheduled transactions.

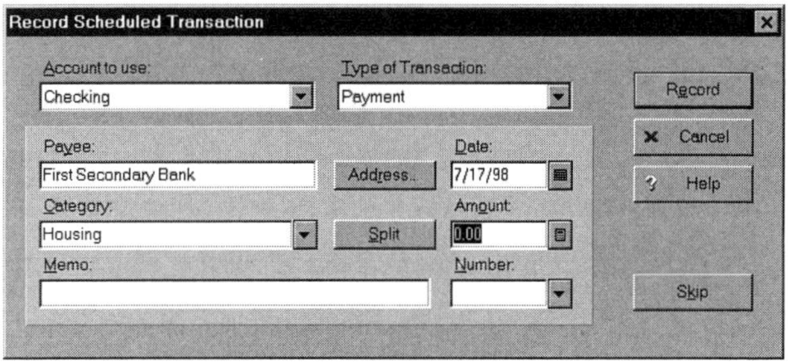

FIGURE 11.3 The Record Scheduled Transaction dialog box.

> **Scheduling vs. Memorizing** Remember that a *scheduled* transaction is different from a *memorized* transaction. In Lesson 8, "Writing Transactions," you learned that Quicken "memorizes" the details of each new transaction, in case you need to recall those details again when posting a similar transaction. The details of *scheduled* transactions, however, are not available when you post a transaction manually.

SCHEDULING GROUPS OF TRANSACTIONS

Suppose you have a situation in which, in the course of managing your account, you always post a handful of related transactions together in one clump—for instance, your home, life, and auto insurance payments, or your monthly paycheck divided among several accounts. You can have Quicken group a set of related transaction types and then have its scheduler post that group regularly as a unit rather than separately. This technique makes related transactions easier to track.

For you to group a set of transactions, all the members of your set must first be *memorized* (previously posted manually; see Lesson 8). Select Memorized Transaction from the Lists menu to see whether all your transactions to be grouped appear in that list. (The list appears as Transactions in your QuickTabs.)

Now that you've verified that the transactions you want to group are memorized, you're ready to begin. To create a new transaction group, do the following:

1. First, switch back to the Scheduled Transaction List. Then, from the Scheduled Transaction List button bar, click New. Quicken displays the Create Scheduled Transaction dialog box.
2. Click Group. Quicken displays the Create Transaction Group dialog box (shown in Figure 11.4).

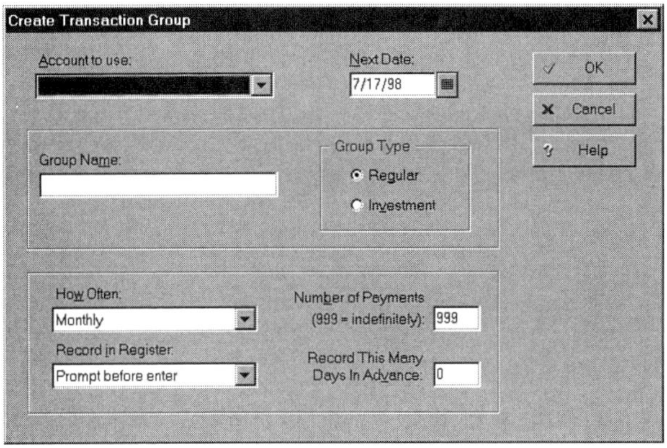

FIGURE 11.4 The Create Transaction Group dialog box.

3. From the Account to Use list box, choose the account to which the transaction applies.
4. Enter a name for the group in the Group Name text box.
5. Under Next Date, enter the next day on the calendar on which this category of transaction is to take place.
6. Choose the length of the period between these transactions from the list marked How Often. By default, Monthly is chosen.

7. By default, Quicken continues to record this transaction periodically for as long as it's installed on your computer. To change this so that Quicken records only a finite number of periods, type that number into the field marked Number of Payments.

8. By default, Quicken prompts you before posting this transaction group. If you don't want this interruption, choose Automatically enter from the list marked Record in Register.

9. An Investment group is one that pertains to your investments; all other groups are considered Regular. In the Group Type frame, choose Regular or Investment.

10. Under Record This Many Days In Advance, enter the number of days in advance you want this transaction recorded.

11. Click OK. Quicken displays a list of transactions memorized thus far, as shown in Figure 11.5. You're now ready to select the transactions you want in this new group.

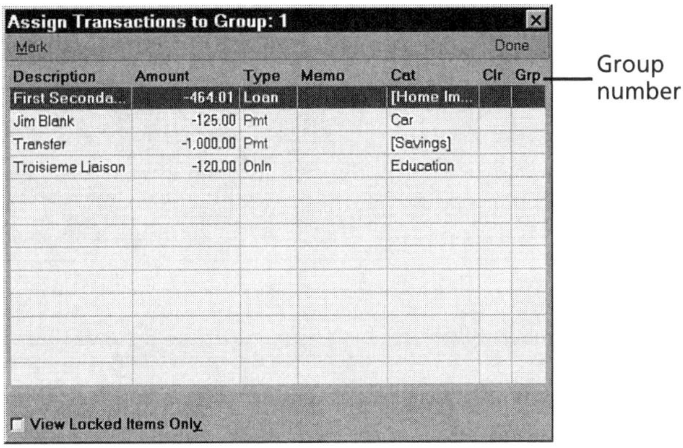

FIGURE 11.5 Choose any of these memorized transactions for the group.

12. Choose a transaction you want to add to the group, and then click Mark. Quicken adds the group number to the Grp (group) column in the list. Repeat this step for as many transactions as you are adding to the group.

13. Click Done. The group is recorded in the Scheduled Transaction List, with the chosen transactions associated with it.

CONTROLLING THE CALENDAR DIRECTLY

One of Quicken's most useful features is tucked away in a far-off menu selection. It is the Financial Calendar, and it shows you your account history on a calendar rather than the standard, sometimes-confusing register format. To see this calendar, open the Features menu, select Reminders, and select Financial Calendar. A sample month is shown in Figure 11.6.

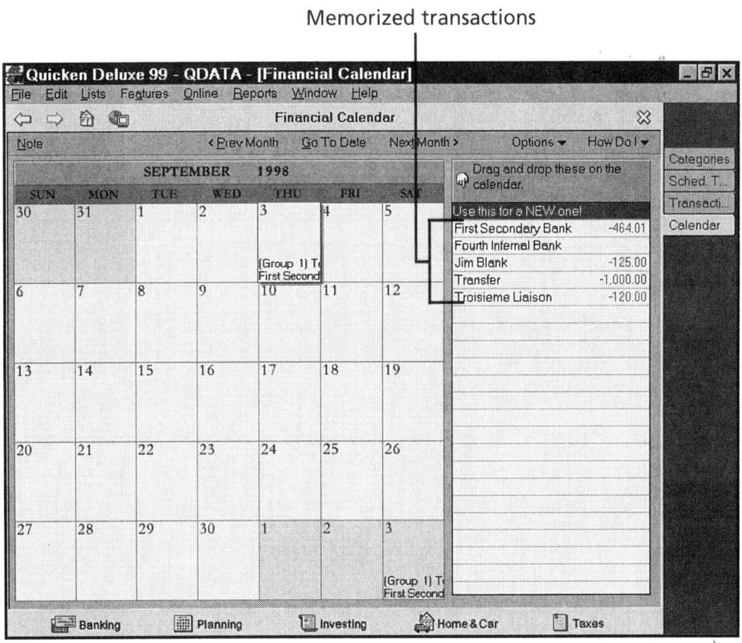

FIGURE 11.6 Quicken's Financial Calendar.

Rather than manage all your transactions from a list or set of lists, you can post them and view them using the Financial Calendar:

- To see the transactions posted for any one day—past, present, or future—double-click that day. Quicken displays the short transaction list shown in Figure 11.7. From here, you can add, edit, or delete a transaction, or change the scheduling for a future payment to the present time by clicking Pay Now.

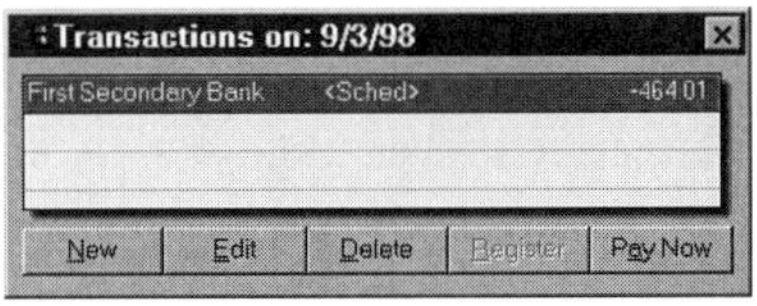

FIGURE 11.7 A short transaction list from the Calendar.

- To browse through the months, click Prev Month or Next Month. Or click Go To Date to enter a specific date to be shown in the Calendar.
- Memorized transactions are shown in the list to the right of the calendar. To post one of these transactions, click and drag it from the list to the day in which it is to be officially posted, and then release the mouse button. The New Transaction dialog provides an opportunity to make any needed changes; if no changes are necessary, you can just click OK. (If you dragged the transaction into the wrong date, just click Cancel and start over.)
- To add a note to yourself, right-click the day, and from the pop-up menu, select Note. Type your note and click Save. A note icon appears in the upper-right corner of the day in the Calendar. To read the note, click this icon.

In this lesson, you learned how to add transactions that take place automatically using a schedule or calendar. In the next lesson, you see how to set up a budget for future expenditures.

LESSON 12

CREATING AND MAINTAINING A BUDGET

In this lesson, you learn how Quicken utilizes the information you've already entered into your accounts to set up a formal budget, which helps you reduce and restrict future expenditures.

LEARNING THE FOUR MAIN CATEGORY GROUPS

The entire purpose of a budget is to help you not to spend more money than you've allocated for any given period. Logic tells you it isn't possible to spend more money than is available; but in practice, well… A Quicken budget can help you limit yourself to spending only what you know you can.

A Quicken Budget sheet, shown in Figure 12.1, is divided into columns, each of which represents a spending period.

To bring up this sheet for the first time, open the Features menu, select Planning, and select Budgets. A dialog box is displayed, indicating what you are about to do and giving you a few pointers. Click OK. You won't see this dialog box the next time.

In the Budget sheet, the divisions of each column, shown in rows, represent how moneys are distributed among the various Quicken transaction categories. *Category groups* encompass the various transaction categories maintained by Quicken (covered in Lesson 6, "Working with Categories"). The following are the meanings of Quicken's four main category groups:

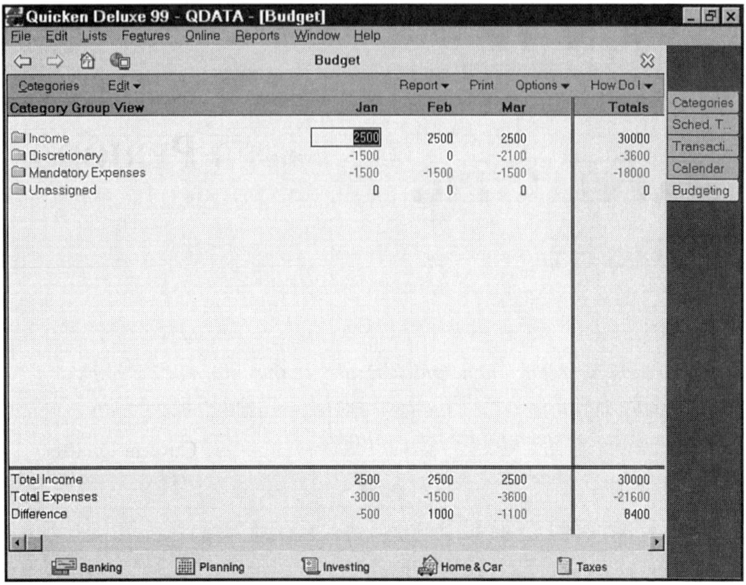

FIGURE 12.1 Quicken's budgetary worksheet.

- *Income* (green). Represents those transactions whose categories are not expenses—for example, your salary, dividends from stock, and interest from a bank account.
- *Discretionary* (red). Those expenses over which you have some nature of control. In other words, you can opt not to incur them—for example, expenses for clothing, restaurants, movie tickets, and charitable donations.
- *Mandatory Expenses* (red). Those over which you do not have control, meaning that you must pay them—for example, utilities, mortgage payments, insurance premiums, and license taxes.
- *Unassigned* (red). Those categories (either income or expenses) you do not want to include under any of the other category groups. You will probably not use this category group yourself, because you don't exactly want to be spending money on things not in your budget. However, if you use AutoCreate to create your budget (as explained later in this lesson), an amount might

appear here (created from an estimate of repeated transactions that have not been assigned a category).

CHANGING THE BUDGETING PERIODS

By default, the Quicken Budget sheet is set for monthly accounting periods. To change this period, do the following:

1. On the button bar, click Options.
2. To change the budgeting period from monthly to quarterly, select Display Quarters.
3. To set up the Budget sheet to account for *one period* rather than a series, select Display Current Month, Display Current Quarter, or Display Current Year.

SUBDIVIDING THE BUDGET INTO CATEGORIES

When you enter a transaction, as you learned in Lesson 6, recording the category to which the transaction belongs helps you keep track of related transactions later. At first, the budget lists only the main category *groups*. You can select which subcategories you want listed in your budget by following these steps:

> **Total Control** Even if you plan to use AutoCreate to create your budget, you might want to control which categories you budget for. Following these steps allows you to do just that.

1. On the button bar, click Categories. Quicken displays the Select Categories to Include dialog box, shown in Figure 12.2.
2. The list shows all currently recognized categories and subcategories for income (the type shown in green) and expenses (in red), as well as bank transactions (in blue). Click once on each category you want the Budget sheet to explicitly account for.

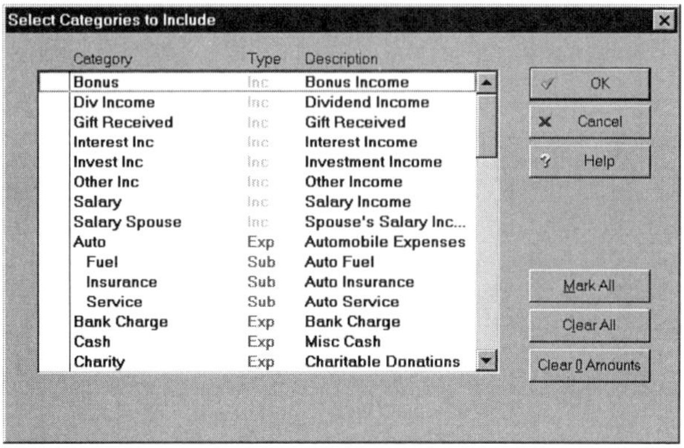

FIGURE 12.2 The Select Categories to Include dialog box.

3. Click OK. Quicken automatically shows categories under the budget division to which they belong.

Category groups that contain explicit categories now are marked in the list with a folder icon. As in Windows Explorer, you can expand or collapse the list of categories by clicking this icon.

REASSIGNING CATEGORICAL DIVISIONS

If you've created any categories of your own, then at that time you told Quicken whether the category represented an income, a mandatory expense, or a discretionary expense. However, Quicken's understanding of the groups to which its own categories belong is derived from common accounting situations. Your own situation might be uncommon, in which case, if you're using any of Quicken's built-in categories, you might need to inform Quicken that, for instance, one category should not be designated Discretionary but instead should be Mandatory. To change the groups to which categories belong, do the following:

1. On the button bar, click Options, followed by Category Groups. Quicken displays the Assign Category Groups dialog box, shown in Figure 12.3.

2. The list at left shows all currently recognized categories, next to the groups to which they belong. At right, another list shows the currently recognized category groups. To assign or reassign a

category to a group, first choose the group from the right list, and then choose the category from the left list (you can choose more than one). Then click Assign Category to Group.

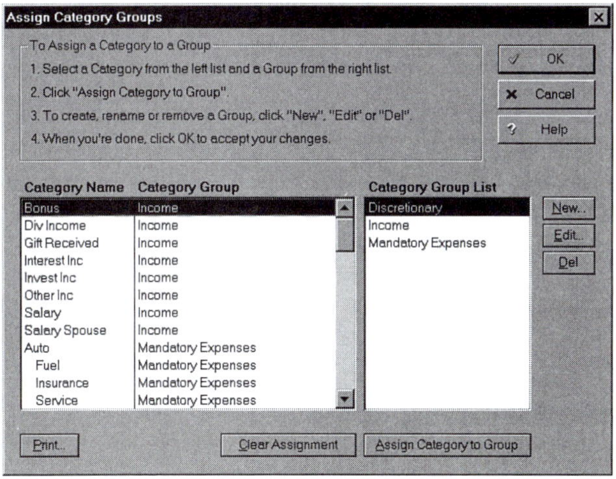

FIGURE 12.3 The Assign Category Groups dialog box.

3. To remove a category assignment, choose the category from the left list, and then click Clear Assignment. The category becomes unassigned.
4. To add a group, click New. In the Create Category Group dialog box that follows, enter a new group name and click OK. The new group is entered into the Category Group List.
5. When you have finished making changes, click OK to finalize them.

> **Don't Mix Your Sources!** You should not assign categories representing *income* plus categories representing *expenses* to any single category group. Quicken treats the group as either an income or an expense group depending on the first category enrolled into it. Besides, such a mixed grouping doesn't make sense.

ENTERING BUDGET VALUES

When the Budget sheet is first displayed, all its budgeted amounts are set to zero. These amounts are supposed to be discretionary—which means that Quicken does not lift them from existing recorded transactions. Instead, they're set by you, so it's up to you to enter real values in place of the zeroes. If you want to have Quicken create a budget based on past transactions and their amounts, see the section "Basing a New Budget on Existing Transactions," later in this lesson.

> **Know Your Income** In the creation of your budget, Quicken assumes either that you have a fixed income or that you know, with a relative degree of certainty, how much income you expect to receive, and when.

You can manipulate the values in the Budget sheet in the following ways:

- To enter a value into the cell, click once on the cell. The cursor blinks at that location, and the text within the cell (normally just 0) is highlighted. Anything you type now overwrites the contents. When the value you've entered is correct, press Enter. The cursor moves to the next cell to the right, or down to the first cell of the next row if it is already at the end of a row.

  Note that when you enter an amount into an expense category or a category group, Quicken rewrites that amount as a *debit*, in red prefixed with a negative sign (–). This is not an error; this is merely to contrast incoming from outgoing amounts.

- To fill all the cells in a row with the same value, type the value and press Enter. Then right-click the value. From the pop-up menu, select Fill Row Right, and click Yes in the dialog box.

- To have Quicken account for a category *biweekly* (every two weeks) rather than the period currently used by the Budget sheet, right-click a value in the *row* where the biweekly period applies, and then from the pop-up menu, select 2-Week. Quicken brings up the Set Up Two-Week Budget dialog box, shown in Figure 12.4. Enter a biweekly amount into the field marked Amount, and then in the field marked Every Two Weeks Starting enter a date from which Quicken is to begin counting two-week periods. After you click OK, you won't see these two-week periods in the Budget sheet, though the figures shown for the chosen category are adjusted to reflect biweekly changes.

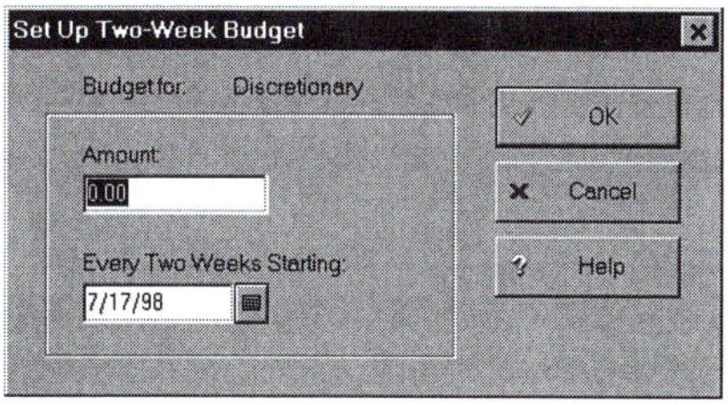

FIGURE 12.4 The Set Up Two-Week Budget dialog box.

Don't Just Jump Right In! When you enter a budget value for a category *group* (not a category unto itself) whose folder icon appears closed in the Budget sheet, the difference between the value already attributed to that group and the value you entered is applied to a separately created category called Other.

For example, if Income reads 205 and you edit it to read 200, then when you expand the Income group to display its included categories, the values for all the categories remain as they were, but a new entry appears under the Other category, reading -5. So when you're changing the budgeted value for a category group such as Income that includes subcategories, change the value of one of its subcategories rather than the total for the group.

BASING A NEW BUDGET ON EXISTING TRANSACTIONS

You can save yourself a lot of time and effort by having Quicken create a template for your budget, if you will, based on historical transactions you've already entered into Quicken. The program can total your past transactions and present a budget based on those figures. You can then modify these numbers to reflect the type of money-management adjustments you want to make for yourself in the future. To have Quicken create this budget template, do the following:

1. On the button bar, click Edit, followed by Autocreate. Quicken displays the Automatically Create Budget dialog box (shown in Figure 12.5).

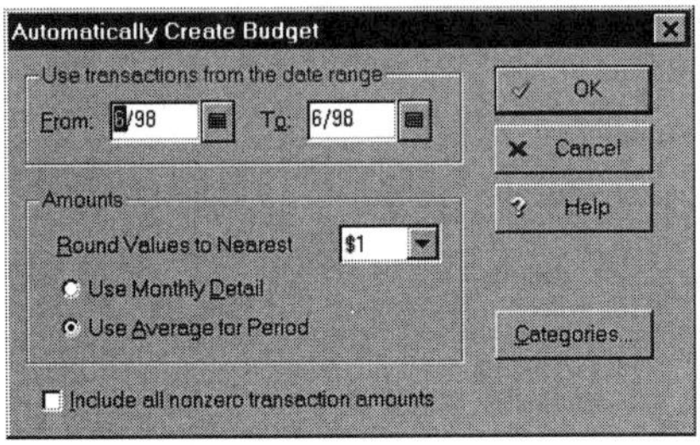

FIGURE 12.5 The Automatically Create Budget dialog box.

2. In the upper frame of the dialog box, enter the beginning and ending dates of the range of transactions on which you want your new budget to be based.
3. To have Quicken base the amounts for each budget period on an average of the amounts for all the periods in the given range, leave the option set for Use Average for Period. Otherwise, to have Quicken base your budget on precisely the numbers as they appear in your register, select the option marked Use Monthly Detail.
4. By default, Quicken rounds its budget amounts to the nearest dollar. To have Quicken round those amounts to a higher denomination, choose that denomination from the list marked Round Values to Nearest.
5. Click OK. Quicken takes a moment to project a budget for you. Feel free to change the budget in any way you choose. It's yours!

In this lesson, you learned how to enter a formalized budget into Quicken. In the next lesson, you learn how to create detailed, automated reports, including a finalized budget report.

LESSON 13

WORKING WITH REPORTS AND GRAPHS

In this lesson, you learn how to create formal reports and detailed graphs with your Quicken data.

COMMON TYPES OF QUICKEN REPORTS

Graphs and reports are the payoff that comes from using Quicken. After you've input all your important data and checked it for correctness, generating a very telling report or graph is usually a one-step process. Because Quicken isn't really a graphics generation program, your objective with reports and graphs isn't to design the appearance of your report; instead, the point is for Quicken to provide you with its perspective of what constitutes proper design.

Quicken 99 Deluxe Edition supports 29 types of preformatted reports, all of which are described under Report Types in Quicken Help. The following descriptions of some of these types might be of use to you:

- *Cash Flow Report* (Reports, Planning, Cash Flow). Details all incoming and outgoing moneys for any given set of transaction categories, for any given time period. This is different from a balance sheet, which shows current assets and liabilities.

- *Itemized Categories Report* (Reports, Planning, Itemized Categories). Details all transactions that have taken place for any given set of transaction categories, for any given period, organized by category.

- *Tax Summary Report* (Reports, Taxes, Tax Summary). Lists all transactions over a given period for all categories in which tax plays a role.
- *Net Worth Report* (Reports, Planning, Net Worth). Works very much like a balance sheet, showing a status report of your assets based on your current bank account and investment values, versus your liabilities based on your outstanding loans, credit debts, and debts to other institutions.
- *Tax Schedule Report* (Reports, Taxes, Tax Schedule). Lists information that can be copied directly to your IRS tax forms, such as deductible items for Schedule C, and charitable donations for Schedule A.
- *Missing Checks Report* (Reports, Banking, Missing Checks). Shows listings for checks posted to your register that have not yet been accounted for on your bank statement, along with checks that cannot be reconciled because they were posted with the same check number.
- *Comparison Report* (Reports, Planning, Comparison). A cash-flow report that compares incoming and outgoing moneys for two different time periods and yields the differences between the two periods.

GENERATING A REPORT

Quicken provides many types of reports you can produce—29 of them, in fact. Here, I show you how to create the most common type of report, called the Accounts Balances report. However, after creating this report, feel free to follow these same general steps to create any other report you want.

Now, on to our example—feel free to follow along! To bring up the Account Balances report, do the following:

1. From the Reports menu, select Banking, followed by Account Balances. Quicken displays the Create Report screen, shown in Figure 13.1.

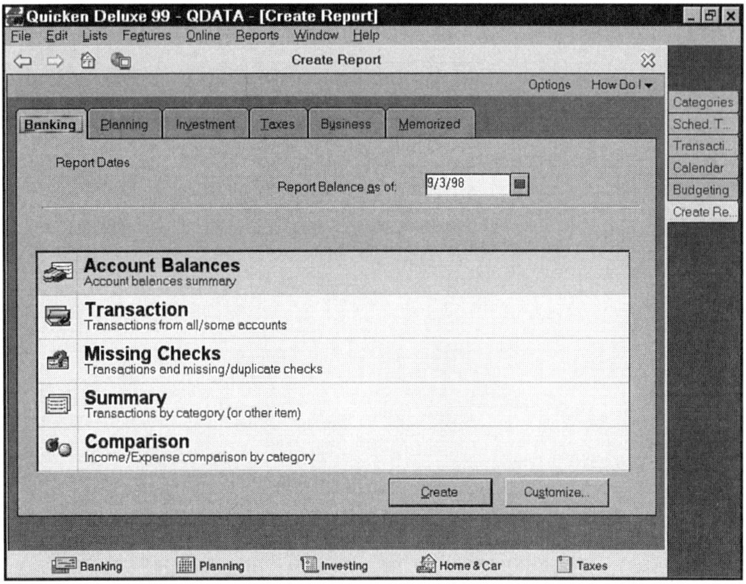

FIGURE 13.1 The Create Report screen.

2. Here you can change your mind as to the category and name of report you want Quicken to show. The upper portion of the dialog box shows parameters particular to the report you've chosen. You can leave these as they are or customize them now. (You can also change these options later, after the report is generated.)

3. With the report you've selected from the main menu bar already chosen (in this case, Account Balances), click Create to bring up the Account Balances report.

As shown in Figure 13.2, an Account Balances Report is laid out like a formal balance sheet. It's divided into two halves, the upper half listing the value of your assets, and the lower half listing your liabilities. On a business's balance sheet, normally, the total of the two must equal zero or the accounts are wrong. But this isn't a business's balance sheet; instead, it simply weighs what you *have* against what you *owe*. The imbalance is not an indication that something's wrong with Quicken, or even that anything is necessarily wrong at all.

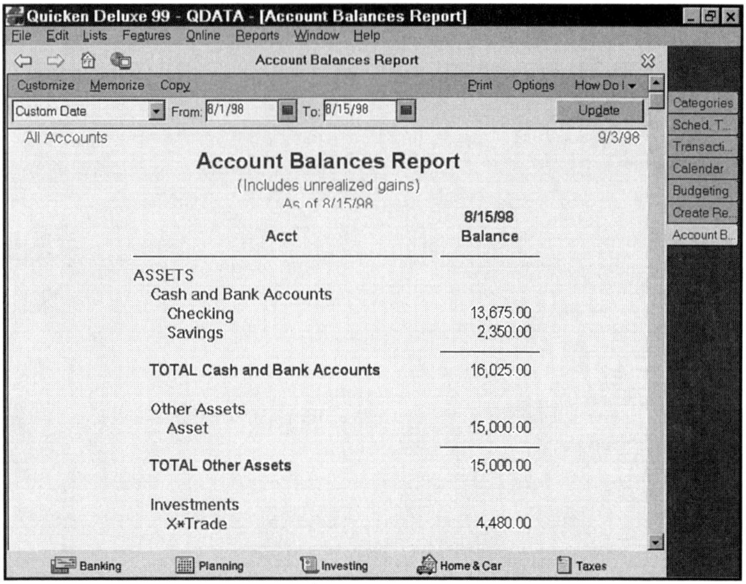

FIGURE 13.2 An Account Balances Report weighs what you have against what you owe.

CHANGING A REPORT'S PARAMETERS

To alter or tailor the parameters of your report, do the following:

1. To have the report cover a general range of time, such as Year to Date, Last Year, or Current Year, choose that time period from the leftmost drop-down list. For our example, try choosing Last Month from the list.

2. To change the specific range of time that the report covers, enter the start and end dates in the fields marked From and To. Because you've already selected Last Month, you don't need to change the dates here, although you can if you want. For example, to show only half the month, you could change the To box to the 15th.

3. After you make the changes you want, click the Update button.

For More Information Many of the items listed in a Quicken report are taken from entries in a register or an account. You'll notice that your mouse pointer becomes a magnifying glass with a **Z** inside it whenever an item in a report is linked to a register or an account entry. Unfortunately, the Account Balances report does not feature any lines like this, but if you create a Transaction report, for example, then when you bring your mouse pointer over most of the line items, you see the magnifying glass.

Double-clicking one of these items too often displays the QuickZoom Report window with the detailed breakdown of that line item. Double-click the item again, and you see the actual register or account entry. (If the item represents only a single entry in the register, you usually skip the QuickZoom window altogether.) Return to the original report window by clicking its tab on the right.

Budget Reports In Lesson 12, "Creating and Maintaining a Budget," you saw how to generate a budget for yourself by entering data into a Budget sheet. The payoff from all that hard work comes from Quicken's Budget Reports, which you can generate quite easily. The standard Budget report (Reports, Planning, Budget) compares the total income and expenditures for the year against the budgeted income and expenditures, and yields the difference between the two. The Monthly Budget report (Reports, Planning, Monthly Budget) displays the same information broken down month by month.

PRINTING A REPORT

To print the currently visible report, do the following:

1. On the button bar, click Print. Quicken displays the Print dialog box (shown in Figure 13.3).

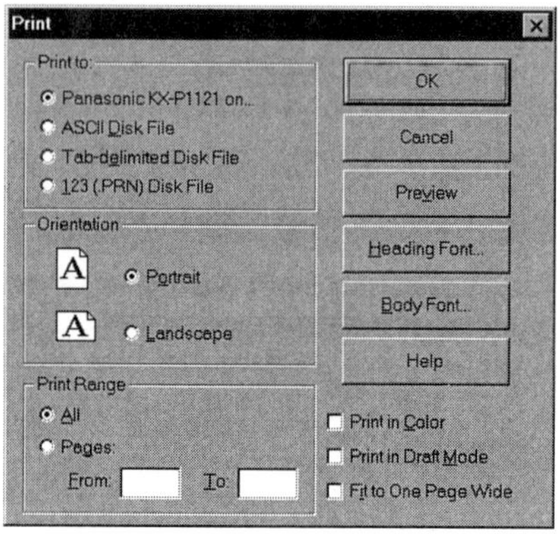

FIGURE 13.3 Quicken's version of the Print dialog box.

2. To change the orientation of the page, set the option marked Landscape.
3. To change Quicken's choice of fonts for the report heading or textual body, click Heading Font or Body Font, and choose a new font from the Font dialog box that appears.
4. To see the page exactly as it will be printed, click Preview.
5. From the Print Preview window, click Print to begin the print process.

MEMORIZING REPORTS

In Quicken, a *memorized report* is one whose parameters have been stored for future recall so that you don't have to re-create the same report with the same features each time. A memorized report might include a column or set of columns for This Month, but for a memorized report that is recalled *next* month, you can have Quicken set This Month to the current month. So it isn't necessarily the facts and figures that you're having Quicken memorize; Quicken doesn't take a snapshot of the report unless that's specifically what you request it to do.

Take, for instance, the Account Balances report described earlier. You can set up such a report to display, month-by-month, your total balances from the past 12 months up to now, or perhaps for the first six months of last year. After you've set up those reports just the way you want them, you can have Quicken memorize them so that you don't have to set them up again. But these two reports are different from one another: the first report deals with a relative time period (a 12-month period relative to now), and the second deals with a specific time period (the first 6 months of 1998). Quicken can memorize both, as long as you tell it whether to memorize them for a relative time period or a specific one.

You can, for example, memorize a customized report that changes when the data you enter into the register changes. For instance, a Missing Checks report (Reports, Banking, Missing Checks) shows a list of all transactions on the Checking register that have yet to be listed in a formal bank statement, or that appear not to have cleared. You can have Quicken memorize a report for a certain six-month period. After a check has cleared, however, it is no longer shown even in the memorized report, because what is memorized is not the data itself but the way the report gathers that data.

To have Quicken memorize a report, do the following:

1. After you have your report exactly the way you want it to appear in the future (except for the data, of course), on the button bar, click Memorize. Quicken displays the Memorize Report dialog box (shown in Figure 13.4).

2. Under Title, give the report a name you'll remember. You'll see this name again when you recall the memorized report.

3. Under Report Dates, choose how you want Quicken to memorize the dates used in this report. To have the dates reflect a generally specified period of time, such as This Month (which is always current) or Year to Date (assuming that "to Date" means "up to today"), set the option for Named Range.

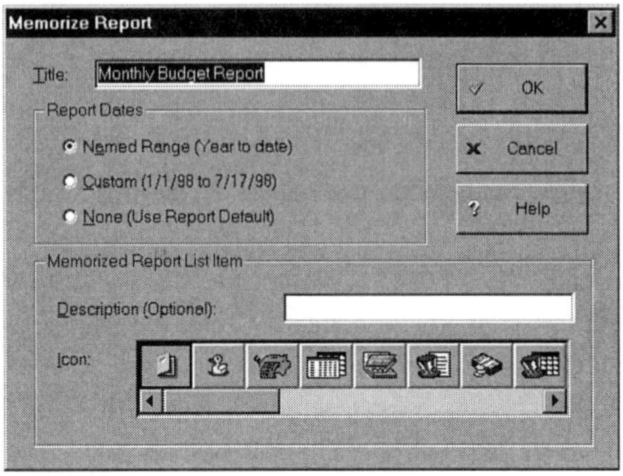

FIGURE 13.4 The Memorize Report dialog box.

4. To have Quicken memorize the dates specifically used for this report and recall those dates later regardless of how much time has passed, set the option for Custom. Otherwise, to simply have Quicken remember whatever you told it when you set the report's options in the Create Report screen or in the report's own toolbar, set the option for None.

5. Optionally, you can enter a description of the report (for when memorized reports come up in a detailed list) in the field marked Description. Also, you can give the report its own commemorative icon by choosing that icon from the scrollable list.

6. Click OK. Quicken now memorizes your report for later recall.

The whole point of memorizing a report is in being able to recall it later. To recall a memorized report, do the following:

1. From the Reports menu, select Memorized Reports. (This selection is visible only if one or more reports have been memorized.)

Further Customization Other options pertaining to customizing the appearance and content of a report—especially if you intend to have Quicken memorize it—are available from the Report's button bar. Simply click Customize.

2. From the Create Report screen, enter any parameters necessary for this report. These changes are in effect only for the report you see onscreen; they do not change the memorized report.
3. Click Create. The memorized report is displayed.

EASYANSWER REPORTS

In addition to Quicken's standard array of 29 complex reports, Intuit has added a set of simple statements that answer fundamental questions about your financial status. These so-called *EasyAnswer Reports* are designed to be called up with a few simple steps, outlined here:

1. From the Reports menu, select EasyAnswer Reports. Quicken displays the EasyAnswer Reports & Graphs dialog box, shown in Figure 13.5.

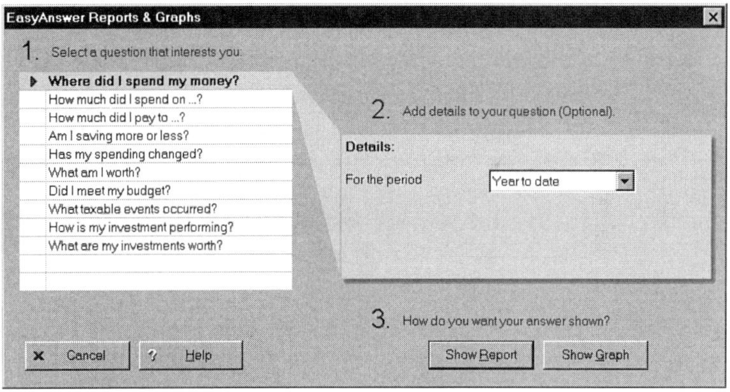

FIGURE 13.5 The EasyAnswer Reports & Graphs dialog box.

2. The list under numeral **1** shows questions that these reports are designed to answer. Choose a question from this list.
3. Numeral **2** shows parameters that are specific to the question you chose; select the options you want.
4. To bring up a textual report, click Show Report. Quicken displays the report that responds to your chosen question. Otherwise, to bring up a detailed, more-colorful graph, click Show Graph.

TYPES OF QUICKEN GRAPHS

Quicken comes complete with five types of useful graphs, the three most common of which are described here:

- *Income and Expense Graph.* A two-part contraption that features a bar chart that tracks your sources of income versus your major expenses categorically, plus a pie chart that divides the entirety of your expenses into those categories that absorb your income.
- *Budget Variance Graph.* Depicts the major categories of your expenditures for a given period versus the amount you originally budgeted for those categories.
- *Net Worth Graph.* A combination line/bar chart that shows the cumulative total values of your accounts and assets over time.

Graphs in Quicken Centers When you start Quicken each time, it takes you to the Quicken Home Page, which is composed of content gathered from your accounts and register, your Quicken CD-ROM, and Intuit's Web site. The Quicken Home Page is arranged like a series of articles in a newspaper, in which Quicken is the self-appointed editor-in-chief. You'll notice from time to time that Quicken informs you of certain aspects of your financial situation, by way of graphs and reports built directly into the page. You didn't put these items there; Quicken simply "thought" you might be interested in them. You learn more about this topic and other Quicken Financial Centers in the next lesson.

PROJECTING GRAPHS

The Quicken series of graphs attempts to show in pictures what is often difficult to convey with columns full of numbers. You should consider Quicken's graphs to be always available; simply call them up with a menu command. Figure 13.6 shows the Net Worth graph, which plots your assets (above the zero line) versus your liabilities (below the zero line) on a month-to-month scale.

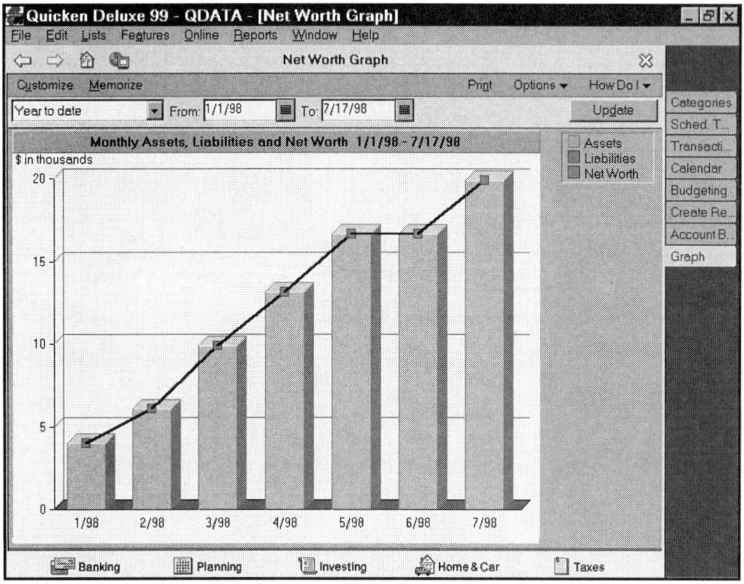

FIGURE 13.6 A line graph charting one's net worth over time.

To pull up a graph, do the following:

1. From the Reports menu, select Graphs and then select the name of the graph you want to see. Quicken displays the Create Graph dialog box highlighting the one you selected, similar to that shown in Figure 13.7.
2. Here you have an opportunity to change your mind about which kind of graph you want. Your choices regarding the time period that the graph is to cover are presented in the top frame of this dialog box. (These same choices are also available through the graph's button bar, so you can change the graph at any time.)
3. Click Create. Quicken displays the chosen graph.

> **Manual Updates** Whenever you make any changes to the parameters of a graph using the button bar, be sure to click the Update button to see the results of your changes.

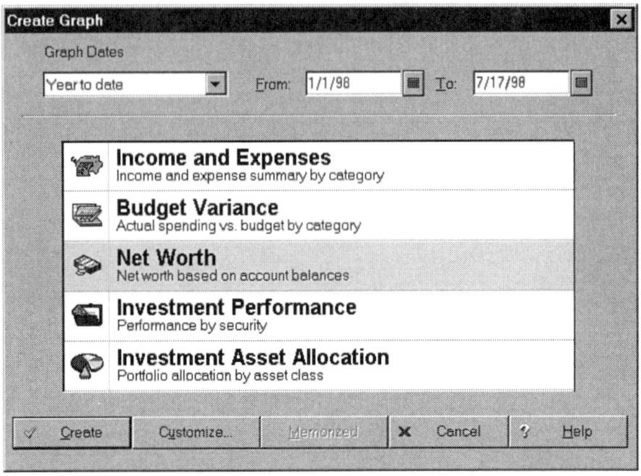

FIGURE 13.7 The Create Graph dialog box.

MEMORIZING A GRAPH

Changing the parameters for a graph is exactly the same process as it is for a report. For example, you might customize the Net Worth graph to have it show just May, June, July, and August, as I did in Figure 13.6. To do that, simply open the From box and select May 1, and then open the To box and select August 31. Then click Update.

After you have a graph that is useful to you in your everyday work, you can have Quicken memorize that graph. For example, you might have Quicken memorize your May-to-August Net Worth graph. Again, this process is similar to the way Quicken memorizes a report.

To memorize a graph, do the following:

1. On the button bar, click Memorize. The Memorize Graph dialog box appears.
2. Enter a name you'll remember later in the field marked Graph Name.
3. Click OK.

To have Quicken recall a memorized graph, do the following:

1. From the Reports menu, select Graphs and then select Memorized Graphs. Quicken displays the Memorized Graphs sheet.
2. Double-click the name of the graph you want to see. Quicken displays the Recall Memorized Graph dialog box.
3. Unless you want to make any changes to the parameters of the memorized graph now, just click OK. Quicken displays the graph you chose.

In this lesson, you learned how Quicken provides you with meaningful information by way of reports and graphs. In the next lesson, you see how another feature called Financial Centers gives you even more graphical information, in a manner that is more pointed, and that often really hits home.

Lesson 14

Using Quicken Deluxe 99's Financial Centers

In this lesson, you learn how Quicken can be used to arrange financial information in more of a magazine or newspaper format that you can utilize more readily.

The Quicken Home Page

If you're smart (and you must be, because you're reading this book), you probably also read a financial or trade periodical such as *BusinessWeek*, *Fortune*, or *Information Week*. You know full well the value of being able to find an interesting or even a crucial piece of information by looking through a well-laid-out summary page.

The programmers at Intuit took note of this situation and have responded by integrating a feature called *Financial Centers* into Quicken 99. Replacements for an earlier feature called Snapshots, Financial Centers contain graphical and summary information that has been gleaned from your accounts and register, and they mix that with information from the CD-ROM and from Intuit's World Wide Web site.

One of the first Financial Centers you encounter is the Quicken Home Page, which you see each time you start Quicken. Designed much like a Web page, it features "columns," in a sense, that contain useful and pertinent financial information. Figure 14.1 shows how the Quicken Home Page might appear.

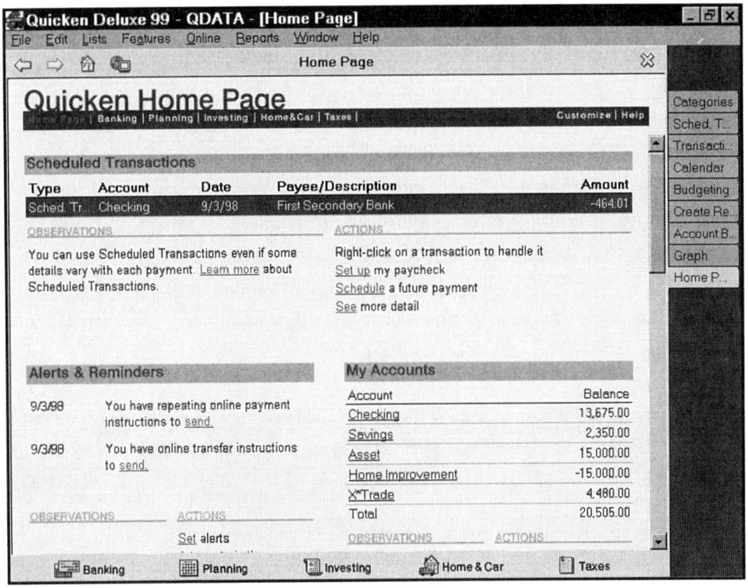

FIGURE 14.1 The Quicken Home Page.

NAVIGATING A FINANCIAL CENTER

If you're familiar with a Web browser, you understand the concept of the *hyperlink*. Certain underscored passages of text, more brightly colored than the rest, act like buttons. When you click one of these passages, Quicken takes you to another page or feature of the program.

For example, under My Accounts on the Quicken Home Page, you might find a bullet point that reads Reconcile an account. Clicking the underlined portion has the same effect as choosing Banking, Reconcile from the Features menu. So here, the Quicken Home Page is steering you toward a feature of the program you might not have seen before.

Elsewhere, under Credit Card Analysis, you find a link marked Plan to reduce my debt. When you click the word Plan, Quicken takes you to the Debt Reduction screen. If you've already made a debt reduction plan (see Lesson 15, "Using the Debt Reduction Planner"), you see Quicken's ongoing progress graph; otherwise, Quicken brings up the wizard that leads you in the process of generating your own debt reduction plan.

In other Financial Center pages, such as the Tax Center page (which you can get to through the Features, Centers, Tax Center command), you might see the first column of an article written by an accredited source on behalf of Intuit. It's under the heading of Did You Know? and you might have to scroll to the bottom of the page to see it. Figure 14.2 shows an example from Quicken's Tax Center. The source of this article is Intuit's Web site, but you don't have to be online to see this headline. Intuit feeds it, if you will, to your copy of Quicken each time you use Quicken to log on (see Lesson 23, "Using Quicken Deluxe 99 on the Internet"). So your Tax Center probably won't show *this* particular article, but it might show one like it, and perhaps in the same place.

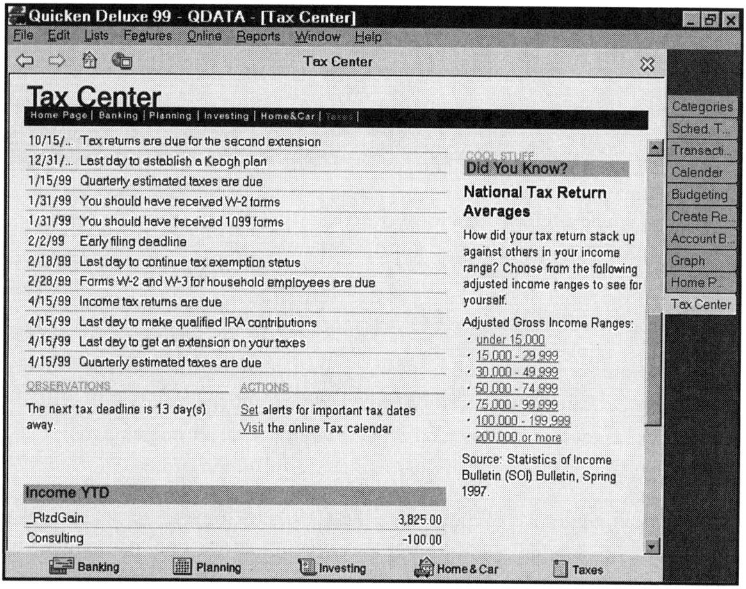

FIGURE 14.2 An informative article found on the Tax Center page.

If you have already logged on to the Internet, when you click the link that, in this example, is marked Common Charity Tax Questions, Quicken again displays the Internet screen and takes you to the full text of the article. If you have yet to log on, you see a dialog box letting you know that Quicken is about to connect to the Internet. You can choose to continue with the connection or Cancel. Quicken handles the business of downloading the article for you, just as a Web browser does.

> **There's Some Place Like Home** Intuit has a special Web site just for Quicken users, called Quicken.com. You learn much more about it in the latter part of this book. Like other Web sites, Quicken.com has a home page, but it is not the same as the so-called Quicken Home Page with which much of this lesson is concerned.

CUSTOMIZING THE QUICKEN HOME PAGE

When you first see the Quicken Home Page, some of the articles shown might not pertain to you. To substitute these articles for some whose subjects are more pertinent to you, do the following:

1. From the Quicken Home Page, from the box of choices in the banner along the top, click Customize, and from the pop-up menu, select Customize this view. Quicken displays the Customize View dialog box (shown in Figure 14.3).

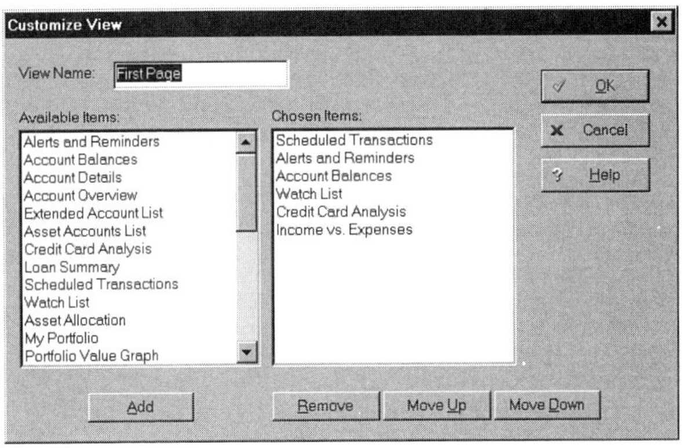

FIGURE 14.3 The Customize View dialog box.

2. The list marked Available Items shows all articles that Quicken is capable of typesetting within the Quicken Home Page. To the

right of that, the list marked Chosen Items shows those items that the Quicken Home Page is currently displaying. To choose new items, select the ones you want from the Available Items list and then click Add. To select more than one item from the Available Items list, hold down the Ctrl key and choose the items you want to add.

3. To remove unnecessary or unwanted items from the Quicken Home Page, choose those items from the Chosen Items list and then click Remove.
4. The items in the right list are displayed in the general order in which they will appear in the Quicken Home Page. To move an article more toward the front, choose that article and then click Move Up. Likewise, to move an item lower in the list, choose the article and click Move Down.
5. Click OK to finalize your choices.

> **You CAN Take It With You** To print a copy of any Financial Center page, right-click any blank area of that page, and from the pop-up menu, select Print this view.

OTHER FINANCIAL CENTERS

Quicken provides five other Financial Center pages for Banking, Planning, Investing, Home & Car, and Tax. You can access all these pages by selecting Centers from the Features menu, and selecting the page name from the submenu.

As you continue to use Quicken, some of the articles featured will be replaced with new and up-to-date articles, *as long as* you continue to use Intuit's Web site through Quicken's Internet screen. So if you register your software and then subscribe to Quicken.com, the content provided by Intuit will be integrated into your own financial information. The result is the next best thing to a financial magazine published exclusively for you.

You Can Customize Only the Quicken Home Page
The layout for the other five Financial Center pages is determined entirely by Quicken; you cannot customize those pages.

In this lesson, you were introduced to the informative capabilities of Quicken's Financial Centers. In the next lesson, you learn how to reduce your debts systematically and painlessly.

LESSON 15

USING THE DEBT REDUCTION PLANNER

In this lesson, you learn about the Debt Reduction Planner, whose job is to set up a debt repayment regimen for you.

YOUR DEBT

The net worth of many of the world's great corporations today is negative—less than some ordinary individuals—and yet they remain capable of acquiring some of the world's other great corporations. Debt, for these companies, is considered simply the equal and opposite reaction that comes from conducting what, for them, is business. One tool they use to eliminate debt is creative accounting.

For you, however, debt is certainly a burden; and with just the right degree of spotlight applied to it by your creditors, it becomes shameful, a punishment, a retribution for some unknown wrong you might have committed against some unknown party. It is no accident that financial institutions know just how to shine their spotlights on your guilt, because that guilt is just what they need to depress you enough that you spend more and go into further debt.

You do not have creative accounting at your disposal. So in light of the fact that you need a tool to help balance your money flow, Quicken provides the Debt Reduction Planner. (Figure 15.1 shows how this special feature appears after data is already entered into it.)

The Planner is capable of comparing the debt repayment plan it creates for you against the plan you've currently been on. Chances are, you might not be on such a plan right now, or you wouldn't need this feature anyway. But even if you can give Quicken just a rough estimate of how much you think you could pay your creditors per month, given the plan in your own head, you can see graphically how Quicken distributes the burden fairly and reduces your higher-interest debt more readily.

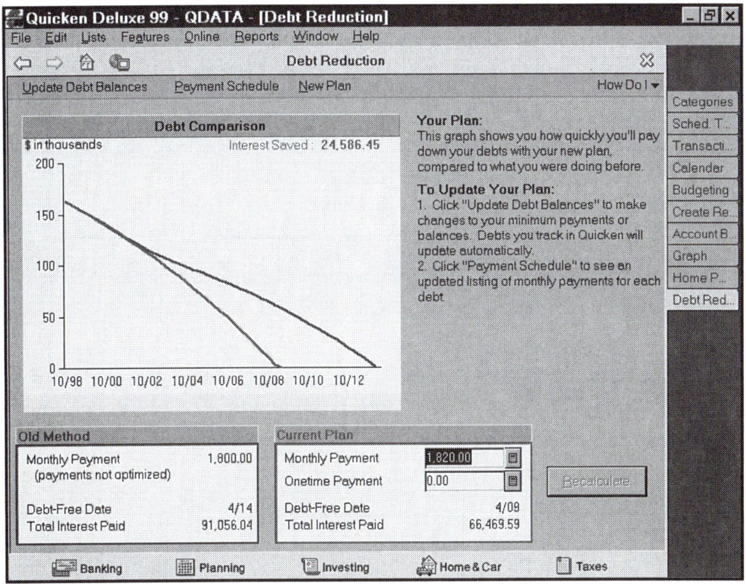

FIGURE 15.1 The result of the Debt Reduction Planner.

> **Where a Budget Would Come In Handy** Lesson 12, "Creating and Maintaining a Budget," discussed how to set up your own budget. In one sense, the Debt Reduction Planner can give you some points as to how to set up a Budget sheet. On the other hand, late in the data-entry process for the Debt Reduction Planner, Quicken attempts to use information from your Budget sheet in giving you an opportunity to reduce your spending even further. So although this approach seems counterproductive on the surface, you might find it useful to produce a preliminary budget using the procedure outlined in Lesson 12 *before* you refine that budget using the following procedures.

THE DEBTS TAB

The Debt Reduction Planner is, in actuality, a report generator. So you must do quite a bit of up-front work before you start to see results. This section discusses in detail how to set up the Planner. It assumes that you've used the processes laid out in Lesson 12 to set up a preliminary Budget sheet, from which the Planner will glean some of its information.

> **Multimedia Spoken Here** To get the most out of the Debt Reduction Planner, you should put your Quicken 99 CD into the CD-ROM drive. From time to time, you're presented with one-minute videos that explain what's going on.

To begin, from the Features menu select Planning, and then select Debt Reduction Planner. Quicken displays the first tab of the Debt Reduction dialog box. Click Next to begin.

NAVIGATING THROUGH THE SCREENS

The Debt Reduction Planner comes to you by way of a multiple-screen dialog box with lots of tabs. Keep these things in mind when navigating it:

- Click Next to go to the next screen.
- To retrace your steps and return to a previous screen, click Back.
- When you first bring up the dialog box, you are prevented from clicking any of the other tabs; however, as you progress through the screens, you can click a tab to go *back* to a page you've already seen.

OPERATING THE VIDEOS

As you use the Debt Reduction Planner, Quicken provides you with additional explanations by way of full-motion videos with sound (with your CD in the drive). These videos are indicated by long buttons with a short title—such as Why start reducing debt today?—and an icon that looks like the letter Q in a movie clip. Just click one of these buttons at any time to see a video. The video appears in a tiny window, with tools you can use to control the video play:

- The long, horizontal slider bar indicates where you are with respect to the entirety of the video. To go back (or forward), drag the slider along the bar. The left portion of the slider represents the beginning of the video; the right portion, the end.
- To start the video again, click the right-arrow Play button on the *left* of the console. As the video plays, this button changes to a Pause button, which you can click at any time.
- To stop and "rewind" the video at any time, click the black-square Stop button to the right of the Pause button.
- You won't see the little Click on Next... prompt when the video stops playing; you'll just need to remember to click Next when nothing's happening, to proceed to the next step.

ENTERING THE NAMES OF YOUR CREDITORS

Quicken tries to enter as much background data as it can from your accounts and your register into the Debt Reduction dialog box. But for the Planner to be complete, it still gives you the opportunity to add more data yourself. For instance, Figure 15.2 shows one of the first screens of the Planner dialog, where you enter the names of your creditors, along with how much you currently owe each one.

This screen gives you explicit instructions about what you need to do, along with numbered steps. These steps do *not* tell you how to add data, although the process here is pretty self-explanatory. For instance, to add a new creditor to the screen shown in Figure 15.2, click Add. Quicken displays the Edit Debt Reduction dialog box, shown in Figure 15.3.

Despite the title, you're not entering a debt reduction; instead, you're entering the name of a creditor, how much you owe that creditor total (not counting interest), how much you pay this creditor per month, and the rate of interest you're charged for this debt. (If your payment period is biweekly, you need to calculate a monthly equivalent.)

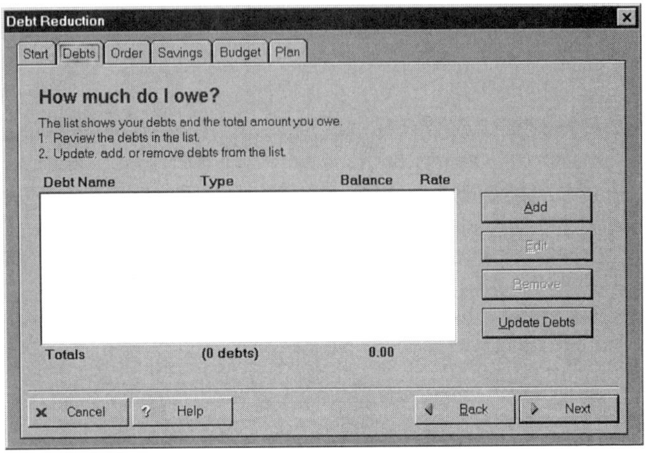

FIGURE 15.2 Where you enter the names of your creditors.

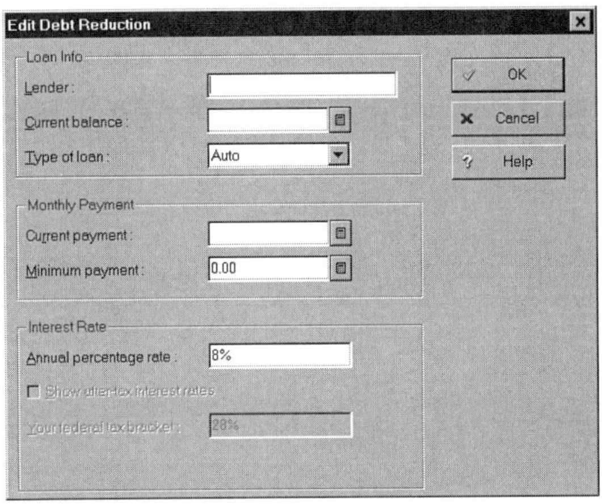

FIGURE 15.3 The Edit Debt Reduction dialog box.

DEALING WITH PERIODIC STATUS REPORTS

Some of the screens you encounter are entirely for review purposes, such as the How am I doing now? screen (shown in Figure 15.4). Here, you simply review the data as it appears, and click Next to proceed.

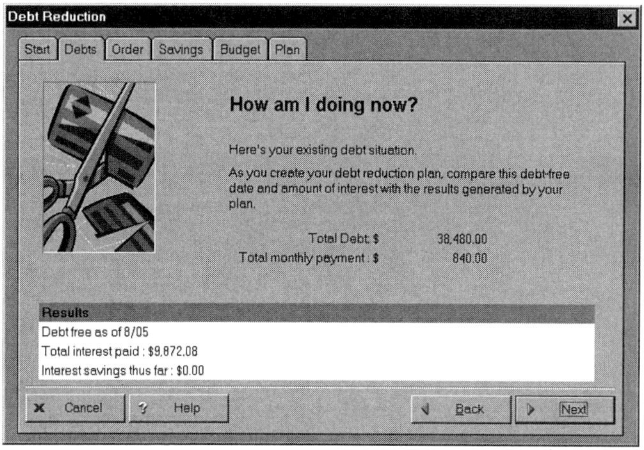

FIGURE 15.4 One example of a periodic status report.

REDUCING DEBT—QUICKEN'S WAY

A few screens later, at the beginning of the set of screens grouped by the Order tab, Quicken shows you its *optimized* order of payment (shown in Figure 15.5), which it suggests as the crux of a new payment plan. You might be astounded at how much interest money you can save, even if it takes a few decades to save it. For instance, if you could redistribute as much as $150 per month from your 30-year mortgage to your credit cards (given today's common interest rates), you could find yourself saving up to $25,000.

When you get to the screen shown in Figure 15.5, you're given the opportunity to shift the payment order from what Quicken suggests to what you prefer. To do this, check the box marked Change Payment Order? and click Next. Then follow the instructions on the next screen that comes up. You might try this just to see how much extra money you'd have to pay if the order of payment were shifted just slightly. But chances are that you'll prefer to stick with the order Quicken suggested to begin with. In such a case, click Reset to Optimized Order, and then click Back.

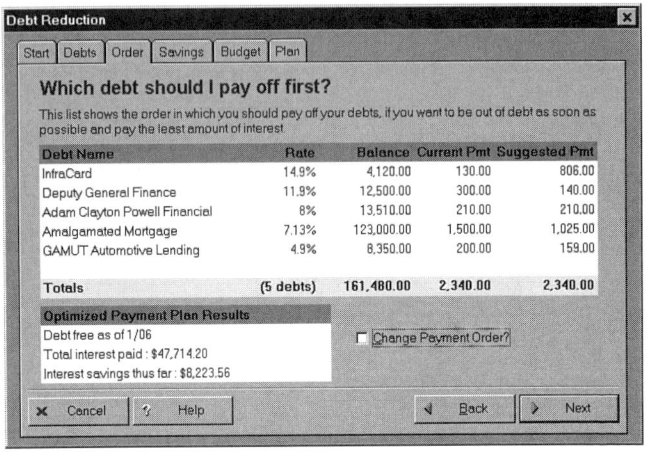

FIGURE 15.5 How a simple shift in payment could save you thousands.

THE SAVINGS TAB

The purpose of the screens grouped by the Savings tab is to give you the opportunity to plan to pay down some of your debt using money currently in your savings accounts. Figure 15.6 shows the first screen of the Savings tab, which basically shows how much savings you have now and asks how much you want to apply toward your debt now.

The theory here is that you would actually be better off reducing the amount of your money that earns a low rate of interest than accumulating savings while your debt is accruing a higher rate of interest. If you don't have much in savings now, this might not be the case. Besides, the savings figure shown here is true only at present and does not reflect the value of your savings account in the future.

To experiment with your current savings, enter a test sacrifice amount into the field marked Onetime amount you would like to apply to reduce your debt, and then click Recalculate. Under the Results frame, check out Interest savings thus far to see how much less money you would be paying. You might have to enter a high amount here in the Onetime account box to save more in interest than you would be spending. Otherwise, to leave your savings alone, just click Next to proceed.

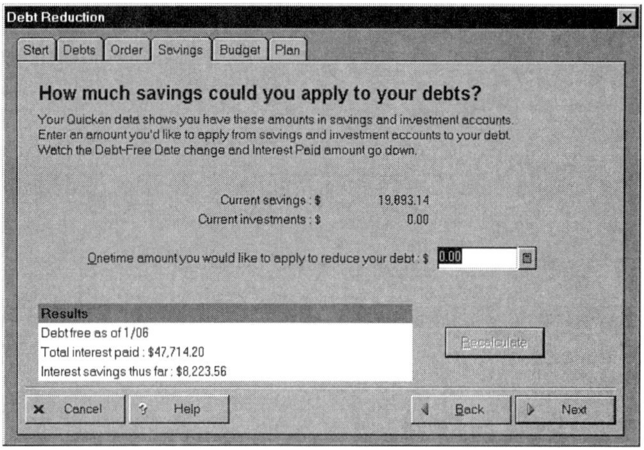

FIGURE 15.6 How much of your savings can you apply now?

THE BUDGET TAB

The purpose of the data-entry screen under the Budget tab, shown in Figure 15.7, is to give you an opportunity to make budget cuts and apply the savings from those cuts to reduce your debt. In Lesson 12, you saw how to set up a budget for yourself. Here, Quicken applies some of the information gleaned from your budget, as well as from your existing accounts, to determine how much discretionary expenditures you have currently.

This screen isn't self-explanatory, so an explanation of how you use it follows:

1. From one of the drop-down list boxes under the column marked Quicken Category, choose a discretionary expense category. The average expenditure per month, based on either your existing accounts or your budget, appears in the column beside it marked Average monthly spending.
2. In the column marked Amount to cut back, enter an arbitrary value that represents how much you believe you will be able to reduce this expenditure (probably less than 100%, to be realistic).

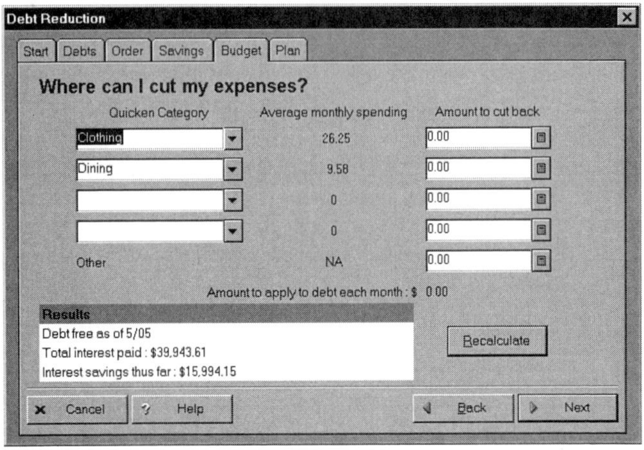

FIGURE 15.7 Putting discretionary expenses on the chopping block.

3. Click Recalculate to see how your cuts affect the figures in the Results frame at the lower left.

4. Click Next to proceed to the next page.

THE PLAN TAB

The sole purpose of the Plan tab is to give you a full report on the plan you're about to finalize. You can read the document here or print it. Included are the steps that Quicken suggests you should take, based on the information you've given it, plus details of the first 12 months of payments that, when printed, can serve as payment coupons for your records.

When you click Next, then finally click Done, Quicken projects a graph showing how rapidly you'll be reducing your debt under the new plan (in green), as opposed to under your existing plan (in blue). Here's what you can do from the Debt Reduction screen:

- To change the amount of your total monthly debt payment, or the amount of savings you want to apply to your debt, enter your revised figures into the fields in the Current Plan frame, and then click Recalculate. The graph changes accordingly.

- If your current balance or minimum payment with any creditor is adjusted along the way (unforeseen circumstances can cause this to happen), you can adjust those figures by clicking Update Debt Balances on the button bar, clicking Yes, and then entering those adjusted figures into the Update Debt Balances dialog box.
- To review all your payments, select Payment Schedule from the button bar. The dialog box details the entire schedule. To print this schedule, click Print.
- To start over from the beginning, click New Plan.

Now, when you select Features, Planning, Debt Reduction Planner, you're taken straight to this graph so that you can examine your plan in progress.

In this lesson, you learned how you can put Quicken to use in coordinating a system for reducing your debt. Next, you are introduced to Quicken's features for managing your loans.

LESSON 16

MANAGING LOANS WITH QUICKEN DELUXE 99

In this lesson, you're shown how to enter information about your outstanding loans into Quicken, and how Quicken helps you manage them.

ENTERING LOAN INFORMATION

The most important way in which Quicken helps you manage your loan information is in reminding you to pay the proper amount *on time*. Quicken has some other welcome features as well, but as this lesson illustrates, none is more critical to your peace of mind than Quicken's capability to regulate when you pay and how much.

> **Either a Borrower or a Lender Be** The way Quicken understands a loan account, you aren't necessarily the lendee. You can also be the lender, in which case, your loan account is treated as an income account. Whether you're the lender or the lendee, you use the same procedure detailed in this lesson to enter and keep track of your loan data.

If you've peeked ahead, you might have noticed a step number 27, and then looked back to the cover to make sure it really does contain the word "Quicken." Entering information about a loan into Quicken isn't really a difficult process. It is, however, a *long* process. So make sure that you can set your other tasks aside for a while before you begin—because after you start, you can't really stop (unless you cancel out of the wizard, in which case you have to start all over again the next time).

To save some time with this process, make sure that you have on hand all the *paper* information you can gather. If you're the lendee, gather the loan agreement papers that the bank or lending institution had you sign. Find where it mentions the principal amount of the loan, the term of the loan (how long before it's paid off), and the rate or rates of interest. If there's a balloon payment at the end, try to find out how much that payment will be. If you've made payments toward this loan already, have your check register or canceled check stubs on hand. If the loan is for the purchase of some *asset* (such as a car, a boat, or an RV), make sure that you have the bill of sale, or the "pink sheets." If you're the lender, have your loan contract ready. (It's not a verbal contract, is it?) Ready to begin? Good. Now, although this is a long process, I'll try to break it up a bit so that you don't lose your mind (I mean, your place).

INITIALIZING THE LOAN

To discover the benefit of having Quicken manage your loans, do the following:

1. Open the Features menu, select Bills, and then select Loans. Quicken brings up the View Loans screen.
2. On the View Loans button bar, click New. The first page of the Loan Setup Wizard is displayed. Click Next.
3. Set the option that defines *your* role with respect to the loan account—Borrow Money or Lend Money. Then click Next.
4. If you used the process outlined in Lesson 4, "Creating Accounts," to set up an account that happens to be a loan account, you might want this Loans screen to refer to this existing data. (This way, you won't need to reenter your loan data.) If so, select the option marked Existing Account, and then choose the name of the account from the drop-down list beside it. Otherwise, leave the option set for New Account, and then type a name for this loan account in the field beside it. Click Next.
5. The next screen is asking whether this is a brand-new loan *for you*. (We know it's new to Quicken.) If you've been managing this loan yourself for a while, you've already made a few payments. In that case, leave the option set to No. If you've just initiated this loan yourself, and you've never made a payment, set

the option to Yes. How you respond to this screen affects the order in which the steps to follow are processed, so remember whether you answer Yes or No. To continue, click Next.

ENTERING THE MAIN DOLLAR AMOUNTS

At this point, Quicken has started a new loan account for you. It's blank, but it's there.

To continue, follow the next set of steps:

6. The two fields in the next screen ask you when you entered into the loan agreement, and the amount of money you borrowed/lent (also called the *principal*). Enter those values into their respective fields, and click Next.
7. The next question asks whether there will be a final, massive payment—called a *balloon payment*—when your loan comes to term. (Many lenders prefer deferring payment on much of your principal until the end of the loan period, as opposed to asking for a larger down payment.) Answer this question and then click Next.

> **Compounding the Problem** One confusing aspect of some loans is that the period used to determine when interest is compounded is different from the period in which you're billed. Most often, interest is compounded monthly; but still, you can be billed biweekly or twice monthly.
>
> Keep in mind also that a loan whose *term* is 36 months does not necessarily compound its interest monthly, nor are its payments necessarily due monthly. You encounter these distinctions in steps 9–11 of this procedure.

8. The next screen asks for the length, or *term*, of the loan. This refers to the total amount of time you are expected to be making

payments on this loan. Most often, the term of a loan is a certain number of years, months, or even weeks; but sometimes (rarely) a loan is calculated in terms of how many payments the loan requires, regardless of the time between them.

From the drop-down list, choose either the interval of time used to measure the term, or Payments if there is no such interval. Then to the left of that list, enter the number of those intervals—for instance, "5 Years," "36 Months," or "15 Payments." Then click Next.

9. If in step 7 you answered No, then skip over to Step 10. But if you answered Yes, you have the type of loan whose term is shorter than its *amortized* length. In other words, you might be making payments whose value is an amount that would normally apply to a 30-year term, but the loan might be due in 7 years. This means that at the end of the seven-year term, all the remaining principal is due. So here Quicken is asking you how many years the term of this loan would be if you were allowed to pay it out without a balloon payment. If you know the answer, enter it in the field marked Amortized Length. If you don't know, Quicken might be able to estimate it for you based on the amount of your monthly payment, so set the option for Please Calculate the Amortized Length For Me. Click Next.

10. You're asked how often payments are expected. You leave the option set for Standard Period if a payment comes due at the end of some interval of time; then you select that interval from the drop-down list beside the option. Otherwise, if the loan merely calls for a fixed number of payments per year, set the option for Other Period, and then enter that number in the adjacent field. Click Next.

11. This screen asks you when interest is compounded. In other words, how often during the term of the loan is accrued interest tacked onto the total amount owed? Choose an interval of time from the drop-down list, and then click Next.

DETERMINING INTEREST AND PAYMENT AMOUNTS

Quicken can calculate for you the amount of each loan payment per period, if you don't know that information now. It *helps* to know it, but if you don't, all is not lost.

To continue, follow the next set of steps:

12. If in step 5 you answered Yes, skip to step 14. If you answered No, at this point, Quicken asks you when the first payment on the loan is scheduled. After you click Next, you're asked whether you know the amount of the first payment. This is not the same as the monthly payment; it's also known as the *down payment*. If you leave the option set here to Yes and click Next, you're asked what that payment is. Enter that amount in the field marked Payment Amount (P+I), and then click Next. (The term P+I is short for principal plus interest.)
13. The next screen asks you for the interest rate. Here, you enter a *percentage* value; you can type the % or leave it off. But you should *not* enter the interest rate as a decimal value, the way you'd enter it into a pocket calculator. So an interest rate of seven-and-one-eighth percent appears as 7.125%. Click Next and skip to step 18.
14. If in step 5 you answered Yes, then with the information you've given Quicken thus far, it should now be able to determine the current balance (present value) of the loan. If you don't know the balance, set the option to No, click Next, and skip to step 16. If you have that value in front of you, leave the option set to Yes and click Next.
15. This screen asks you the current balance. If you have a statement showing your current balance, that number is current only as of the date of that statement—even if it is your most recent statement. So enter the date of the statement in the field marked Current Balance Date, and then enter the balance itself under Current Balance Amount. Click Next.
16. You're asked when the next payment is due. Enter that date here, and click Next.

17. If you answered No in step 5, skip to step 18. Otherwise, at this point, Quicken should be able to calculate the value of your next payment. But if you know that information, you can leave the option set to Yes, click Next, and then in the next screen enter that payment amount in the field and click Next again. Otherwise, set the option to No and click Next. Now go back to step 13.

REVIEWING YOUR ENTRIES

Now comes the first screen in the set grouped by the Summary tab. Although the next three screens contain several controls, they are simply provided for your review only. They indicate the selections you made earlier. If you goofed somehow or somewhere, you can correct yourself now before you finalize your loan account.

To continue, follow the next set of steps:

18. Use the Next button to browse through the screens belonging to the Summary tab, and make any corrections you see necessary.
19. When you reach the third Summary screen, click Done. Quicken brings up the Set Up Loan Payment dialog box, shown in Figure 16.1.

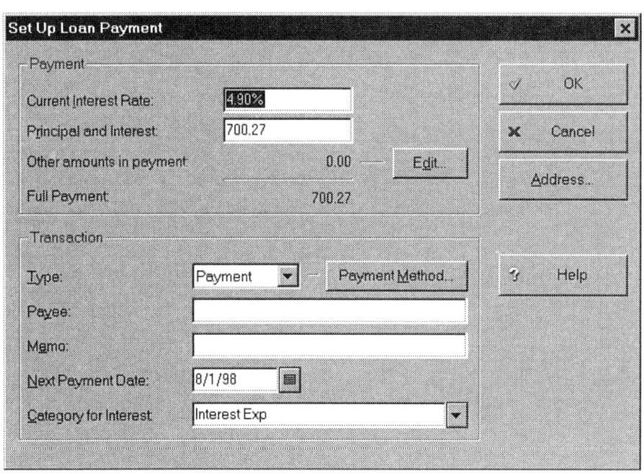

FIGURE 16.1 The Set Up Loan Payment dialog box.

INITIALIZING THE FIRST LOAN PAYMENT

At this point, the Loan Setup Wizard exits the stage, and the Set Up Loan Payment dialog box takes charge. Quicken knows the most important information about this payment, but one thing it doesn't know is *who gets the money*?

To continue, follow the next set of steps:

20. The information Quicken has already filled into the fields is what it has calculated for you based on the data you gave it earlier. The fields you need to fill in here are Payee (to whom the checks get made out) and Memo (in case you need to make a note to yourself).
21. To change the payment amount, enter that amount in the field marked Principal and Interest.
22. In the list marked Type, choose whether payments on this loan are to be made out manually as Payment (by you, assuming that you're the lendee) or automatically as Print Check, allowing Quicken to print the check for you.
23. By default, Quicken reminds you to make the payment every month, and the details of the payment are recalled as one of Quicken's memorized transactions (see Lesson 5, "Recording Transactions"). Alternatively, you can have Quicken make loan payments for you automatically. If you'd rather just let Quicken notify you when a payment is due, skip to step 27. Otherwise, click Payment Method. Quicken brings up the Select Payment Method dialog box, shown in Figure 16.2.
24. To have Quicken initiate the transaction automatically each period, set the option for Scheduled Transaction. Then under the For Scheduled Transactions frame, choose whether Quicken should prompt you first from the list box marked Register Entry; choose the account from which payments are made from the list box marked Account to Pay From; and set the number of Days in Advance to make out the payment, in the field so marked.
25. If you've already set up Quicken to handle transactions over the Internet (see Lesson 23, "Using Quicken Deluxe 99 on the Internet"), then to have Quicken make payment transactions

online through your electronic bank, set the option for Repeating Online Payment. Click OK to continue.

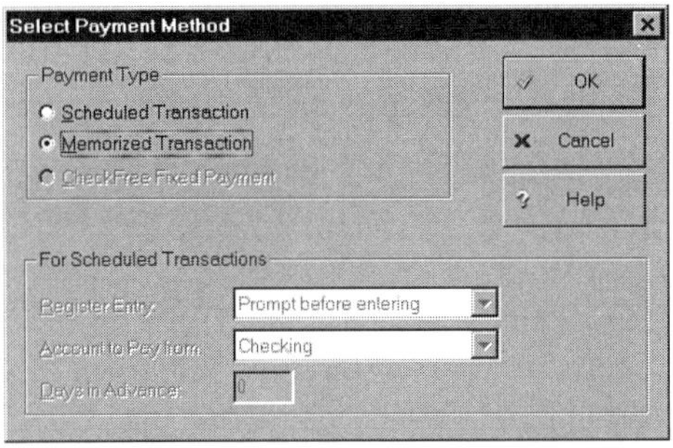

FIGURE 16.2 The Select Payment Method dialog box.

26. Back in the Set Up Loan Payment dialog box, the default setting for Category for Interest is set to Interest Exp, which is the category Quicken sets up to handle interest-related (tax-deductible) expenses. This is probably the right category in any event; but if you've set up one of your own that's more specific, choose that category from the list box and click OK.
27. Quicken now asks whether you want to associate an asset (house, car, boat) with this loan. If you click Yes, you're taken to the Asset Account Setup dialog box—which is a separate procedure that I cover later, in just a few paragraphs. If no assets are associated with this loan, click No. In a moment, you see Quicken's report on the loan in the View Loans screen, shown in Figure 16.3.

SETTING UP AN ASSET ACCOUNT

Earlier, you saw that toward the end of setting up your loan account, you could associate that loan with an asset. For Quicken to understand what an asset is, it needs a separate account to define it. Assuming that you told Quicken in step 27 of the preceding procedure to set up an asset account, from that point you should take the following steps:

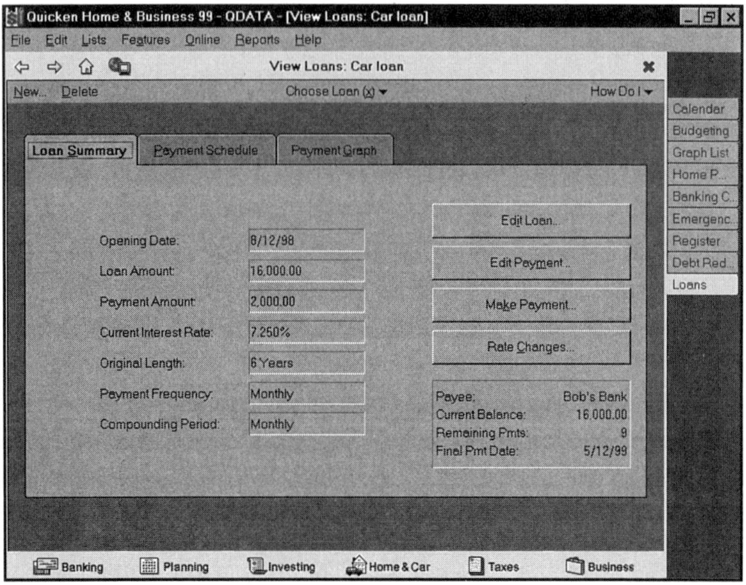

FIGURE 16.3 The newly completed View Loans screen.

1. You see a screen that asks you to name and describe the asset account. Enter these two items into their respective fields, and then click Next.

2. Here, you're asked how much your asset is worth. Technically, this is the same as the *present value* of the asset; this does not refer to the value of the debt associated with the asset, or of the debenture used to secure the debt, or to any measure of the value of the loan. In less technical terms, this is the "face value" of the asset. If you don't know this value, set the option to No, click Next, and then skip to step 4. Otherwise, leave the option set to Yes, and then click Next.

3. When the next screen asks for a date, it's actually asking for the most current date in which the asset has been evaluated. Suppose you know for certain that today, the asset is worth $16,000. In that case, you'd leave the date field marked As of Date as is, because it reads "today," and then you would enter that value in the field marked Value. If you've owned the asset for even a

short while, however, devaluation might have taken place. In such a case, you might be better off entering the face value of the asset at the time you took possession of it and then changing the date field to read the date when you took possession. Click Next.

4. The next screen is a summary showing the data you've entered thus far and giving you a chance to change it before committing it to the new asset account. Click Done when you're certain the data is correct.

MANAGING THE LOAN ACCOUNT

From this point on, selecting Features, Bills, Loans takes you to the View Loans screen. Following are the key things you can do from this screen:

- If you have more than one loan account, then when Quicken first brings up the View Loans screen, it shows the first loan in its list of loan accounts. To view another loan, from the button bar, select Choose Loan, followed by the name of the loan account.
- To set up a new loan account, select New from the button bar, and then go through the process outlined earlier in this lesson.
- The Loan Summary tab shows the important data associated with the loan account. To change this data, click Edit Loan. You should recognize the dialog box for changing your loan data from the Summary portion of Loan Setup.
- To change data associated with how payments are made, click Edit Payment. The Edit Loan Payment dialog box that comes up is identical to the Set Up Loan Payment dialog box shown back in Figure 16.1.
- After you've set up your loan account for memorized payments, Quicken notifies you when it's time to make a payment. At that point (or sooner, if you prefer) from the dialog box in the middle of the View Loans screen, click Make Payment. You're asked whether this is to be your Regular payment (of the amount and at the time scheduled) or an Extra payment over and above what you're scheduled to pay. For a regular payment, Quicken

displays the dialog box shown in Figure 16.4 (the Make Extra Payment dialog box is no different except for its title).

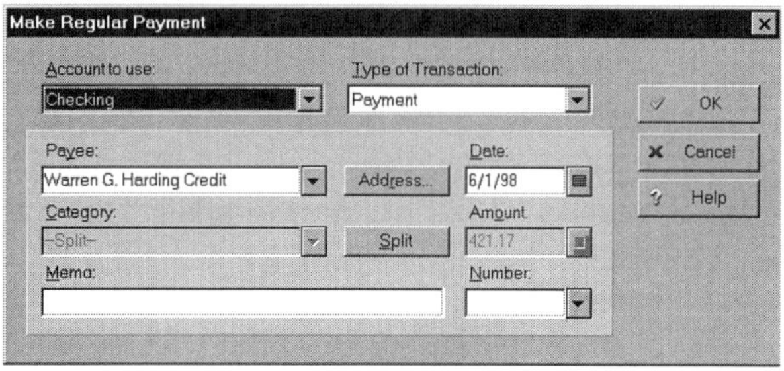

FIGURE 16.4 Where you register regular payments on your loan account.

- In the Make Regular Payment or Make Extra Payment dialog box, under Type of Transaction, you can select whether this is a regular Payment made out by you, a Print Check that Quicken is to print for you, or an Online Pmt (payment) made through your electronic bank. Under Number, enter the number on the check used to make the payment, or choose Next Check Num to have Quicken figure out that number for you. The rest of the data here should reflect the data that Quicken has calculated for the loan, so click OK to proceed.
- To review those times when the interest rate on the loan has changed, click Rate Changes in the Loan Summary tab. Quicken pulls up a list of those changes, at the top of which always is the initial interest rate on the loan even if there have been no changes.
- To review the totals for the payments remaining on the loan, click the Payment Schedule tab. The list details which part of each payment goes toward principal, and which part, interest.
- To see a graph showing how your loan balance declines as your interest paid rises, click the Payment Graph tab.

In this lesson, you saw how to set up a loan account, how to set up an asset account to go with it, and the features Quicken provides for managing loan accounts. In the next lesson, you look at the Financial Calculators—worksheets that give you some valuable pointers on how to plan, invest, and save.

LESSON 17

USING THE FINANCIAL CALCULATORS

In this lesson, you experiment with the Financial Calculators—simple dialog boxes that solve common finance-oriented formulas.

HOW TO OPERATE A FINANCIAL CALCULATOR

The purpose of Quicken's Financial Calculators is to give you some insight into your planning, by enabling you to see the most common formulas. These Calculators don't have any effect on your accounts or register. They simply enable you to experiment with different financial scenarios to see whether there's more you can save, a better way to invest, or a simpler way to plan for your children's college.

Follow these steps to use any of the Financial Calculators:

1. Open the Features menu, select Planning, select Financial Calculators, and then select the name of the calculator you want to use.
2. A dialog box appears with controls you can use to enter input data for the formula.
3. Click Calculate to bring up a window that lists the results of that formula, generally in the form of a table.
4. From here, you can click Print to have Quicken send that table to your printer. You can go back to entering data for new formulas, or you can click Done to exit the Calculator.

THE LOAN CALCULATOR

You can use the Loan Calculator to solve for either of two results:

- The amount you'd pay per month for a loan of a given amount, at a fixed interest rate (Payment Per Period)
- The amount of a loan extended for a given period of time, at a fixed interest rate (Loan Amount, the previous formula in reverse)

Figure 17.1 shows the Loan Calculator window. Follow these steps to use it:

1. Choose the formula to solve for from the frame marked Calculate for.
2. In the upper frame marked Loan Information, enter the fixed rate of interest as a percentage, the number of years in the loan, the number of payment periods within the year (12 if monthly, 2 if semi-annually), and the interval of time for which interest is compounded (daily, monthly, or semi-annually).
3. At the top and bottom of the frame are the value of the loan and the value of each individual payment, respectively. Of these two, when you can edit one, you're solving for the other; notice that when you switch the option under Loan Information, the editable status of these two fields flip-flops. Click Calculate to have Quicken solve for the desired value.

   To see a list of all the payments in the schedule that would make up the loan you've entered into the calculator, click Schedule. The list divides that part of the payment that goes toward principal and the part that is interest and also keeps a running tally of the principal balance after each payment.
4. Click Print to print out this list, or Close to dismiss the list.

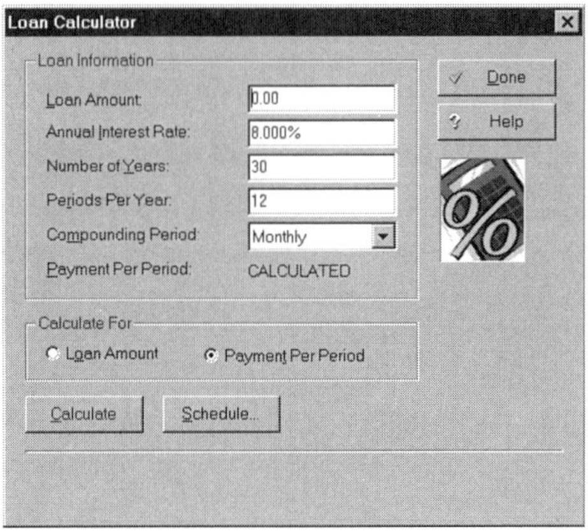

FIGURE 17.1 The Loan Calculator helps you calculate the amount of your loan payments.

THE REFINANCE CALCULATOR

The purpose of the Refinance Calculator is to aid you in determining whether it would be a good idea to refinance your existing mortgage. This calculator, shown in Figure 17.2, is divided into three frames. You solve for the items in each of these frames, marked CALCULATED. Follow these steps:

1. In the Existing Mortgage frame, enter your current monthly payment plus the amount that you pay that is entered into escrow each month.
2. In the Proposed Mortgage frame, enter data about the mortgage plan that you're currently investigating (or hoping for). All you need is the amount of the mortgage, the number of years in the term, and the fixed interest rate. (Sorry, adjustable rates aren't accounted for here.)
3. Click Calculate, and you see what your monthly payment (P+I) would be under the new plan, plus the difference between the two.
4. In order to know for sure whether you're really saving the money indicated in the Proposed Mortgage frame, you need to

enter the expenses you'll incur in acquiring the new mortgage. Total up all your Mortgage Closing Costs and enter that figure in the frame so marked.

5. Enter the amount of points that you would have to pay down in order to achieve the interest rate you entered in the Proposed Mortgage frame.
6. When you click Calculate, you see your actual closing costs (taking points into account), plus the number of months you'd need to sustain your new mortgage before you actually begin to see savings over your current plan (months to break even).

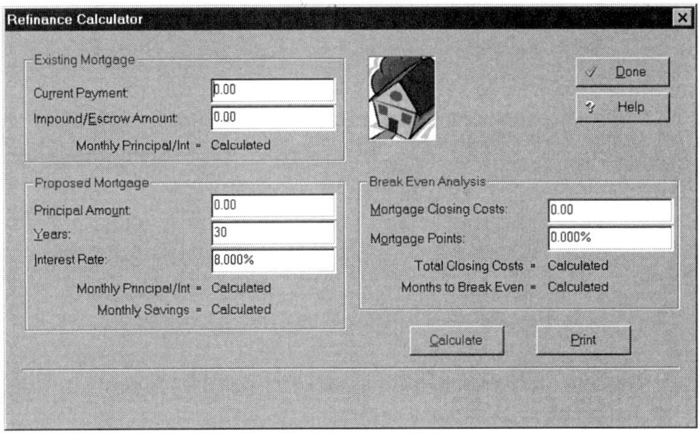

FIGURE 17.2 The Refinance Calculator helps you decide whether to refinance your current mortgage.

THE SAVINGS CALCULATOR

The premise of the Savings Calculator, shown in Figure 17.3, is to solve for any of the three most common questions asked about a savings account:

- How much you would need to open a savings account if you plan to contribute a certain amount and have a goal amount in mind after a given period of time (Opening Savings Balance).

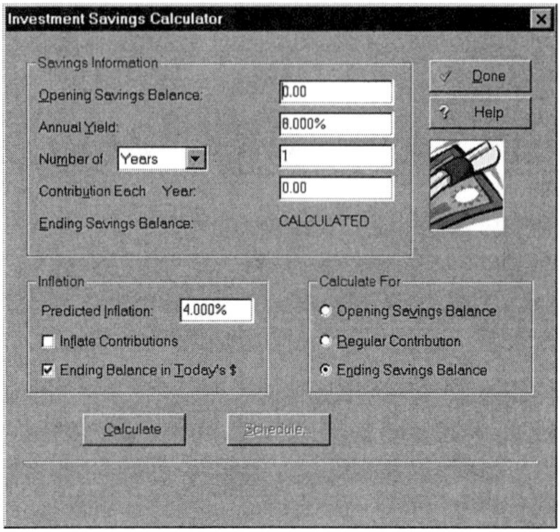

FIGURE 17.3 The Savings Calculator helps you plan your savings accounts.

- How much you would need to contribute to your savings account each year if you open it with a certain amount, and have a goal amount in mind after a given period of time (Regular Contribution)
- The value of your savings account after a given period of time if you open it now with a certain amount, and contribute a given amount to it regularly (Ending Savings Balance)

As with the Loan calculator, when you choose a value to solve for in the Calculate For frame, one of the input fields becomes uneditable and is marked CALCULATED. This mark indicates where the result will appear when you click Calculate.

You enter your key data into the Savings Information frame. Note that the default interval of time for the term of your account is set to Years; you can change that to Weeks, Months, or Quarters. In the Inflation frame, you enter an estimate on how much the annual rate of inflation (nowadays gauged using the Producer Price Index) can reduce the *value*, if not the amount, of your savings. Of course, this estimate assumes that inflation growth stays steady over the course of your account, which has rarely happened in the history of America. You can assume here, however, a *median* interest rate after all the peaks and pits in the real PPI are ironed out.

Say you're solving for Ending Savings Balance. With an inflation estimate entered, check Ending Balance in Today's $. If the *value* of your future savings account were handed to you *now*, the figure under Ending Savings Balance would be the amount of dollars you would receive. Note how a 3 percent inflation rate acting on a 30-year account can cut the dollar *amount* by more than half. You can reduce the effects of this a bit by checking Inflate Contributions. This creates a schedule where the amount of your periodic contribution is also adjusted for the rate of inflation, which may dampen the blow but probably won't eliminate it.

THE COLLEGE CALCULATOR

The College Calculator works very similarly to the Savings Calculator (see Figure 17.4). It can solve for any of the following:

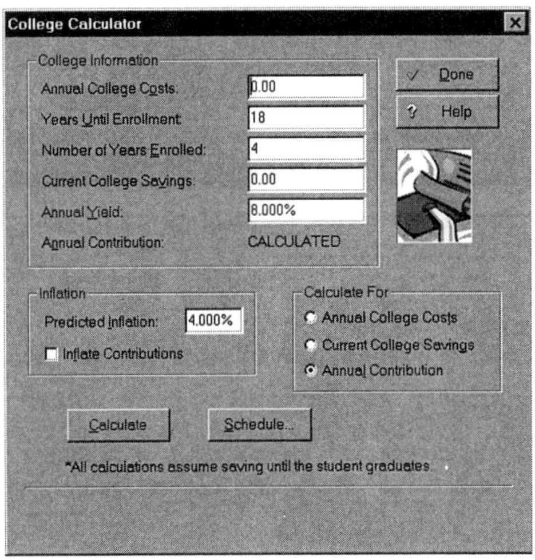

FIGURE 17.4 The College Calculator helps you plan for college tuition.

- How much college, in terms of dollar value, you could afford if you opened your savings account now, and contributed a given amount every year until it became time to enroll (Annual College Costs)

- How much you would need to open your savings account now if you contributed a given amount every year, assuming you've been quoted a tuition figure (Current College Savings)
- How much you would need to contribute to your savings account annually if you opened it now with a given amount, assuming you've been quoted a tuition figure (Annual Contribution)

> **Ah, Inflation** One difference with the College Calculator is that it always adjusts for the inflation estimate entered under Predicted Inflation. (You can enter a 0 here to turn inflation off.) This is important, because college costs have recently tended to increase faster than the rate of inflation. If you're solving for Annual College Costs, you'll have more dollars in your account than the tally shows, but the *value* of those dollars in terms of today's currency is what's shown under Annual College Costs. To try to compensate for the value reduction, check Inflate Contributions to have Quicken increase the amount of your annual contributions by the given rate of inflation.

THE RETIREMENT CALCULATOR

The same savings principles are applied again with the Retirement Calculator, shown in Figure 17.5. Here, you can solve for the following:

- How much you would need to open a retirement account now with a given fixed-interest rate, to which you contribute a given amount every year, if you intend to withdraw from that account for a given number of years after your retirement age and earn a certain goal income amount (Current Savings)
- How much you would need to contribute annually to a retirement account opened now with a certain amount, at a given fixed interest rate, if you intend to withdraw from that account

for a given number of years after your retirement age and earn a certain goal income amount (Annual Contribution)

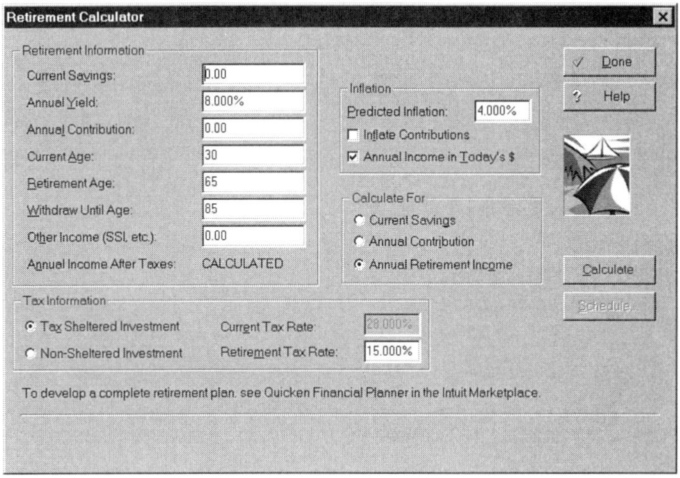

FIGURE 17.5 The Retirement Calculator helps you plan for your future.

- How much you would be earning in retirement income if you opened an account now with a certain amount, at a fixed interest rate, if you intend to withdraw from that account for a given number of years after your retirement age (Annual Retirement Income)

In the Retirement Information frame, you enter how old you are now, the age you want to be when you retire, the age you think you'll be when you stop withdrawing from your account, plus an estimate of your annual income from other sources such as Social Security. Adjusting the final tally for inflation is an option; check Annual Income in Today's $ to do so.

One key addition to this Calculator is the Tax Information frame. Not all retirement accounts are tax deductible. Hopefully, your contributions won't be taxed; by default, the option marked Tax Sheltered Investment is set. In such a case, only the Retirement Tax Rate field is editable. This represents the rate at which your annual retirement income will be taxed when it is withdrawn from the account. If your contributions are still treated as income during the year you've made them, set the option for Non-Sheltered Investment, and then enter your current income tax rate in the field marked Current Tax Rate.

In this lesson, you've been introduced to five useful problem solvers brought to you by Quicken. In the next lesson, you see how you can use Quicken to keep track of the addresses of the institutions with which you do business.

LESSON 18

WORKING WITH THE FINANCIAL ADDRESS BOOK

In this lesson, you see how you can gain access to the database where Quicken keeps its list of names and addresses.

OPENING THE FINANCIAL ADDRESS BOOK

Whenever Quicken memorizes a transaction or enrolls a new scheduled transaction, the names and addresses of the companies with which you do business—associates, creditors, debtors—are kept in a database. You have access to this database through a tool called the Financial Address Book, whose main window is shown in Figure 18.1.

You open the Financial Address Book's main window by selecting Track Important Addresses from the Lists menu or clicking the AddrBk button on the Quicken iconbar. In this window, you see a list of everyone with whom Quicken has had to deal thus far. You can use this list for your own purposes, and even add entries to the list.

ADDING A NEW ENTRY

To add a new name and address to Quicken's internal database, do the following:

1. In the Address Book's iconbar, click New. The cursor appears in the Last Name field in the entry form in the lower portion of the window.
2. Enter data into each field. Press Tab to move the cursor between fields.

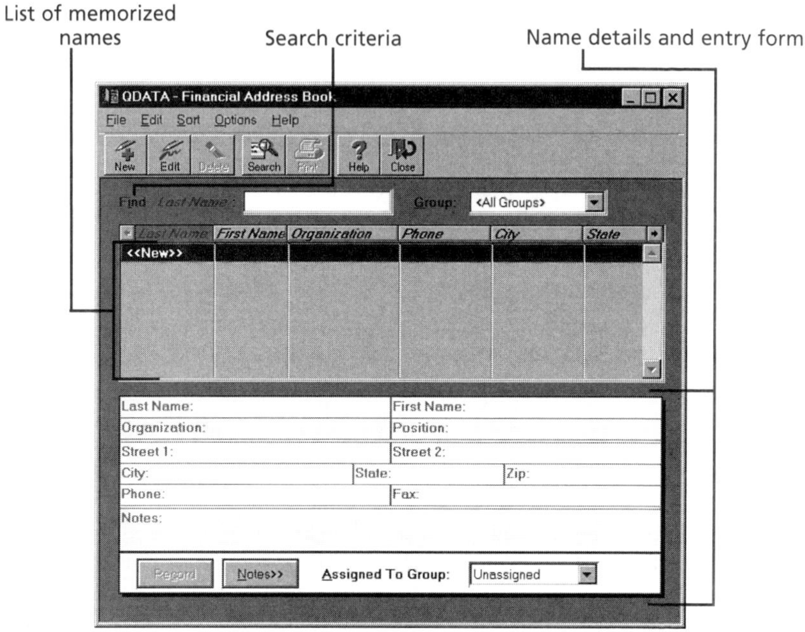

FIGURE 18.1 In the Financial Address Book's main window you can track your transactions.

3. To attribute the name to an Address Book group—usually Quicken, Family, Friends, or Work—choose the name of that group from the list box marked Assigned to Group.
4. Click Record when you're ready to save the name to the database.

EDITING AN EXISTING ENTRY

To make changes to an entry already in the database, do the following:

1. From the main list of names in the upper frame, choose the name you want to edit. The details for this name appear in the lower frame.

2. Click the field you want to edit, and use the cursor to change that field as needed. Continue with all fields that require editing.
3. Click Record to finalize your changes.

SEARCHING FOR ENTRIES

Although the Financial Address Book was designed to serve as a way to access names and addresses used by Quicken 99, it can also be used as a general-purpose filing cabinet for names and addresses. In such circumstances, the subset of records in the Address Book that are actually used by Quicken, belong to a *Group* called Quicken. All of the addresses that you have previously entered into other features of the Quicken program, can be retrieved from the Address Book by choosing Quicken from the list marked Group.

If your Windows screen resolution is 640×480 or 800×600, the upper portion of the Address Book window might not be long enough to display all the contents of an entire record. So when you do search for records in the database, if you can't see what the Address Book has found, then you have to do a search yourself anyway. Use the horizontal scroll bar at the *top* of this list of records rather than at the bottom. With the left- and right-arrows along the top, you can scroll over to reveal the hidden columns.

To search for one entry in the list, follow these steps:

1. In the upper frame, click the header of the column you want the Address Book to search. The sort order changes so that all entries in that chosen column are listed alphabetically or in ascending order for numeric data (telephone numbers, zip codes, and so on).
2. Click in the field marked Find at the top of the window and type what you're looking for. As you type, the Address Book indicates the first entry in the list that matches the field contents. If no matching information is contained in the database, nothing is displayed when you type.

To search for one or more entries whose contents meet a given set of criteria, follow these steps instead:

1. From the Address Book's Iconbar, click Search. The Address Book displays the dialog box shown in Figure 18.2.

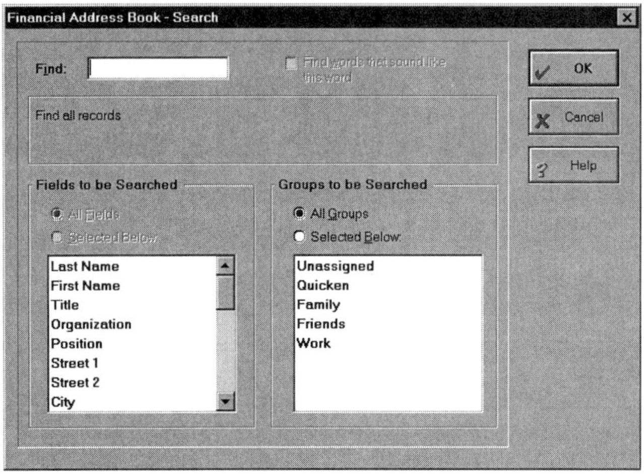

FIGURE 18.2 The Financial Address Book's search facilities.

2. Type what you're looking for in the field marked Find.
3. To have the Address Book search for homonyms (words that sound like the one you've typed, in case you're not certain of the spelling), check Find words that sound like this word.
4. In the frame marked Fields to be Searched, choose any number of fields, or set the option for All Fields.
5. In the frame marked Groups to be Searched, choose any number of groups, or set the option for All Groups. Hold down the Ctrl Key when clicking a group to select multiple groups to search.
6. Click OK to begin. A dialog box indicates how many matching entries were found. When you click OK, the upper frame lists only entries that match the criteria you supplied.

To sort the entries in the upper frame by the contents in any one column alphabetically, in ascending order, click the column header.

Nice Job. Now How Do I Get Rid of It? After you've completed your search, notice that the Group list box at the top of the Address Book window reads Search Result. To clear the search criteria and set the upper frame to show any or all groups, choose another entry from the Group list box.

ADDING GROUPS

Ordinarily, when you add an address to the database using Financial Address Book, by default it becomes a member of the Unassigned group. There are three other groups: Family, Friends, and Work. None of these four groups contain records that are visible to Quicken; which means, if you add a record to a group other than the Quicken group, Quicken won't be able to use it for anything.

Any group you add to the Financial Address Book is therefore only useful to you within the context of the Financial Address Book. To give yourself a new group to work with, do the following:

1. From the Options menu of the Address Book window, select Set Up Groups.
2. Enter the name of your new group in the field marked Add New Group, and then click Record. The group is added to the list marked Available Groups. Repeat for as many groups as you need.
3. Click OK when you are done.

PRINTING ENTRIES

To print any or all entries in the upper frame list, do the following:

1. Choose the group you want to print from the Group list box.
2. Choose any entries in the list that you want included in the print-out, or leave the list alone if you intend to print all entries showing.

3. From the toolbar, click Print.
4. If in Step 2 you selected addresses to be singled out, set the option for Selected addresses. Choose the format for the printout from the Print drop-down menu. (Format examples include Address Book, Phone Book, Labels, Rolodex, and Envelope.)
5. Click OK to begin the printing process.

To Close And Not To Close When you exit the Quicken 99 application, if the Financial Address Book window is open, you'll notice it remains open. This is because the Address Book is a separate program, and must be exited independently of Quicken. To do that, select Exit from the Address Book's File menu.

In this lesson, you learned how to access and manage Quicken's internal database of names and addresses. In the next lesson, you learn about the features of Quicken that relate to your taxes.

LESSON 19

PREPARING TAXES WITH QUICKEN DELUXE 99

In this lesson, you see how to better organize your financial data within Quicken to prepare for tax time.

ASSOCIATING QUICKEN CATEGORIES WITH TAX FORM LINE ITEMS

As you are probably aware, Quicken cannot do your taxes. Intuit makes another program called TurboTax for that job. The tax-related features of Quicken deal with organizing your financial data for filling out your forms when the time comes for you (or TurboTax) to do so. Additionally,

> **Start by Centering Yourself** Quicken's Tax Center (introduced in Lesson 14, "Using Quicken Deluxe 99's Financial Centers") acts as a sort of home page for all of Quicken's tax-oriented features and information. All these features are laid out for you in an easy-to-find, magazine-page format. You might find it easier to access the Tax Center from the menu bar (Features, Centers, Tax Center) and use that as your home base. You're shown important dates you need to know (not just April 15); and if you go online to the Quicken home page (http://www.quicken.com) regularly, you see updated articles, tips, and other timely information.

Quicken gives you some pointers on how to prepare for April 15, and how to best apply your refund when you get one.

As you know, Quicken organizes all of its transactions into categories (for example, Salary, Groceries, Insurance) and subcategories (such as, Doctor as a subcategory of Medical, or Fuel as a subcategory of Auto). When you're filling out your tax forms, some, though probably not all, of your expense-related data, and certainly all of your income-related data, is of interest to the IRS. Quicken knows how to reconcile its own categories against its database of IRS tax form line items—for the most part.

Some of your expenses might be tax-deductible. You might want to mention those expenses on IRS Form Schedule A (Itemized Deductions) or C (Income from Self Employment). Right out of the box, Quicken does not have enough information about the organization of your finances or small business to conclude which of your expenses qualify as income deductions. Quicken should know which expenses from your categories are truly deductible so that it can report to you (or TurboTax) the amounts to enter on your tax forms.

Quicken might already know this information, but you won't know for certain until you look for yourself. To do this, you need to access a feature called the Tax Link Assistant. There, you see all of Quicken's categories, including those you added yourself. The Tax Link Assistant also lists all of the tax form line items that Quicken tracks. This feature enables you to see the pairings between the two lists whenever categorical information might be pertinent to your tax forms. You can make changes to accommodate your own financial or business structure.

> **Why You?** The job of figuring out why certain Quicken categories have been or should be delegated to certain tax form line items, might not be easy for you. It's an intimidating process, but so is reading the Federal Tax Code. You might want to consult a tax specialist or the U.S. Internal Revenue Service (yes, them!) before you start trying to make sense of Quicken's Tax Link Assistant.

The following procedure is the easiest for using Tax Link Assistant to make sure that Quicken is keeping track of all the right things:

1. From the Features menu, select Taxes, Set Up for Taxes. Quicken displays the Tax Link Assistant dialog box shown in Figure 19.1.

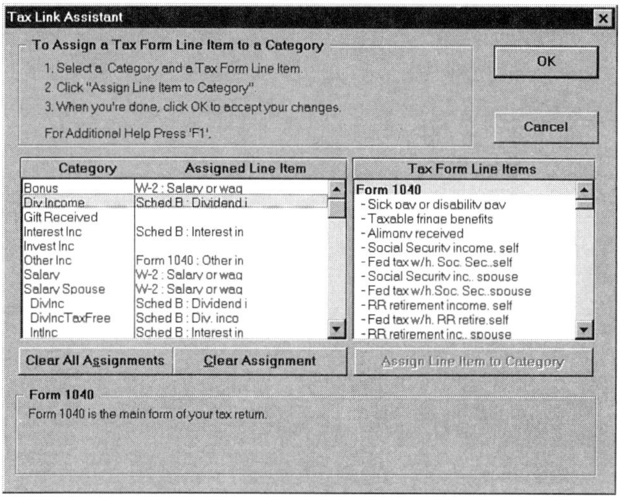

FIGURE 19.1 In the Tax Link Assistant dialog box tell Quicken what to track.

2. In the Assigned Line Item column, you find the IRS form and line to which each category applies, if any. To see more information on a Category, double-click it.

3. The Tax Form Line Items list contains a very long list of recognized line items, organized in order of the forms to which they belong—Form 1040 first, followed by Schedules, and so on. To find out more about a particular line item, click the item, and read its description at the bottom of the dialog box.

4. To have Quicken start over from scratch, click Clear All Assignments. *Do this only on the advice of a knowledgeable tax specialist or attorney.* Starting over is a rough process.

5. To assign a category to a line item, choose a category from the Category list, and a line item from the Tax Forms Line Items list, and then click Assign Line Item to Category.

6. To remove an assignment from a Quicken category and leave it blank, choose the category from the Category list and click Clear Assignment. You do *not* need to do this to reassign a category to a different line item.
7. If at any time something goes wrong, there is one out—Click Cancel.
8. When all the assignments you've made have been checked for accuracy, click OK.

USING THE TAX DEDUCTION FINDER

The most common reason why people consult tax specialists is to find out whether they are including enough deductions on their tax return. Quicken knows about many of these deductions and might be able to uncover some deductions you weren't aware of. It knows the (relatively) simpler rules concerning your eligibility for deductions.

To use the Tax Deduction Finder, do the following:

1. From the Features menu, select Taxes, Tax Deduction Finder. Quicken displays a Welcome dialog box. Click OK. Following that, Quicken displays the Deduction Finder screen (shown in Figure 19.2).
2. Under Choose a deduction type, select a category pertinent to the type of deduction you're searching for. Your choices are Employee, Homeowner, Individual, Investor, Medical, and Self-Employed.
3. Select an item in the Choose a deduction list. Quicken displays a list of questions in the frame marked 3.
4. Answer *all* these yes/no questions by clicking the appropriate box, Y or N. The Deduction Finder will not work unless you answer every question about the chosen category.
5. To learn more about the current deduction category, click More Information; then read the dialog box that opens.
6. To have Quicken start tracking information about the chosen category from here on out, click Create a Category. Then click OK from the dialog box that follows.

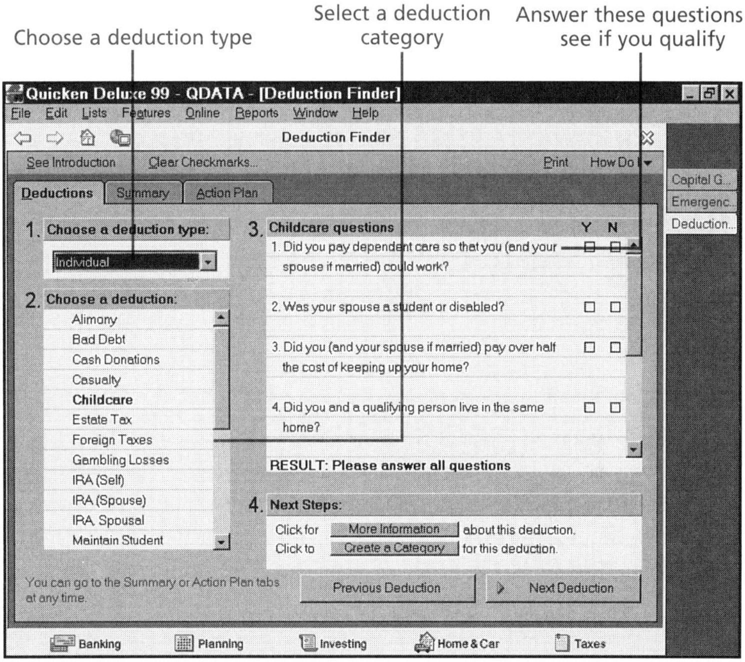

FIGURE 19.2 The Deduction Finder screen helps you determine which deductions you can take.

7. When you've answered all questions, click Next Deduction. Quicken proceeds to the next item in the Choose a deduction list.

8. To start over from scratch, click Clear Checkmarks on the button bar.

9. After you cover all the deduction categories pertinent to the deduction type you selected in Choose a deduction type, click the Summary tab. Quicken shows a report listing the number of deductions for which you are eligible.

10. To read Quicken's final report on your deductions, click the Action Plan tab. This page contains information you should keep on hand when you're filling out your tax forms. To be able to use this information later, click Print to make a hard copy of this page.

In this lesson, you learned how to help Quicken use the financial information it tracks for you when it comes time to file your tax forms. In the next lesson, you learn how the Tax Planner can give you a ballpark figure of what you owe or what you are owed.

Lesson 20

Working with the Tax Planner

In this lesson, you learn how to use the Tax Planner to estimate how much tax you might have to pay, how much tax has been withheld, or how much refund you can expect to receive. Later, you also see how to estimate a capital gains tax.

Initial Setup

The real purpose of Quicken's Tax Planner is to give you a ballpark estimate for the final figures on your Federal Form 1040. In the Tax Planner, you enter your income for the previous tax year plus those deductions that you currently know about. Some of the Tax Planner's information can be gleaned from your Quicken accounts. The Tax Planner is no substitute for TurboTax, but it can give you a heads-up before you find yourself owing more than you'd saved for.

> **Planning for the Planner** Although Quicken recommends that you get your tax-related papers in order before you start to use the Tax Planner, you might find it easier to let the Tax Planner tell you what information you need to organize. Remember, the Tax Planner is just a tax estimator, so it's better to use it prior to tax time.

You access the Tax Planner by selecting Features from the menu bar, followed by Taxes, and then Tax Planner. The main Tax Planner window opens (see Figure 20.1). Operating the Tax Planner involves several small, interrelated processes, which are discussed here one at a time.

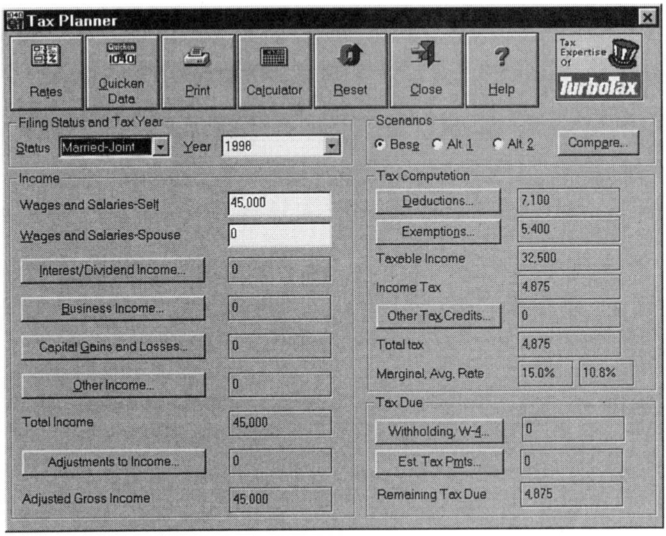

FIGURE 20.1 The Tax Planner Planner window on startup.

There are a few steps you should take before you begin entering your income from the previous year into the Tax Planner. Those steps are listed here:

1. Select your filing status from the Status drop-down list; then choose the year for which you're filing taxes from the Year drop-down list box.

2. Click Rates on the Iconbar. Quicken displays the Tax Rates and Filing Status dialog box.

3. Review the tax bracket percentages provided here, to make sure they coincide with the percentages shown in your Federal Form 1040 instructions. If they don't match, adjust them accordingly.

4. Click OK.

Have Quicken. Use Quicken To tell the Tax Planner to import as much data as it can from your Quicken accounts, click the Quicken Data icon in the Tax Planner's Iconbar, and then click OK. You don't need to have your Quicken accounts finalized and up-to-date to use the Tax Planner; although if your accounts are current, you have no real need to duplicate your data entry efforts either.

ENTERING YOUR INCOME

Now it's time to estimate your unadjusted gross income. Follow these steps:

1. In the Wages and Salaries text box, enter the amount of your earnings as reported on your Form W-2. Remember, this includes tips. If your filing status is Married Filing Jointly, enter your spouse's income in the field just below.
2. If you earned taxable interest on your savings accounts, or any kind of dividend from ownership of securities or from cash accounts you hold in a credit union (reported to you on your Form 1099-INT), click Interest/Dividend Income and enter your income from interest and dividends separately. Quicken totals them.
3. If you're the sole proprietor of or a partner in a business, and you file a Schedule C with your tax return, click Business Income and enter your best guess estimate of revenue and expenses. (If your business is in generating intellectual property, such as being an author, artist, or musician, you have no cost of goods sold.) Click OK when you're ready to proceed.
4. If you sold securities or investment properties during the previous tax year, you might owe capital gains tax. (A more detailed way to estimate this tax is discussed later in this lesson.) If you need help finding out how much, click Calculator on the iconbar. To enter what you earned from securities, click Capital Gains and Losses. Quicken brings up the Schedule D dialog box.

Determine the *net* gains from the sale of your assets for the four categories listed by subtracting your losses from your gains. (For example, the cost of the stock when you bought it minus the cost when you sold it, plus broker costs.) Then enter the results in the fields in the Capital Gains/Losses dialog box. The second column of fields applies to you only if you qualify for the Alternative Minimum Tax. If you do qualify, check the Alternative Tax box to activate these fields. Click OK to continue.

> **Getting Out the Calculator** To bring up the Windows Calculator accessory, click Calculator in the Tax Planner's iconbar, *prior to displaying the Capital Gains/Losses dialog box.*

5. Click Other Income to see whether any other income categories apply to you. If you received any kind of taxable distributions from pension or unemployment, Social Security benefits, alimony, or taxable state tax refunds, enter those amounts in the corresponding fields.

   If you received income from real estate, rents, partnerships, royalties (not on intellectual property), or trusts, click Schedule E Income, and then enter your revenues from those items into their corresponding fields and click OK.

   If you had profit or loss from your farm, click Schedule F Income—Farm, enter your revenues and expenses in their appropriate fields, and click OK.

   After you review your other income categories and have entered all the appropriate data you currently have on hand, click OK.

ADJUSTING YOUR INCOME

Next, you make the first round of adjustments to the income figures you provided thus far and arrive at an estimate of your adjusted gross income. Do the following:

1. In the Tax Planner window, click Adjustments to Income. Quicken displays the Adjustments to Income dialog box.
2. The dialog box shows categories of expenditures that the Federal Government has decided are truly reductions in your income rather than everyday expenses. If you have amounts that apply to any of these categories, enter them in their corresponding fields and then click OK.

EXEMPTIONS, DEDUCTIONS, AND CREDITS

With the adjustments to your income entered, it's time to decide how much of the remaining income figure is actually taxable by the Federal Government. Reductions come in three flavors:

- *Exemptions*. Reductions to your taxable income that are granted to you and your dependents just for being alive.
- *Deductions*. Reductions that come about as a result of your financial situation, although you are granted a minimum deduction by virtue of your filing status.
- *Credits*. These are not reductions in your taxable income, but reductions in your *tax*. If you qualify, a credit is just that much less tax you have to pay.

No matter who you are, you do have some of these adjustments coming to you. To estimate how much, do the following:

1. Click Deductions. Quicken displays the Itemized (Schedule A) and Standardized Deductions dialog box shown in Figure 20.2.
2. In the Standardized Deductions dialog box, you determine whether your itemized deductions are greater than the standard deduction you already deserve. In the Standard Deduction frame, check those deductions for which you qualify. Then in the frame marked Itemized Deductions (Schedule A), enter those deductions you know you can itemize thus far.

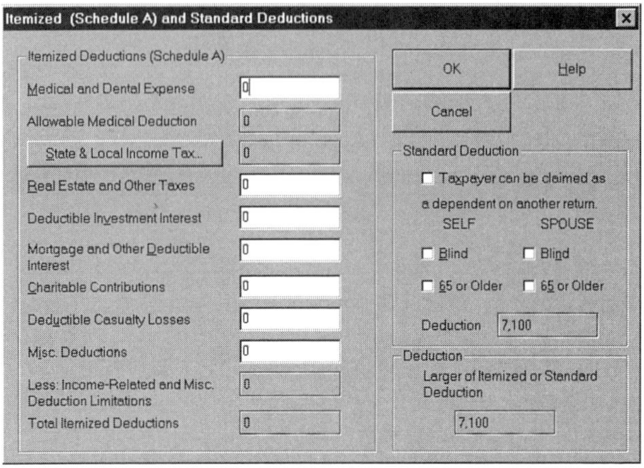

FIGURE 20.2 The Itemized (Schedule A) and Standard Deductions dialog box you choose which deductions to take.

If you haven't figured out what you can itemize yet, don't worry. You can come back to the Tax Planner to enter those figures later. Use the Standard Deduction for now. (To claim tax withheld as a deduction, click State & Local Income Tax, complete the dialog box that appears, and then click OK to close that dialog box.) Click OK to proceed.

3. If you have any dependents, click Exemptions, enter the number of Dependents, and then click OK.
4. If the instructions for your Federal Form 1040 state that you are eligible for tax credits, use the worksheet provided with your instructions to figure the amount of those credits. Then click Other Tax Credits, enter that amount in the field marked Credits, and then click OK.

ASSESSING YOUR TAX

At this point, the Tax Planner should have an idea of how much you owe the IRS. But it's possible that the IRS might already have some of this money, by virtue of employer withholding or quarterly payments you might already have made. To tell the Tax Planner how much of your tax you've paid, do the following:

1. If you have tax withheld, click Withholding, W-4. If the year for which you're calculating tax has already passed, enter the total amount withheld for both you and your spouse in the Withholdings to Date text boxes.

   If the tax year for which you're estimating has yet to expire (in other words, it's not yet December 31), enter the date you expect to receive your next regular paycheck. Then choose how often you receive a paycheck from the list box marked Pay Period, enter how much of your paycheck is withheld each period. Click OK to continue.

2. If you've already made payments to the IRS, which should be accounted for here, click Est. Tax Pmts. (estimated tax payments). In the dialog box, if you've already made payments with those handy 1040-ES coupons, enter the total of those payments in the first field. If the tax year isn't over, and there are some payments yet to be made, enter the amount of those payments in the second field. Finally, if last year you carried over part or all of your tax refund to this year, enter the portion of that amount you want to apply to this year's taxes in the third field. Click OK when done.

At this time, the Tax Planner should have a realistic estimate for you of how much you owe or how much you're owed. The figure doesn't boast its presence much. It's the field in the lower-right corner of the Tax Planner window. If you owe tax, the amount is shown as **Remaining Tax Due**. If you're due some money back from the IRS, the field is marked **Refund Due**.

Whenever you exit the Tax Planner by clicking the Close button in its iconbar, the figures you entered are saved automatically and are recalled whenever you bring up the window again. To clear all figures you entered and start over, click Reset.

Case in Point You can use the Tax Planner to compare up to three different ways to file your taxes. Suppose, for instance, you want to compare Married Filing Jointly to Married Filing Separately. Sometimes the taxes are the same, but sometimes not. In the Scenarios frame, the option is currently set to Base. This means that the figures you entered apply to the base or main scenario. To switch to one or the other alternative scenarios, so you can enter different (though still legal) figures to see what happens, set the option for Alt. 1 or Alt. 2. Then to compare your scenarios, click Compare to see the final tallies from all three scenarios side-by-side. Click OK to close the Comparison box.

ESTIMATING CAPITAL GAINS TAX

As promised, here is how you can get a clearer picture of the tax you might owe as a result of the sale of a security or investment. The feature that provides this is the Capital Gains Estimator, shown in Figure 20.3. You access this feature by selecting Quicken's Features menu, Taxes, Estimate Capital Gains.

You need to have accounts for the securities you intend to sell in Quicken to work with them in the Capital Gains Estimator. Those securities that Quicken is currently tracking appear in the Current Holdings frame in the lower frame of the Estimator window. With those accounts active, here is how you use the Estimator:

1. Click Tax Rates. Quicken displays the Select Tax Rates dialog box.
2. Set the option that corresponds to the tax rate brackets that currently apply to you, according to the instructions for Federal Schedule D. Click OK to continue.
3. Click the *name* of the stock that you plan to sell. (Do not click an individual lot.) Click Add. The Add to Scenario dialog box appears.

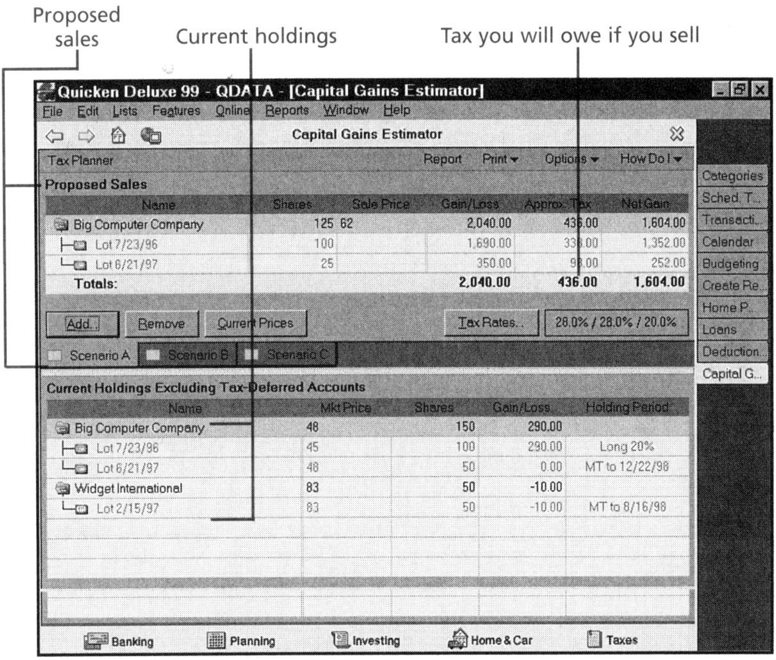

FIGURE 20.3 The Capital Gains Estimator screen works with securities that Quicken is tracking.

4. Enter the number of shares you propose to sell (some or all), followed by your proposed sale price (arbitrary), and then click OK. Quicken adds your proposed sale to the upper frame. The important column here is Approx. Tax, which shows how much tax you would need to reserve for the IRS.
5. Repeat from Step 3 for all securities that you intend to sell.

In this lesson, you learned how to estimate, with a reasonable degree of accuracy, the tax you owe or the refund you'll receive for a given tax year. In the next lesson, you learn about the benefits of keeping a home inventory.

Lesson 21

Using Quicken Deluxe 99 Home Inventory

In this lesson, you learn about a valuable extension program—Home Inventory. This program helps you make sense of your personal assets and can help you find tax deductions, reduce your insurance payments, increase the power of your insurance policies, and acquire home improvement loans.

Accessing Home Inventory

Home Inventory is an extension program that ships as part of Quicken 99. In essence, it's a little dedicated database manager. It's dedicated to a portion of your finances that the other parts of Quicken don't deal with—the state of your *fixed assets.*

You access Home Inventory by selecting the Features menu, followed by Planning, Quicken Home Inventory. The Welcome screen opens. Click Continue. You see the main data-entry screen (see Figure 21.1).

The Home Inventory database is already configured with a set of locations representing places or rooms in your house. On the right is a list of items that commonly belong to a specific category, such as Furnishings or Electronics. These items don't necessarily represent everything found in your home, just those things that a reasonable person might expect if he were looking for something in that category.

Before you start entering data into Home Inventory, you need to have at least a rough idea of the following:

- Those items in your home whose value is significant enough for them to be mentioned explicitly in an insurance policy

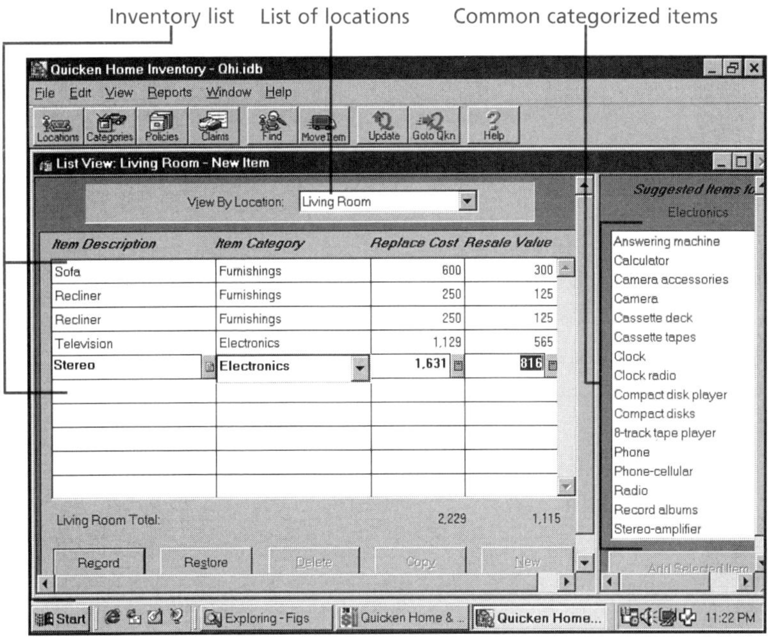

FIGURE 21.1 The home base of Quicken Home Inventory suggests common inventoried items.

- The locations of those valuable items, or at least those places where they belong
- The coverage and deductible provided for in your home insurance policies, and whether any claims have been placed against those policies

MANAGING THE LOCATIONS LIST

To make sure that Home Inventory's list of locations corresponds to the architecture of your house *before* you start entering inventory items, you might want to tweak its Locations list. Follow these steps:

1. Click Locations in the iconbar. Home Inventory displays the Locations dialog box shown in Figure 21.2.

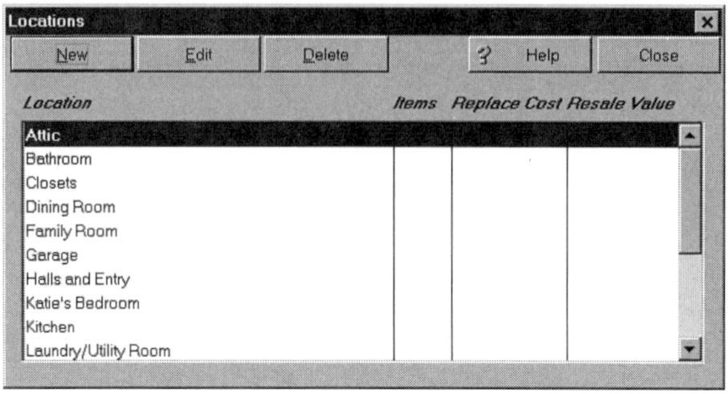

FIGURE 21.2 The Locations dialog box helps you go through your possessions room by room.

2. To add a new location to the list, click New. Then in the dialog box that opens, type a new name in the Location field and click OK.
3. To rename an existing location in the list, choose that location and click Edit. In the dialog box that opens, type a new name and click OK.
4. To delete a location from the list, choose that location and click Delete. Then Click OK in the verification dialog box that opens.
5. Click Close to finalize your changes.

MANAGING THE CATEGORIES LIST

Home Inventory keeps track of how much you own that belongs to a given category. The way you organize your assets of value in your mind might be different than the way Home Inventory has chosen. You can revise the Categories list before you start entering inventory items. To edit the Categories list, do the following:

1. Click Categories in the iconbar. Home Inventory displays the Categories dialog box, which is similar to the Locations dialog box profiled previously.
2. To add a new category to the list, click New; then in the dialog box that opens, type a new name in the lone field and click OK.

If that category already exists, Quicken does not warn you, but instead adds a duplicate category. You might want to check the list before adding a new categories.

3. To rename an existing category in the list, choose that category and click Edit. In the dialog box that opens, type a new name in the lone field and click OK.
4. To delete a category from the list, choose that category, and click Delete. Then click OK in the verification dialog box that opens.
5. Click Close to finalize your changes.

Becoming Unassigned When you enter an item into your Home Inventory list and later delete the category or location to which you assigned that item, the item shows up in the Categories list as belonging to a category or location called Unassigned.

ENTERING AN INVENTORY ITEM

With the Categories and Locations lists the way you want them, you can now begin entering inventory items. Do the following:

1. In the Item Description column, in the first blank row below the last entry, click the blue page icon. The display switches to Detail view (see Figure 21.3).
2. Here you enter as much history about the item as you have available to you. The Description field is mandatory; you need to enter a name for the item there. After that, the most important items are in the upper-right column—the date of purchase, how much you purchased it for, the estimated replacement cost, and the estimated resale value.
3. Choose the item's Category and Location.
4. If the item is covered under one of your current insurance policies, in the list box marked Ins. Policy, choose the term that best describes how that item is covered.

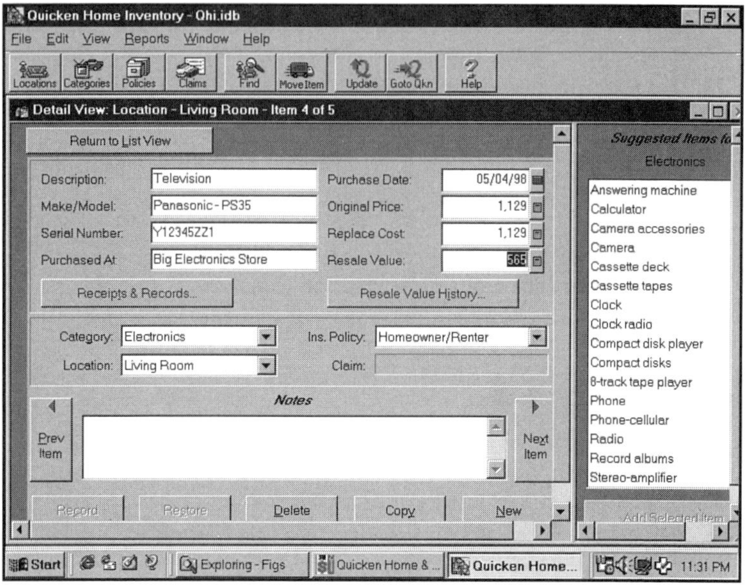

FIGURE 21.3 Enter a new inventory item in Detail view.

5. If you have any receipts or other papers that verify the value of the item, click Receipts & Records. Then in the dialog box that opens, check the boxes next to the listings for all the types of papers you have on hand. Click OK to continue.

6. If you know that the item has been sold for a specific value in the past, enter the sales history for that item. Click Resale Value History. The dialog box that opens shows all events pertaining to the sale of the item, in chronological order. To enter a new event, click New, and then enter the date and value of the sale. Click OK and click Close to continue.

7. To finalize your entry, click Record. To add another item, click New and repeat steps 2–7. To see your entries in list form, click Return to List View.

ENTERING YOUR INSURANCE DATA

Quicken's Home Inventory program is capable of generating detailed reports for both you and your insurance agent. For those reports to be more accurate, you should enter some data about your policies and the claims you've made on those policies thus far into Home Inventory.

POLICY DATA

To access Home Inventory's data about your insurance policies, do the following:

1. Click Policies on the iconbar. Quicken displays the Policies dialog box.
2. Listed in the Policies dialog box are descriptions for three generalized policies, plus a category for Unassigned. To add a policy entry, click New, and then enter as much pertinent information about the policy as you can, including a descriptive Policy Name (the only mandatory field), plus the name and address of your agent. Then click OK.
3. To change the data about a policy, choose its name from the list and click Edit. Update all relevant fields, and then click OK.
4. To delete a policy entry, choose its name from the list; click Delete, and then click OK in the verification message that follows.
5. Click Close to finalize your changes.

CLAIMS DATA

To record data about a claim you placed on a policy at any time during the history of that policy, from Home Inventory's iconbar, click Claims. Quicken displays the Claims dialog box. The dialog box shows all claims recorded for all your policies thus far. To add a new claim, do the following:

1. Click New. Quicken displays the New Claim Instructions message box. Click OK. Quicken then displays the New Claim dialog box (shown in Figure 21.4).

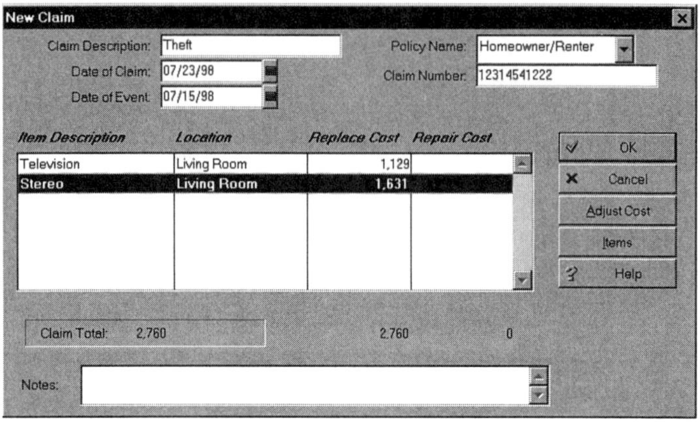

FIGURE 21.4 The New Claim dialog box helps you to keep track of all items in a new claim.

2. Start by entering a descriptive name for the claim in the field marked Claim Description.
3. Choose the name of the policy against which the claim was placed from the list box marked Policy Name.
4. To enter the item or items that are the subject of the claim, click Items. The dialog box that opens lists all items in inventory. From this list, choose all the items that apply, and then click OK.
5. If the coverage amount for an item is different than its listed worth, click Adjust Cost. Then choose whether the claim covers replacement or repair. Next, enter the associated cost and click OK.
6. When the claim is complete, in the New Claim dialog box, click OK. Quicken asks whether you want to see a report about the claim you entered; click Yes to see the report.

GENERATING INVENTORY REPORTS

The payoff from entering all these items into the database comes in the form of detailed inventory reports. All of these reports are available from Home Inventory's Reports menu. The six reports supported are as follows:

- *Inventory Value Summary.* Lists in columns the replacement cost, resale value, date of purchase, and purchase price of all items in inventory. Items are organized by your choice of category, location, or associated policy.
- *Inventory Detail.* Lists all important data about all items entered into inventory and can also be organized by category, location, or policy.
- *Insurance Coverage Summary.* This is like the Inventory Value Summary, except that items can be organized by the specific insurance policy that covers them. The report also adds some information about each policy.
- *Insurance Coverage Detail.* This is also formatted like Inventory Detail, except that items listed can be organized by specific policy.
- *Insurance Claim Summary.* This is like the Insurance Coverage Summary, except that it boils down the contents to just those items against which claims have been made.
- *Insurance Claim Detail.* This is like Insurance Coverage Detail, except that only items against which claims have been placed are shown.

To view a report, select it from the Quicken Home Inventory Reports menu. To print a report, click Print on the iconbar.

In this lesson, you learned how to organize the records of the assets you keep in your home and insure against fire, theft, or loss. In the next lesson, you learn how to organize your own financial records in case something should happen to you.

Lesson 22

Working with the Emergency Records Organizer

In this lesson, you learn how to create a database of vitally important information about yourself, to be used in the event that someone you love or trust might have to act on your behalf someday.

Records Categories

The objective of the Emergency Records Organizer (ERO) is to help you generate reports that others can use in the event that you're not present for a critical event, or that you are incapacitated. Your financial, legal, and medical data all come into play here, as well as important data about your spouse and family.

ERO keeps track of vital data pertinent to the following categories:

- *Adults' Emergency Info.* Contains data about who should be contacted in an emergency situation involving the adult members of the family.
- *Children's Emergency Info.* Contains data about who should be contacted in the event of an emergency involving any of the children in the family, where the adult members cannot be contacted or are unavailable.
- *Adults' Important Info.* Contains the general data that you would normally fill out at the top of an employment or medical form, plus information about your business, marriage, education, and military history.

- *Children's Important Info.* Contains the type of data you would enter into a form for your child's school or doctor.
- *Personal & Legal Docs.* Deals with the identification, categorical content, and location of your most important vital documents, such as your birth certificate, wills, and passport.
- *Accounts.* Describes the financial accounts (checking, savings, credit) you hold with various institutions. Much of this data can be gleaned from your existing Quicken accounts.
- *Income.* Identifies your sources of income and the names of responsible parties in authority at those sources.
- *Invest and Retirement.* Contains data about your securities holdings and retirement accounts. Again, some of this information can be copied from your existing Quicken accounts data.
- *Home/Auto/Property.* Deals with your most important possessions, such as your car, recreational vehicles, the contents of your safety deposit box, and even your pets.
- *Insurance.* Lists data about your current policies, such as contact location about your agents, and the extent to which your home and life are insured.
- *Mortgage/Loans.* Deals with your home mortgage, and your home, auto, and tuition loans.

Each category of data has associated subcategories or *topics*, and each of those has an entry form. Not every category or topic may apply to you, and some information may be of a type you would rather not share with anyone else. ERO is nonjudgmental; you can enter as much or as little data as you like.

ENTERING VITAL DATA

The process of entering data into ERO is mostly one of entering data into forms—dull, but uneventful. To load ERO with your vital data, do the following:

1. From the Features menu, select Planning, followed by Emergency Records Organizer. Quicken displays the ERO

screen, which is divided into three tabs. The first tab is an introductory page.

2. Click the Create/Update Records tab. The ERO screen appears as shown in Figure 22.1.

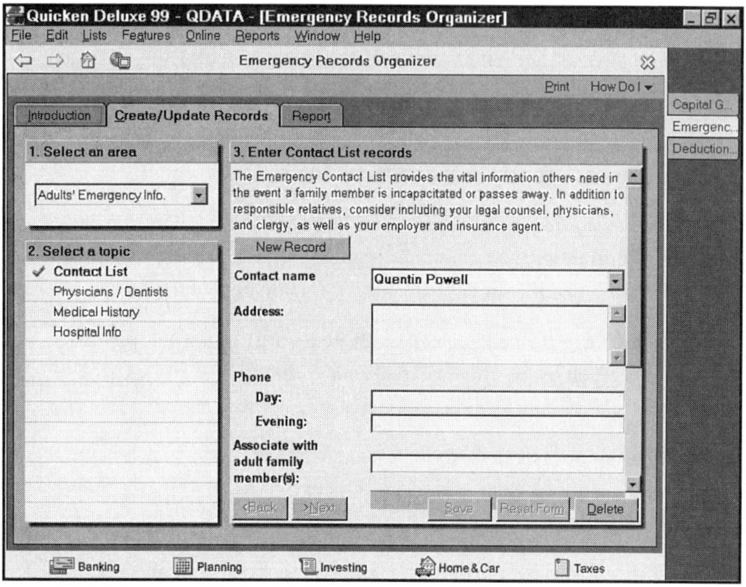

FIGURE 22.1 In ERO's data-entry screen create emergency records.

3. In the frame marked 1, choose a category for which you want to enter data.

4. The list marked 2 shows all topics associated with the chosen category. A green check mark beside a topic indicates that information already exists for that topic. To enter information for a topic, choose that topic from the list. The entry form for that topic appears in the frame marked 3.

5. If data already exists for the chosen topic, you can simply type over that data if it needs to be updated. However, it's possible for ERO to maintain more than one set of data for the chosen topic—for example, more than one contact if your child is in an emergency, or if you have more than one checking account. In

those cases, the New Record button is enabled. Click this button to clear the form so that you can enter a new record; the existing record is retained.

> **Browsing Multiple Records** When more than one record exists for a topic, the Back and Next buttons at the bottom of the ERO screen become available. Use these buttons to browse back to the previous record or forward to the next record for the chosen topic.

6. Enter as much data as is applicable to you for the given topic. Press Tab to navigate between fields.
7. To abort data entry for a record and start over, click Cancel. The ERO screen does not go away; the form is simply cleared.
8. To delete a record, from the lower-right corner of the ERO screen, click Delete.
9. To finalize your new record, click Save.
10. Repeat this process for as many topics and categories as you like.

GENERATING REPORTS

You probably should not expect a friend, relative, or guardian to learn to use Quicken just to access your emergency records. Instead, you should print your records to paper—which everyone knows how to use. ERO generates the following five types of reports:

- *Emergency Report*. Lists those people who can be contacted in case of an emergency, and also lists some sources that those contacts may require, such as your doctor or lawyer.
- *Caretaker Report*. Can be given to someone taking care of your home and family in your absence—for instance, a babysitter. It doesn't give away any of your financial data; it just lets that person know whom to contact.

- *Survivor's Report.* This is to be given to someone in the most extreme of circumstances and lists the crucial data about your vital contacts, your bank accounts, your investment advisors or brokers, and your creditors.
- *Summary of Records Entered Report.* An overview of all data you entered into ERO.
- *Detail Report.* Shows all data you entered into ERO.

To generate and print an ERO report, do the following:

1. In the ERO screen, click the Report tab. The Report page comes up with the Emergency Report, as shown in Figure 22.2.

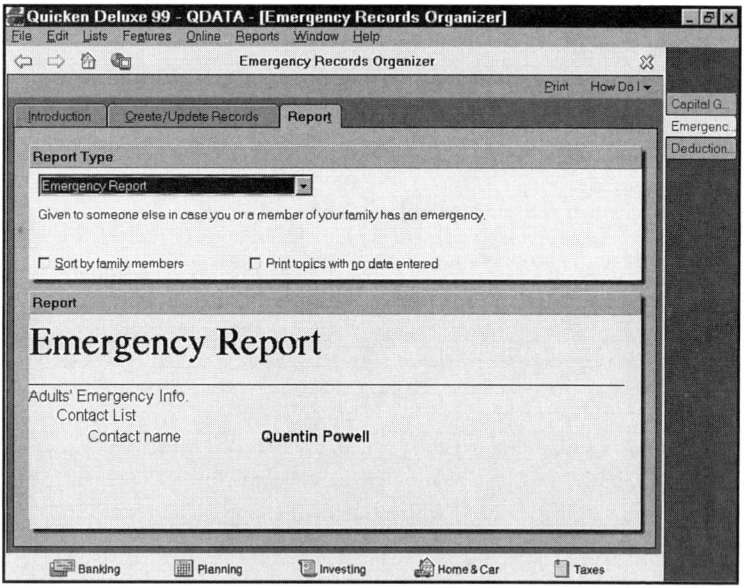

FIGURE 22.2 This ERO's Report page shows an Emergency Report.

2. Unless you want the Emergency Report, choose a report from the list box marked Report Type.

3. To print the chosen report, from the inset menu of the ERO screen, select Print. The report is immediately sent to the printer.

In this lesson, you learned how Quicken can organize your vital data in case of emergencies. Next, you learn how Quicken can be put to work for you via the Internet.

LESSON 23

USING QUICKEN DELUXE 99 ON THE INTERNET

In this lesson, you learn how Quicken gets its informational content from the Internet and how you can program Quicken to receive updates. You'll see Quicken's main Web site and learn how to use it directly from within Quicken.

When you install Quicken 99, you are given the option to install Internet Explorer 4.01 (IE4). If you use Windows 98, you don't need to install IE4 because it's already part of that operating system. But in any event, IE4 is crucial to much of the operation of Quicken. Besides relying on IE4 to connect it to the Internet, Quicken also uses IE4 as the layout engine for its many Centers and your personal home page. (For more information, see Lesson 14, "Using Quicken Deluxe 99's Financial Centers.")

> **The Call Is Coming From Inside the House!** If your computer connects to the Internet by way of a modem, then you might be surprised to find your computer dialing your Internet service provider all by itself while you're using Quicken. Periodically, Quicken updates its own textual content featured in its many Centers. To accomplish this, Quicken might have to borrow your phone every half hour or so, but it doesn't ask first. To disable this conduct, from the Online menu, select Internet Connection, Options. In the dialog box that opens, in the Background Downloading frame, set the option marked Don't use background downloading, and then click OK.

GOING ONLINE WITH QUICKEN.COM

Think of Quicken.com (pronounced Quicken-dot-com) as an up-to-date financial news center (see Figure 23.1). Here, you'll find the latest business and financial headlines, plus U.S. financial indices. Clicking a headline takes you to the full story, often supplied by Standard & Poor's, a leading financial publisher.

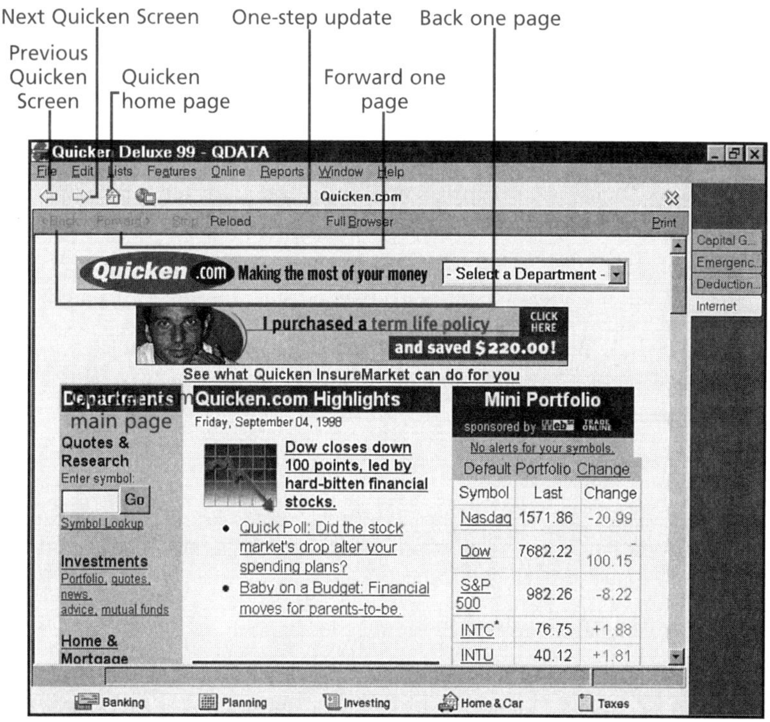

FIGURE 23.1 The home page for Quicken.com contains the latest financial news.

ACCESSING THE MAIN PAGE

To access Quicken.com from within Quicken, do the following:

1. From the Online menu, select Quicken on the Web, Quicken.com.

2. Quicken notifies you that it's about to connect to the Internet. Click OK.

3. If you haven't set up your Internet Connection through Quicken yet, you'll be shown the Internet Connection Setup dialog box. In this case, follow the procedure for this dialog box as covered in Lesson 3, "Finding Help."

4. After a few moments, the home page for Quicken on the Web (not to be confused with your own home page located in the Centers menu) is displayed in Quicken's Internet screen.

NAVIGATING THE INTERNET SCREEN

The Internet screen inside Quicken 99 is Microsoft Internet Explorer in a different guise. So many of the controls you expect to find in IE4 are present here as well; they're just located elsewhere.

- Usually, a brightly colored, underlined passage of text is a hyperlink. When you click it, the Internet screen takes you to another passage of text, often on a different page, which expands upon the same topic.
- To go back to a previously viewed page, select <Back from the button bar.
- To return to a page from which you previously jumped *back*, select Forward> from the button bar.
- If a Web page does not appear to be loading properly, or if loading appears to have stopped prematurely, select Reload.
- To halt the loading of a Web page at any time, click Stop.
- To print the current Web page, select Print from the button bar.
- To bring up the current page in a conventional Internet Explorer window, from the button bar, select Full Browser. The same page you're viewing in the Internet screen opens in a separate IE4 screen; you should notice no difference. Quicken displays a small window containing an icon marked Go back to Quicken. Click this icon to remove the IE4 window.

Not That Back, This Back! It's easy to confuse the left- and right-arrows that appear in the button bar of Quicken's Internet screen, with the Back and Forward buttons that normally control a Web browser. But that is not what the arrow buttons are for. Instead, the arrow buttons (marked by the ToolTips Go Back and Go Forward) take you through the set of open Quicken screens, represented on the right of the Quicken window by the QuickTabs. Likewise, the house icon on the button bar of Quicken screens takes you to the Quicken home page on your own computer (covered in Lesson 14) rather than the home page of Quicken.com.

Everything But URLs The one missing element distinguishing Quicken's Internet screen from a fully-fledged Web browser is a field showing the name (more technically, the Universal Resource Locator, or URL) of the Web page you're currently viewing. On a regular Web browser, you can type a new URL into this field and be taken to the page to which the URL points. When you restrict yourself to the comfortable confines of Quicken.com, this isn't a problem. However, Quicken.com is sponsored by many other companies whose own Web sites are just a click away. If you click one of their ads, you're generally taken to some other page away from Quicken.com. From there, you might be tempted to click an ad and go someplace else, and it is here that you realize that a URL field would be helpful. So whenever you decide to leave Quicken.com and go surfing, it's probably a good idea to select **Full Browser** and go straight to IE4. (See Appendix B, "Using Internet Explorer 4.01," for some pointers on how to use IE4 on its own.)

REGISTERING WITH QUICKEN.COM

Quicken.com can be set up to include some personalized features, such as quotes for stocks or bonds that you currently hold in your portfolio. Quicken.com cannot do this, however, unless it knows more about you so that each time you log on (or more accurately, each time Quicken 99 logs you on), Quicken.com can identify you and pull up news that you want to see.

To register yourself with Quicken.com so that you can personalize some of its features, do the following:

1. From Quicken.com's main page, in the Departments frame, under the Investments category click the Portfolio link.
2. From the Portfolio page that opens, click the Register Now button.
3. In the Registration page, the only fields for which you must supply data are your five-digit ZIP code, your email address, and an arbitrary password. If you want, you can add your name, date of birth, and your sex.
4. Click the Submit Registration button. After a moment, you're taken to Quicken's Portfolio page.

THE QUICKEN.COM PORTFOLIO

After you register, the Quicken.com server can be told which stocks, bonds, mutual funds, futures, averages, or indices you want tracked. Quicken.com can then pull up listings for you automatically whenever you log on.

> **Know Your Ticker Symbols** Before you enter trading issues into your Quicken.com portfolio, you need to know their accepted *ticker symbols*. These are the abbreviations that exclusively identify these issues when their trading values are transmitted over the press wire.

Your default Quicken.com portfolio consists of indices for the NASDAQ, Dow 30, and S&P 500 averages, plus listings for issues that are certainly of interest to Quicken: Intel Corp., Intuit, Microsoft, and Excite (the search engine division of AOL). To enroll a set of ticker symbols into your Quicken.com portfolio, do the following:

1. From the Quicken.com main page, click the Full Portfolio link. You're taken to the Portfolio page.
2. Click the Edit Symbols link.
3. In the big unmarked text field in the center of the page that opens, type the ticker symbols for all the issues and indices you want tracked and delete any symbols you don't care about. Be sure to type a single space between each symbol. Don't worry if symbols wrap over onto another line. Type your symbols in the order you want them to appear in your portfolio list.
4. To change the title of this portfolio from Your Portfolio to something else, type a new title in the field marked Portfolio Name.
5. Click Save Changes. Soon the Portfolio page is resent, and contains fresh listings for the ticker symbols you typed (see Figure 23.2). Now, whenever you log onto Quicken.com, the Mini Portfolio column shows the issues and indices being tracked for you.

Whenever a headline comes in over the wire regarding one of the issues in your portfolio, the Mini Portfolio column on your Quicken.com main page is updated with an exclamation point icon, next to the You have alerts! message. Click the icon to see the headline; perhaps one of the big brokerage firms has updated its rating on the stock from hold to buy.

OTHER QUICKEN WEB PAGES

There are five other Web sites accessible from Quicken 99's Online, Quicken on the Web menu selection:

- *InsureMarket*. Provides you with insights into the insurance market, such as the different categories of policies, and how much coverage you might need or can reasonably afford.

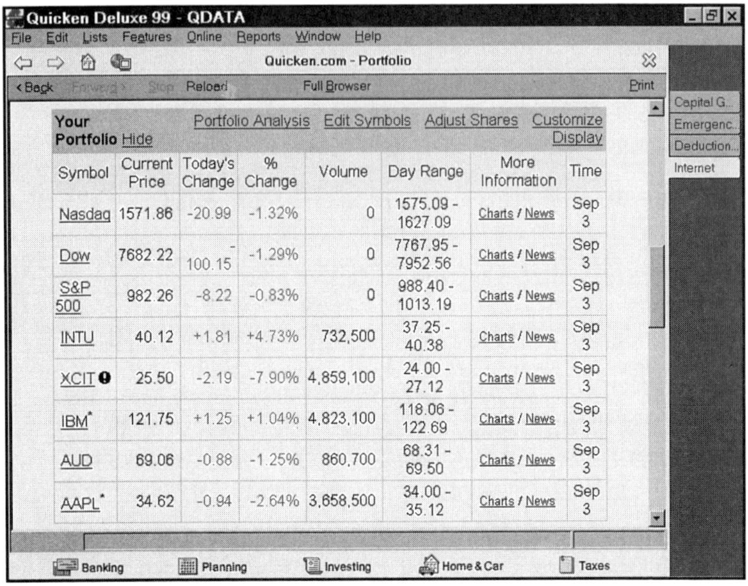

FIGURE 23.2 Customize the portfolio to meet your needs.

- *Mortgage Center*. Offers advice on topics such as whether you would save money by refinancing your home mortgage, or what to expect if you intend to be a first-time homeowner soon.
- *Credit Check*. A fee-based service from which you can order a copy of your credit report.
- *Investment Research*. Gives you a screen from which you can request detailed reports on stocks and mutual funds (also available from Quicken.com's main page).
- *Cash Finder*. Brings together a network of trusted lending institutions to help your small business obtain the funding it needs to get started or to get back on track. After you complete a questionnaire, the Web site generates a finalized report that you can use in formal applications for small business loans.

INITIALIZING ONE STEP UPDATE

For Quicken 99 to be able to refresh its internal bank of financial data, you need to set up its One Step Update feature. Follow these steps:

1. From the Online menu, select One Step Update.
2. In the Welcome dialog box that opens, click Continue.
3. Fill out the Software Registration form, and then click Next.
4. Answer the short questionnaire that follows, and then click Done. Quicken opens the Quicken 99 Download Selection dialog box.
5. The Download Selection list shows those items that you want Quicken to update for you via the Internet. By default, all items have been checked. If you need to, click an item to deselect it. Otherwise, just click Update Now.
6. If Quicken opens the Quicken.com Login dialog box and you've successfully created a portfolio for yourself on Quicken.com or a personalized start page for yourself on Excite's main page, click I Am Registered. Otherwise, click Register Now to register yourself with Quicken.com (as outlined earlier in this lesson).
7. Enter your email address and your Quicken.com password *exactly* as you created it. If you want Quicken to remember this password for next time (why not?) then check Remember who I am. Then click OK. Quicken displays a Download Status dialog box as it updates its internal information. After a few minutes, you see a Download Summary detailing what was downloaded. The underlined entries in this list are hyperlinks; click one of them to be taken straight to the newly refreshed Quicken feature.

From this point on, when you select Online, One Step Update, you're taken directly to the Download Selection list in Step 5.

In this lesson, you saw how to use Quicken's online Web service, Quicken.com. Next, you learn how you can set up Quicken to manage your financial transactions electronically.

LESSON 24

SETTING UP THE ONLINE CENTER

In this lesson, you learn how to set up and use Quicken's central resource for online transactions.

ACCESSING QUICKEN'S ONLINE CENTER

To access Quicken's Online Financial Transaction Center (or Online Center for short), follow these steps:

1. From the Online menu, select Online Financial Services Setup. Quicken brings up the Get Started dialog box.
2. If you have yet to set up an Internet connection with Quicken, click Set Up. Otherwise, to check out those financial institutions that support electronic transactions via Quicken, click Financial Institutions. Quicken displays the Apply for Online Financial Services page, shown in Figure 24.1.
3. To see a report on a financial institution, click its name in the Financial Institution Directory at left. Information on the chosen firm shows up in the frame at right.
4. To see more information from the chosen firm's own Web site, click the link marked Visit our Web site at. When you're done, click <Back until you get back to this page.
5. To bring up an application form for the chosen site, click the Apply Now button. The form comes up in the Internet screen. You might be able to sign up through a secured Web page; in some cases, you might be given a form to print and mail in (mail as in U.S. mail, not email). In any event, the procedure for each institution is different from this point on.

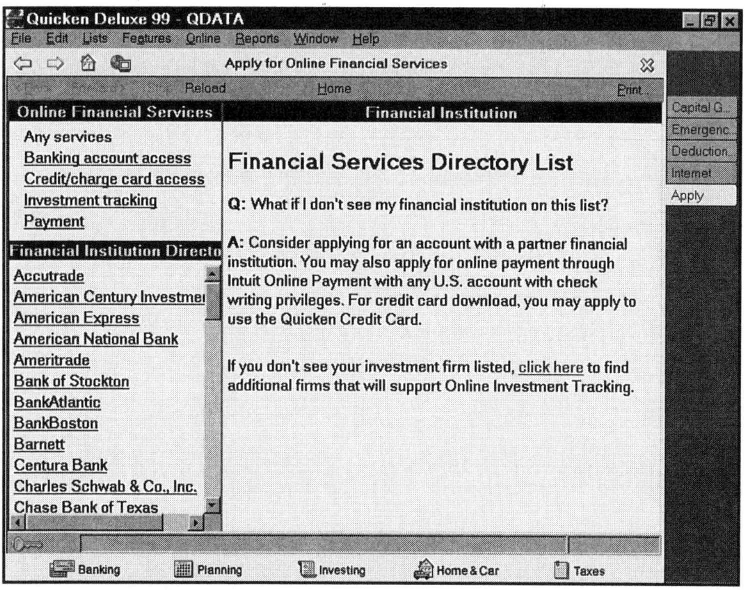

FIGURE 24.1 The Apply for Online Financial Services page.

Whenever you get a response from the financial institution of your choice—be it by email or U.S. mail—you should receive some important numbers. Your account number is one. Another is your customer ID number, which is often your own Social Security number. Yet a third is called a *routing number*. You need all these to enable electronic transactions for your Quicken accounts.

ENABLING ACCOUNTS FOR ONLINE TRANSACTIONS AND INVESTMENTS

This is where you tell Quicken to make your existing accounts Internet ready. To enable a bank account for online transactions, do the following:

1. From the Lists menu, select Account. Quicken brings up the Account List screen.

2. Choose the bank account you want to enable (it will read Bank under the Type column), and from the button bar, select Edit. Quicken brings up the Edit Bank Account dialog box.

3. To make it possible for you to go online to check your account status and balance, in the frame marked Online Information, check the box marked Enable Online Account Access.

4. To make it possible for you to order payments to be made electronically from your bank to your creditors, check the box marked Enable Online Payment.

5. Click Next. Quicken displays the Edit Bank Account dialog box.

6. Verify that your routing number, account number, type of account (checking, savings, money market, or line of credit), and your customer ID are correct. Click Done. Your account is now marked in the Account List with a lightning-bolt icon.

To enable your investment account for online transactions, the process is similar:

1. Choose your investment account from the Account List; then from the button bar, select Edit.

2. In the Edit Investment Account dialog box, check Enable Online Investment, and then click Next.

3. Verify that your account number and your customer ID number are correct, and then click Done. Your investment account now appears with a lightning-bolt icon in the Account List screen.

OVERVIEW OF THE ONLINE CENTER

Over the course of the remaining lessons, you see Quicken from an entirely new perspective—from the point of view of the Online Center. To bring up the Online Center screen, from the Online menu, select Online Center. After you're set up for online transactions, Quicken becomes a nerve center for sensing your personal financial status and monitoring changes in global financial markets. Figure 24.2 shows the Online Center's Payments tab associated with an online bank account with online payments enabled.

With banking institutions like the one shown previously, you can make direct and instantaneous payments from your accounts. You can set up Quicken so that paying your monthly bills becomes a scheduled event that always takes place on time, because Quicken is your agent of payment.

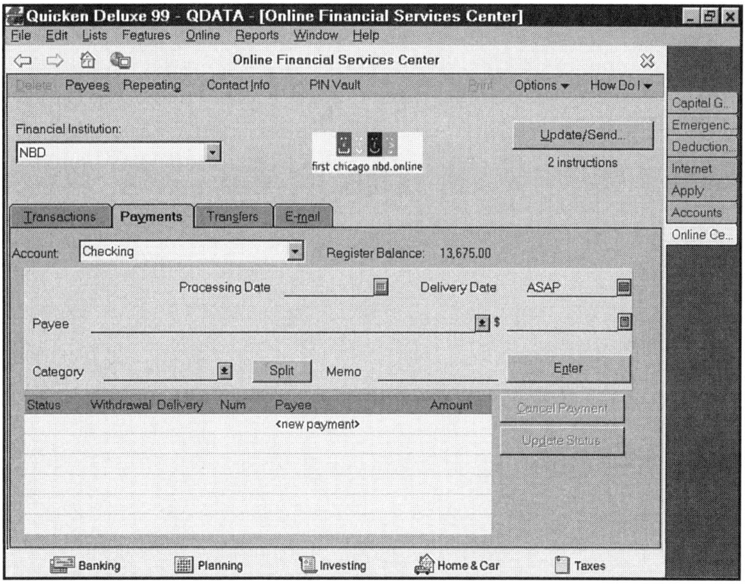

FIGURE 24.2 Where you set up direct electronic payments.

With online trading institutions, you can connect your Quicken investment accounts to your portfolios with such recognized brokers as E*TRADE, Ameritrade, and Suretrade. Let Quicken update you with the financial news you need on the spot, and then sell your shares at precisely the right hour for maximum profits.

In this lesson, you started your journey toward online success by setting up Quicken's Online Center. The next lesson shows how you use the Online Center's banking features.

LESSON 25
BANKING ONLINE

In this lesson, you learn how to use your Internet-enabled Quicken bank accounts. You see how to check your balances and how to make one-time and scheduled online payments.

CHECK YOUR BALANCES

In the preceding lesson, you set up your online bank account. Part of the purpose of the Online Center is to give you a place to download your account balance and transaction statements. As experience has probably taught you, for as long as you've been mailed statements on paper, the bank's perspective on your account and your own perspective often differ. In such cases, it isn't always clear who's at fault, and it isn't always you. Simply because your transaction statement can be made available to you online does not change this state of affairs. You might still receive an incorrect statement or one that simply doesn't coincide with your version of the events…only now you'll receive that statement sooner than ever before.

For this reason, Quicken provides tools that help you reconcile your online bank statements with your Quicken accounts. This is also why Quicken displays your online transaction statements *separately* in the Online Center, instead of simply merging all those transactions into your account database and red-flagging all the discrepancies.

DOWNLOADING YOUR ACCOUNT STATUS

To bring up the Online Center, from the Online menu, select Online Center. To download your account information from your online bank of choice, here's how you begin:

> **You Never Step in the Same River Twice** Intuit's electronic transaction scheme is set up so that participating financial institutions can conduct some business with their clients in their own way. Where their methods differ from one another, there's no one clear set of instructions this book can offer about using those methods.
>
> Also, those methods are subject to change without notice to anyone, including Intuit, but most notably including you. So what this book does instead in those situations is give you an idea of what to expect when you encounter a situation in which the next step is uncertain.

1. Choose your bank from the list box marked Financial Institution. Its logo should appear in the center of the Online Center screen.
2. Click Update/Send. Quicken brings up a list of instructions that it is set to give to your bank.
3. By default, all these instructions are checked. They might include **Download latest cleared transactions and balances** and **Bring my payment information up to date**. Uncheck any instructions you do not need sent, and then click Send.
4. You might see a logon screen asking you for your bank's PIN number. If this is the first time you're logging on, you might be instructed to change your PIN number now, to avoid using one that is documented on paper for someone else to discover. Click OK when you're ready for Quicken to log on.
5. Click the Transactions tab to see the list of downloaded items.

If you have a register screen open and you want to update the records in your register with your bank's recollection of the account, from the button bar select Reconcile. Quicken takes you to the Online Center, from which you can click Update/Send and receive the current transactions list.

UPDATING YOUR REGISTER

After you've downloaded your bank statement, your transactions appear in the Online Center under the Transactions tab. For each transaction, any of the following conditions might be in effect:

- The Online Center might show a transaction that is not currently recorded in your register. In this case, you should add it to the register even if you dispute it. You can make a note of your dispute and then alter the register later when the bank's version of events is corrected.
- A transaction might show up that matches one recorded in your register. No problem there.
- A transaction might show up that is similar to one recorded in your register, but that is for a different amount. You might need to change the register, even if you dispute the amount. You can make a note of the difference and make adjustments later. (It's better than accidentally spending money you don't have someday.)
- A transaction might appear in your register for which the bank has no record. No problem there; your check probably hasn't cleared yet. Treat it as though it did clear, because it might at any time.

To put your register's version of events in accordance with your bank's—disputed or not—do the following:

1. After the Online Center's transactions list has been refreshed, click Compare to Register. Quicken brings up the Register screen but divides it in two. The upper frame shows the ordinary register, and the lower frame shows the recently downloaded transactions.
2. Choose a transaction from the lower frame. If a matching transaction appears in the upper frame, it is highlighted. If the highlighted entry in the register matches the downloaded transaction, check the Clr column in the register to see whether the transaction has already been cleared.

If an **R** (for reconciled) appears in that column, you do not need to record that transaction a second time. In such a case, click Delete in the lower frame. This action removes the transaction from the lower frame list, *not* from the register. If the Clr column is blank, click Accept. This places an **R** in the column, indicating that the transaction has cleared the bank.

3. If a transaction exists in your register that is the only one very similar to the chosen transaction in the lower frame, Quicken places the entry bar around this transaction in the register and marks it as a **Near Match** in the lower frame. This gives you the opportunity to edit the amount to make it coincide with the bank's state of affairs, if you believe that your original entry into the register was in error. Click Accept when the entry is edited to match the downloaded transaction.

4. If no matching transaction is highlighted in the upper frame, the entry bar appears at the bottom of the register as though you were about to record a newly written check. The data from the chosen transaction is automatically copied to the entry bar. Edit this entry as necessary.

   You might want to assign a category to the transaction now. If you have a dispute, you might want to mark that dispute in the Memo field. Click Accept to finalize the entry of the transaction into the register. Note that in the Status column in the lower frame, the transaction has changed from **New** to **Accepted**.

5. Repeat from step 2 for all transactions in the lower frame until all remaining transactions there have been marked **Accepted**. Then click Done.

TRANSFERRING FUNDS BETWEEN ONLINE ACCOUNTS

If you have two or more accounts within Quicken that are set up for online account access, Quicken can manage the entire process of moving funds between those accounts. The simplest method to do this is to *register the transfer first*. Then go into the Online Center and have it initiate the transfer you've registered. This approach seems slightly backward, but it does save a few steps. Here's what you do:

1. From the Lists menu, select Account.
2. In the Account List, double-click the name of the account from which you want to transfer funds. This is the source of the funds, not the destination. Quicken brings up the Register screen for that account and places the entry bar at the bottom.
3. Press Tab to enter today's date and move on to the next field.
4. In the drop-down list that appears in the Num column, choose Online Transfer. Your choice is recorded in this column as **OXfr**.
5. Enter any meaningful Description into that column, and then press Tab.
6. Enter an amount to be transferred, and then press Tab.
7. In the Xfer Acct field, choose the account to which funds are to be transferred. This is the destination.
8. Click the Enter button to register the transfer.
9. From the Online menu, select Online Center.
10. Choose the bank where your accounts are held from the Financial Institution list, and then click the Transfers tab. The Online Center should now appear as depicted in Figure 25.1. In the lower frame, you should see the transfer you just registered. Notice in the Status column that the transfer is marked **Not Sent**.
11. Click Update/Send to have Quicken go online and initiate the transfer. It should take only a few minutes.

Performing the transfer this way saves you from having to download a record of the transfer from the bank and reconcile that record against your register later. Incidentally, the transfer of funds is automatically recorded in the register for the account receiving the funds; you do not need to go into the receiving register to make the amounts match.

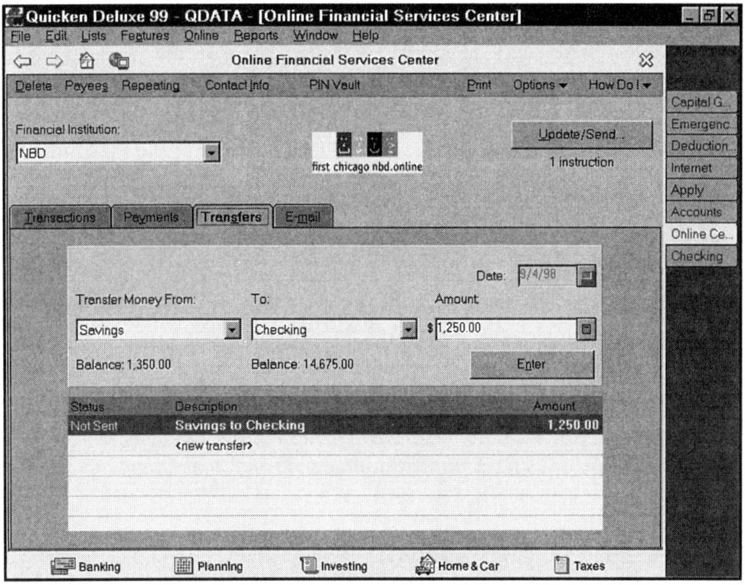

FIGURE 25.1 The Transfers tab of the Online Center.

In this lesson, you learned how to download your bank statement, how to reconcile the accounts therein against your register, and how to transfer funds between two online accounts. The next lesson deals with handling your bills and regular payments through your online bank.

LESSON 26

MANAGING BILLS AND PAYMENTS ONLINE

In this lesson, you learn how Quicken's Online Center can be set up to make payments to your creditors through your electronic bank.

MANAGING ONLINE PAYEES

Not every financial institution is set up to handle online *payments*. Most handle downloading of balances and account information, and transfers of funds between accounts (profiled in the preceding lesson). But some are equipped to actually initiate transactions—in effect, transferring funds from your bank to someone else's. Other banks are equipped with the capability to mail out checks to your designated recipients for you, for a nominal fee.

To bring up the Online Center, select Online Center from the Online menu. To make Quicken 99 ready for making payments, your first step is to inform Quicken as to whom it can possibly pay. You see, your online recipients must have their own payment accounts whose numbers are made public, or at least made known to you. All payees who can be paid electronically must be enrolled in an exclusive list of payees maintained by Quicken's Online Center. If your bank can mail checks, Quicken needs to know your payee's mailing information. After a payee is enrolled, a single payment or a set of recurring payments can be established with the payee as designated recipient.

ENROLLING A NEW PAYEE

To enter your online payees into Quicken, do the following:

1. From the button bar, select Payees. Quicken displays the Online Payee List screen.
2. From the Online Payee List screen's button bar, select New. Quicken displays the Set Up Online Payee dialog box shown in Figure 26.1.

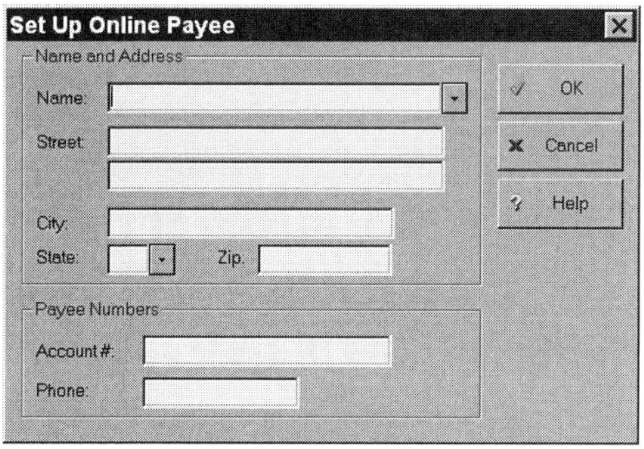

FIGURE 26.1 The Set Up Online Payee dialog box.

3. Enter the payee's mailing information in the frame marked Name and Address.
4. Enter the payee's account number and telephone number (for verification) in the fields in the Payee Numbers frame. These are required fields.
5. Click OK when done. The name is added to the Payee list.

In the Payee list, notice the column marked Lead Time. This refers to the minimum number of days that should elapse between the time a payment is initiated and the time it is received. By default, this time is set for four days.

EDITING AN EXISTING PAYEE

To change any information about an online payee, do the following:

1. In the Online Payee List screen, right-click the payee's name, and from the pop-up menu, select Edit. Quicken brings up the Edit Online Payee dialog box, which is a clone of the one shown earlier in Figure 26.1.
2. Change any information necessary.
3. Click OK to finalize your changes.

You Can't Change a Payee While He's Being Paid If you've scheduled a transaction involving an existing payee, and you have yet to send that transaction to your bank with the Online Center's Update/Send button, then Quicken prevents you from being able to edit that payee's listing until the pending transaction is sent. For this reason, you should be certain to make any changes to payees' addresses before scheduling transactions.

MAKING INDIVIDUAL ONLINE PAYMENTS

Now that Quicken knows whom you can pay and how, you can write a sort of "online check" to this party. You set up a one-time payment to a registered online payee like this:

1. In the Online Center screen, choose your online bank from the upper-left corner list marked Financial Institution.
2. Click the Payments tab. The screen appears as shown in Figure 26.2.
3. In the Account list box, choose an online account to serve as the source of funds.
4. For the "online check," Quicken distinguishes between the Processing Date (today, the date in which the transaction is initiated) and the Delivery Date. This latter date is when the transaction is uploaded to the bank, and it is adjusted based on the given lead time for the designated payee. Despite the fact that

online payments are fast in the processing on your end, they are sometimes slow on the bank's end. So you might want to choose a delivery date that is well in advance of the due date.

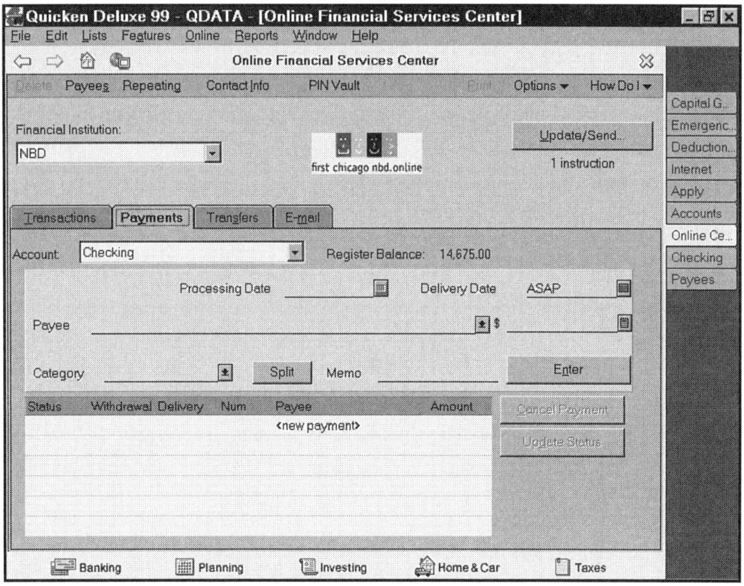

FIGURE 26.2 The Payments tab of the Online Center screen.

5. For the Payee field, use the drop-down button to choose a registered online payee.
6. Enter an amount to pay the designated party in the field marked $.
7. Enter the category for which Quicken should record this payment in its register. To split the paid amount between two or more categories, click Split; then in the Split Transaction Window that comes up, choose multiple categories for the Category column, and distribute the payment amount among them.
8. If necessary, enter text in the Memo field.

9. Click Enter. The payment request is now recorded and ready to be sent to your bank. Click the <new payment> line in the transactions list to wipe the payment form and start a new one.

Immediately after you order an online payment, it becomes listed in the register for the account you chose as the source of funds. This entry appears in the register even before you send your order to the bank with the Online Center's Update/Send button. Any unsent transactions recorded in the register are marked by a telltale blue line above the top row, plus the word **Send** in the Num column.

SETTING UP A REPEATING ONLINE PAYMENT

Perhaps the most clever feature of Quicken's Online Center is the capability for it to make regular electronic payments for you automatically. A repeating payment is a formal scheduled transaction, which shows up on Quicken's Scheduled Transaction List under the Repeating Online tab. To set up a regular repeating payment, do the following:

1. From the button bar of the Online Center screen, select Repeating. Quicken displays the Scheduled Transaction List.
2. If at least one transaction already appears in this list, in the button bar click New to bring up the Create Repeating Online Payment dialog box, shown in Figure 26.3. If this is your first repeating payment, Quicken brings up this dialog box automatically.
3. In the First Payment field, choose the date when the first repeating payment is to be made.
4. Choose the Account from which funds are to be drawn, from the list box so marked.
5. Choose an online Payee from the list box so marked.
6. In the Category field, choose a category for Quicken to associate the payment with.
7. Enter an Amount for each regular payment in the field so marked.

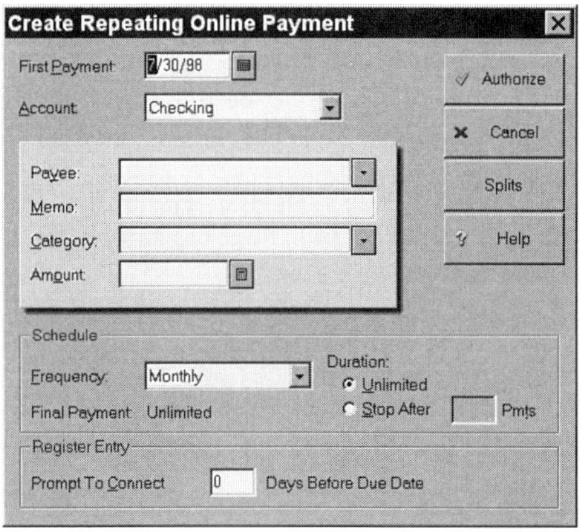

FIGURE 26.3 The Create Repeating Online Payment dialog box.

8. In the Schedule frame, from the list box marked Frequency, choose how often a new payment is to be made out—every two weeks, twice per month, monthly, every two months, quarterly, twice per year, or annually.

9. By default, the Duration option is set to Unlimited, which means that the repeating payment continues until you delete it explicitly. To have the repeating payment terminate itself after a given number of electronic checks, set the option marked Stop After and then enter a number in the field marked Pmts (payments).

10. In the Register Entry frame, the lone field set to 0 means that Quicken does not prompt you to send the payment to your electronic bank. To change this so that you're prompted a given number of days before the set due date of the payment (actually the date in which the payment is presumed to take place), change this number from 0 to a positive value.

11. When your repeating payment is ready to be recorded, click Authorize. Quicken adds the payment to the Scheduled Transaction List.

Repeating transactions do not show up in the Online Center's list of transactions to be sent to the bank until it's time to send them. The Scheduled

Transaction List does not show the individual payments, but instead the record on which those payments are based. Each generated payment based on that repeating transaction appears under the Payments tab of Online Center.

In this lesson, you learned how to schedule one-time and repeating online payments. In the next and final lesson, you see how to use the Online Center to track your investments.

LESSON 27

TRACKING ONLINE INVESTMENTS

In this lesson, you learn about the Online Center's features for tracking and managing your investment accounts.

DOWNLOADING YOUR INVESTMENT TRANSACTIONS

One feature Quicken 99 does *not* have is the capability for you to place your investment and trading orders directly through Quicken. In other words, you can't use Quicken to make a trade, or to buy or sell shares. Intuit is working on this capability, but for now, there's no standard way for a program to communicate using standardized code with an electronic brokerage firm. A common language is needed between the two, and one hasn't been devised yet.

For now, you have to settle for trading using an ordinary Web browser. But this doesn't make Quicken's Online Center useless to you in the investment department. You can use Quicken with some online brokerages to shift funds into and out of your investment accounts, to check the status of your portfolio, and to go over your trading history.

To bring up the Online Center, from the Online menu, select Online Center. In Lesson 4, "Creating Accounts," you saw how to initiate an investment account within Quicken. To download your account information from your online broker of choice, here's how you begin:

1. Choose your broker from the list box marked Financial Institution. Its logo should appear in the center of the Online Center screen.

2. Click Update/Send. Quicken brings up a list of instructions that it is set to give to your broker.
3. By default, all these instructions are checked. They might include **Download latest transactions, balances, and holdings**. Uncheck any instructions you do not need sent.
4. Enter the PIN number given to you by your broker, in the field marked Enter your PIN.
5. Click Send to log on. In a moment, after sending your pending instructions, Quicken downloads an up-to-date list of transactions.
6. Click the Transactions tab to see the list of downloaded items.

RECONCILING FUNDS TRANSFERS

Because trading online takes place over the World Wide Web, it's out of view of Quicken. Quicken won't "know" that a trade has taken place until either you enter that trade into the register for your investment account or you download your trading information into the Online Center. Either method gets the data where it belongs, but the latter method might save you some time. Because your broker records all your transactions anyway, why not copy your data from your broker if you can?

The job of reconciling your broker's statement of your investment account against your own register could end up being simply a job of copying your broker's records to your own. Besides, you really won't know how much you made from a securities transaction until your broker tells you. To check your broker's statement of funds against the register for your investment account, do the following:

1. After the Online Center's transactions list has been refreshed, click Compare to Register. Quicken brings up the Register screen for your investment account but divides it in two. The upper frame shows the ordinary register, and the lower frame shows the recently downloaded transactions.
2. If a transaction involves a trading issue or ticker symbol that Quicken does not recognize, at this point it pulls up the Identify Securities window. At the top of the window is the name of the

security in question as downloaded from your broker. (Different brokers might have different names for the same trading issue.)

Below that is a list of known securities from your Quicken portfolio. If you see the issue in question in that list, choose it and click Yes. Otherwise, just click No, and Quicken creates a new portfolio entry based on the listed security. If no more securities' names are in question, click Next; otherwise, click Done.

3. In the Register screen, choose a transaction from the lower frame. If a matching transaction appears in the upper frame, it is highlighted. If the highlighted entry in the register matches the downloaded transaction, check the Clr column in the register to see whether the transaction has already been cleared. If an **R** (for "reconciled") appears in that column, you do not need to record that transaction a second time. In such a case, click Delete in the lower frame. This action removes the transaction from the lower frame list, *not* from the register. If the Clr column is blank, click Accept. This places an **R** in that column.

4. If a transaction exists in your register that is the only one very similar to the chosen transaction in the lower frame, Quicken places the entry bar around this transaction in the register and marks it as a **Near Match** in the lower frame. This gives you the opportunity to edit the amount to make it coincide with your broker's database, if you believe that your original entry into the register was in error. Click Accept when the entry is edited to match the downloaded transaction.

5. If no matching transaction is highlighted in the upper frame, the entry bar appears at the bottom of the register. The data from the chosen transaction is automatically copied to the entry bar. Edit this entry as necessary. Click Accept to finalize the entry of the transaction into the register. Note that in the Status column in the lower frame, the transaction has changed from **New** to **Accepted**.

6. Repeat from step 3 for all transactions in the lower frame until all remaining transactions there have been marked Accepted.

7. If you linked your investment account to a separate checking account (if your broker allows you to write checks on your

investment account), click Continue. You're taken to the Register screen for that account, where you can reconcile transactions using the method outlined in Lesson 25, "Banking Online," for reconciling bank accounts. If there is no linked checking account, just click Done.

> **Checking Your Balances Only** When you're managing your online investments with the Online Center, the Balances tab shows you the most currently downloaded cash balances for all the accounts held with your chosen broker. The securities issues that yielded these balances are left out of this statement.

Reconciling Securities Holdings

From time to time, your broker's account of the particular securities you hold and Quicken's account might not agree. Earlier in this lesson, you saw how to reconcile transactions involving your investment account. This is different from reconciling your list of holdings with your broker's list of your holdings. To make these lists coincide, do the following:

1. In the Online Center screen, choose your broker from the list box marked Financial Institution.
2. Click the Holdings tab.
3. Choose your investment account from the list box at the upper-left corner of the frame, just below the tabs.
4. From the list box in the middle of the screen (just below the Holdings tab), choose whether you want to reconcile all securities (the default), or just stocks, mutual funds, options, bonds, or securities listed as **Other**.
5. Click Compare to Portfolio. Quicken brings up the Investment screen for your chosen investment account, as shown in Figure 27.1.
6. Choose an issue from the list in the lower frame. Any near match is highlighted in the upper frame, allowing you to edit it. Click the Enter button when your edits look right.

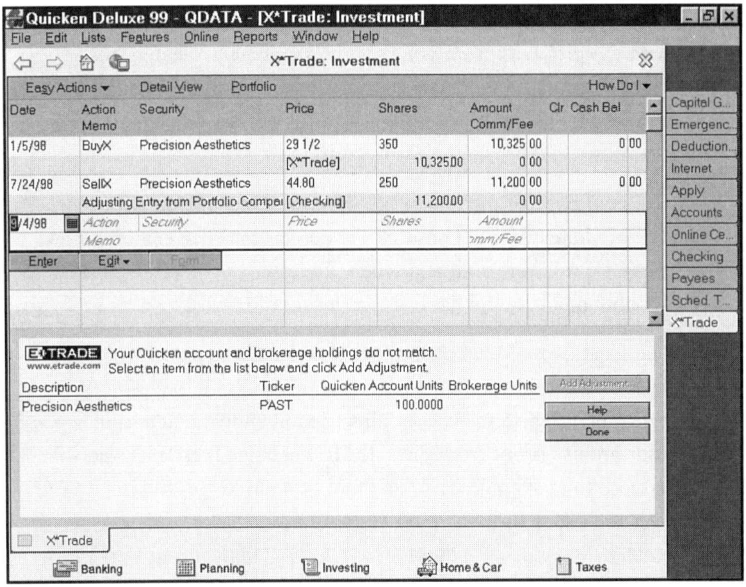

FIGURE 27.1 Reconciling your portfolio.

7. If a transaction exists for the chosen security that is not listed in the register, the data for that transaction is automatically added to the entry bar. Click Add Adjustment to accept that entry. If the adjustment constitutes a sale of shares, Quicken displays the Sell/Remove Shares dialog box. If not, skip to step 11.

Don't Confuse This with a Sell Order When you make an adjustment to your portfolio transactions, any sale of shares you record here should reflect sales that have already been made. Quicken is not an automated broker, so your sale of shares dialog boxes do not elicit information to be transmitted to your broker later. You adjust your account here with transactions that have already taken place.

8. The first question here concerns what Quicken is supposed to do with the proceeds from your sale of shares. To transfer those proceeds into a Quicken account, set the option to Yes, and then choose that account from the list box. Otherwise, leave the option set at No. Click Next to continue.

9. The next page of the dialog box has you enter the data for the sale of shares. If you chose No in step 8, you're asked only how many shares were sold and when. Otherwise, you're also asked for how much, and what the commission fee was.

10. The Cost Basis Method frame deals with how you want Quicken to track the sale value of shares recorded on one line of your Investment register. This pertains to how Quicken determines your precise profit from the sale. To have Quicken track the sale based on the average cost per share purchased for that issue, over the entire time that you've purchased shares of that issue, choose Average Cost, and then click Next and skip to step 14.

    To have Quicken track the sale of the number of shares you've chosen, starting with the oldest lots you purchased and working toward the newest lots, choose Lot Identification and do nothing else with that frame.

    To specify which lots you've sold, rather than have Quicken start at the beginning, choose Lot Identification and then click Specify Lots. Quicken brings up the Specify Lots dialog box (shown in Figure 27.2).

11. In the Selected column, enter the number of shares you're selling from each of your purchased lots. Quicken ensures that your Total Selected tally at the lower left does not exceed the Shares to Sell tally just above it.

12. To have Quicken record the sale of the earliest shares you've purchased (the default), click First Shares In. To have Quicken record just the reverse—those shares you most recently purchased—click Last Shares In.

    To have Quicken record the sale of the *lowest*-valued shares you've ever purchased of this issue, click Maximum Gain. To have Quicken record the sale of the *highest*-valued shares you've purchased (which might be a requirement of your broker, if your broker isn't interested in profits), click Minimum Gain.

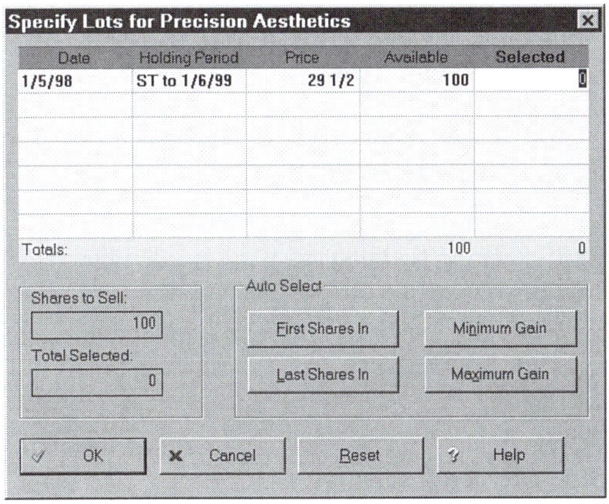

FIGURE 27.2 Telling Quicken specifically which of your shares you're selling.

> **How Quicken Tracks Sales of Securities** You sell shares of stock or mutual funds as all or part of a *lot*. This can be a round lot (a multiple of 100 shares) or an odd lot (any other number). It's possible that the total number of shares in this lot might represent a collection of different lots you've purchased at different times, perhaps at different values. When you have Quicken use an Average Cost basis, Quicken averages the values of all the shares being sold and determines your sales price—and your capital gain—based on that number. When Quicken tracks your sale on the ticker, it looks for this average cost, as well as a sales lot that totals the number of shares you've designated *or greater* (sometimes brokerages pool like-valued sales together). Some brokerage firms do not accept this method, and instead sell a specific lot—generally the oldest lot in your portfolio.

13. When you're done selecting sales lots, click OK. Then in the Sell/Remove Shares dialog box, click Next to proceed.
14. The Summary page lets you review the details of the sale and change them before committing them to Quicken. Click Done when everything looks right.
15. A dialog box tells you that your account and your broker's account are in agreement. Click OK.

In this lesson, you saw how to manage the information about trades that you made through your online broker, using Quicken's Online Center. This is the final lesson. Good luck with Quicken, and may every dollar you earn be earned well.

APPENDIX A

INSTALLING QUICKEN 99

In this appendix, you learn how to install Quicken Deluxe 99 and Microsoft Internet Explorer 4.01.

FOLLOWING THE INSTALLATION STEPS

To install Quicken Deluxe 99, you need the Quicken CD or the program's floppy disks. Quicken's Setup program walks you through the necessary steps to install the program onto your computer's hard disk drive.

The steps in this appendix focus on installing Quicken with the CD, but if you've got floppy disks, you can still follow along, switching disks when prompted.

1. Close all open applications and insert the Quicken CD into your CD-ROM drive.
2. If your computer is set up to automatically run CDs, the AutoRun Windows Application prompt appears, as shown in Figure A.1. Click Yes to continue.

   If AutoRun isn't on, open My Computer, double-click the CD drive's icon, and then double-click the Install icon.

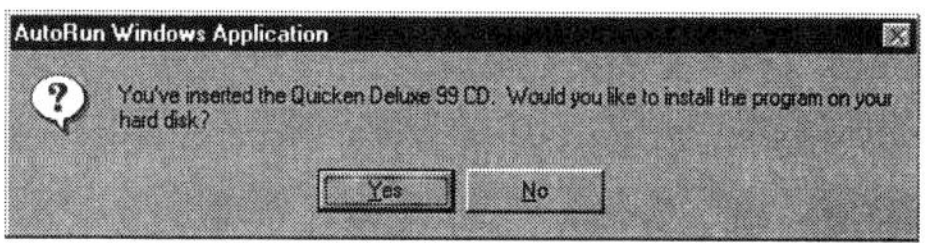

FIGURE A.1 To begin the installation program, click Yes.

3. The first installation dialog box that appears is a Welcome box (see Figure A.2). Click Next to continue.

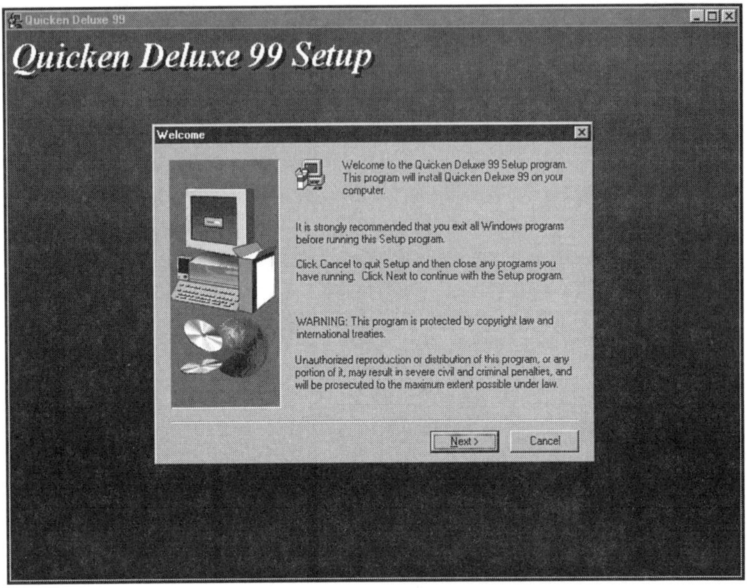

FIGURE A.2 From the Welcome dialog box, click Next to begin.

4. Read the Software License Agreement and click Yes to accept and continue installing.
5. Use the next dialog box to determine a location for the program files (see Figure A.3). By default, Quicken is installed to your main drive, usually C, in the QUICKENW folder. If the default location is okay with you, click Next to continue. If not, click Browse and select another folder to store the program to.
6. Next, choose a type of installation, as shown in Figure A.4. Use the Express installation to install the common options that come with Quicken Deluxe 99. Select Custom if you prefer to install only certain components. For most users, the default Express installation is the way to go; click Next to continue.
7. The next dialog box enables you to select a program folder. To use the default program group, just click Next to continue.
8. The Setup program lists the components to be installed. Click Start Copying to begin saving the files to your computer's hard drive. A gauge appears monitoring the installation's progress.

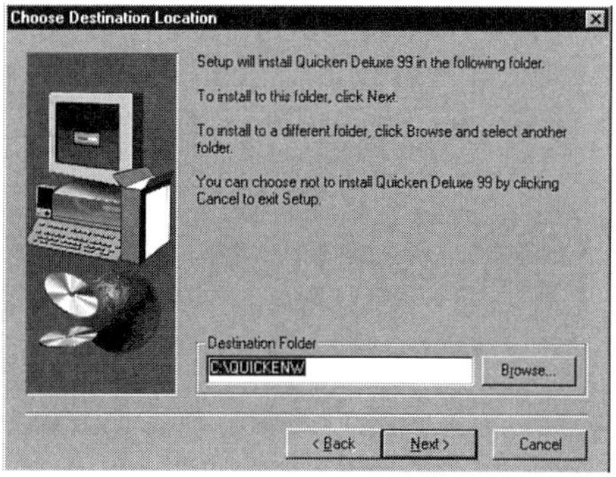

FIGURE A.3 Use the Choose Destination Location box to specify where you want Quicken installed.

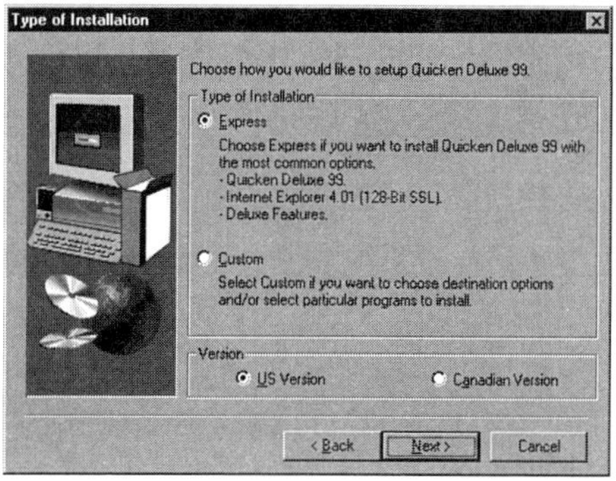

FIGURE A.4 Select from Express or Custom installation.

9. You're prompted when the installation is complete. Click OK and Quicken asks whether you want to install Microsoft Internet Explorer. Click Yes to continue.

10. Internet Explorer Active Setup now takes over to install the browser program, as shown in Figure A.5. Click Next to continue.

11. Read the license agreement and select the I Accept the Agreement option and click Next.

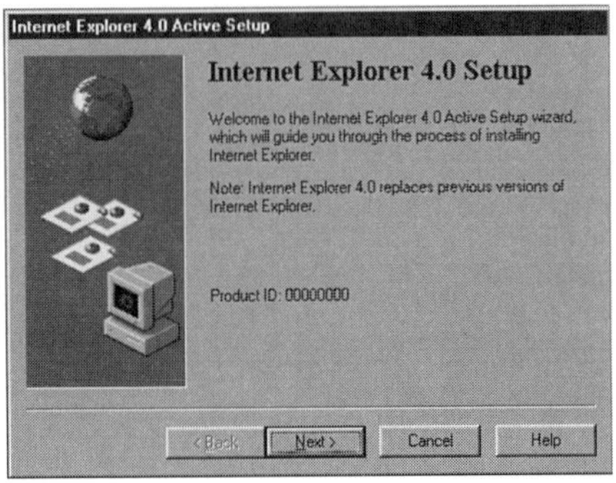

FIGURE A.5 As part of the Quicken installation, you can install Internet Explorer.

12. Choose a destination folder where you want to store the Internet Explorer files. To save the files in the default folder listed, click Next. To change the folder, click Browse and select another folder.

13. Setup begins installing the various Internet Explorer components. When the installation is complete, a prompt box appears telling you so; click OK.

14. To finish installing you must restart your computer. Click Finish and your computer restarts with Quicken and Internet Explorer now installed.

APPENDIX B

USING INTERNET EXPLORER 4.01

In this appendix, you learn the basic skills necessary to use Internet Explorer.

BROWSER BASICS

In a nutshell, Internet Explorer is a Web browser, a program designed specifically for viewing pages found on the World Wide Web (or Web, for short). The Web is just one part of what we call the Internet, that vast, worldwide network of inter-connected computers. By far the most popular aspect of the Internet (besides email), the Web is a collection of documents, called pages, scattered all over the Internet. Each page is linked to others, so you can move from page to page. One minute you may be reading about financial news found on a server (a computer that stores large quantities of data) in Los Angeles, the next you can view the latest local news from a server in Hong Kong.

Web pages use Hypertext Transfer Protocol (or HTTP) technology, which means an underlined link on a page can be clicked and another page appears on your screen for viewing. Links are what make Web pages so easy to use. By moving from link to link, you can view all kinds of information found on the Web.

Each Web document can be identified by its URL (pronounced “Earl”), which stands for Uniform Resource Locator—its address on the Internet. Besides jumping from link to link on a page, you can type in an URL to go directly to that page. (You can find URLs all over the place, in advertising, computer magazines, even your friends might give you some URLs to check out.)

Microsoft Internet Explorer comes bundled with Quicken Deluxe 99. When you install Quicken (see Appendix A), you have the option of installing the latest and greatest version of Internet Explorer, too.

> **Do You Have an Internet Account?** Before you can use Internet Explorer, or any of Quicken's Internet features, you must have a modem and an Internet Service Provider (a company that lets you use their computers to access the Internet). If you don't, you'll need to care for these two crucial elements in order to "go online" with Internet Explorer. To find an Internet Service Provider in your area, try your local Yellow Pages.

OPENING INTERNET EXPLORER

To open Internet Explorer, double-click the Internet Explorer icon on the Windows 95 or 98 desktop. You can also open the browser from within Quicken. If you're connected to the Internet (which is the only way to use Quicken's Internet features or Internet Explorer), click an Internet feature in Quicken to open the Internet window. Click the Full Browser button at the top of the Internet window to open the Web page in the Internet Explorer program window, as shown in Figure B.1.

USING THE INTERNET EXPLORER TOOLS

Like the Quicken program window, the Internet Explorer window has basic window elements, such as a title bar, menu bar, toolbar, scroll bars, and so on. Take a look at the maximized Internet Explorer window to see the various window elements (see Figure B.2).

A new element you might not be familiar with is the Address bar. Use the Address text box to type in the URL of a page you want to view. Click inside the text box and type in the URL, and then press Enter. After a brief moment (depending on the speed of your modem and connection) Internet Explorer displays the page.

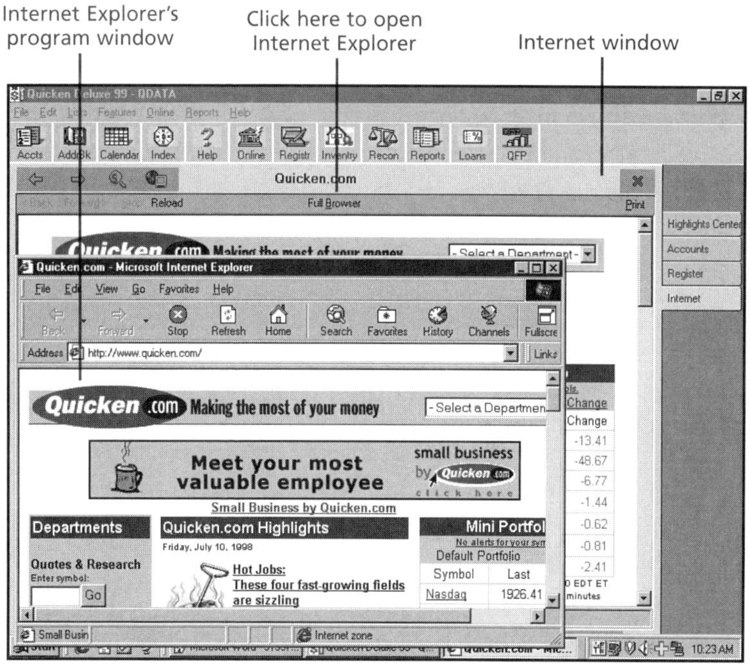

FIGURE B.1 When you open an Internet feature in Quicken, the Internet window opens. To open the Internet Explorer browser window, click the Full Browser button.

Of course, the easiest way to view Web pages is to click links. Links are typically underlined text on a Web page, however, links can also be graphics or buttons. To find out whether text or a graphic is a link, hover your mouse pointer over the item. If the pointer takes the shape of a pointing hand, it's a link.

As you begin viewing Web pages, you can use the navigation buttons on Internet Explorer's toolbar to move back and forth between pages.

Troubles? If the page didn't download correctly, click the Refresh button on the toolbar. This reloads the current page. To stop a page from downloading (when it's taking too long, for example), click the Stop button.

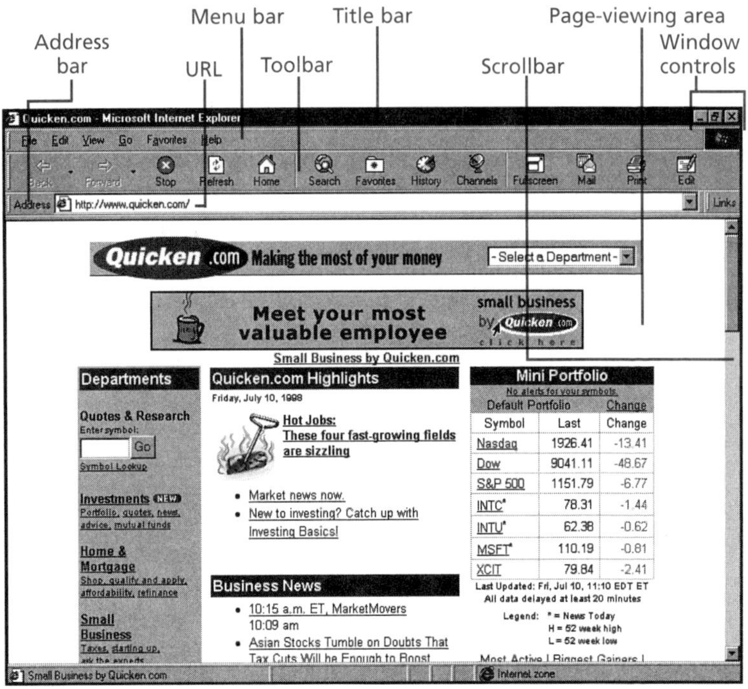

FIGURE B.2 The Internet Explorer window contains many of the same elements found in other Windows programs.

SEARCHING THE WEB

If going from link to link doesn't produce the information you're looking for, try using one of the Web's many search engines (special tools for finding information on the Web).

To conduct a search for information on the Web, click the Search button to open a Search pane, as shown in Figure B.3. Click inside the Search text box and enter the word or words for which you want to look. Press Enter or click the Seek or Start button. (The name of the button varies based on the search engine you're using.)

The search engine used varies from time to time. To use another search engine, click the Choose a Search Engine link at the top of the Search pane.

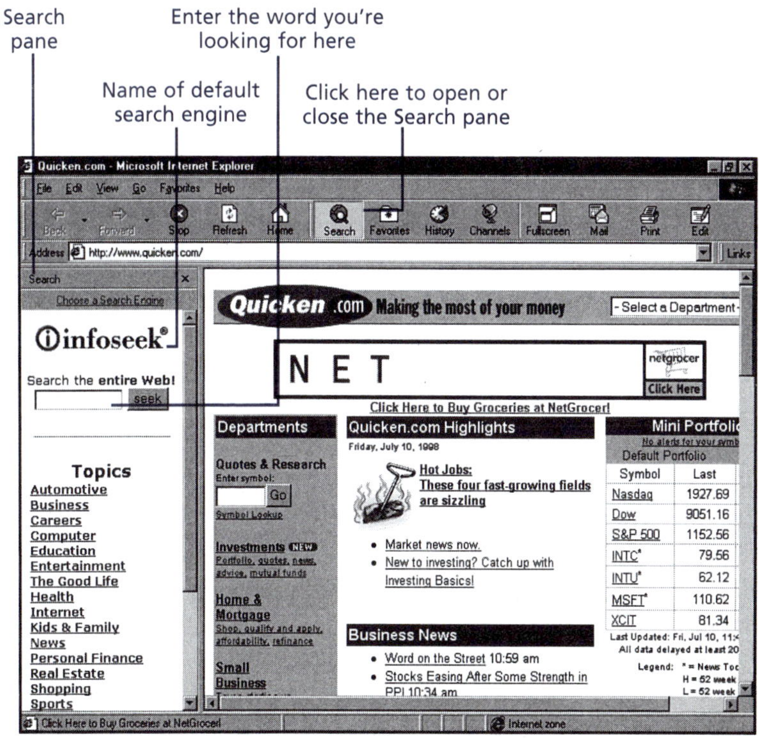

FIGURE B.3 Use a search engine to look up information on the Web.

The results of the search appear as another Web page. Depending on how many matches the database found, you might have a few links to follow, or hundreds.

> **Close the Search Pane** Click the Search button on the Internet Explorer toolbar to close the Search pane.

MARKING FAVORITE WEB PAGES

As you run across Web pages you like (and want to revisit again), mark them as your favorites. This way you can access them again without going through various links or typing in the URL.

To add a page to your Favorites list, display the page, and then open the Favorites menu and select Add to Favorites. This opens the Add Favorite dialog box. Click OK. The next time you want to visit the page, click the Favorites button on the toolbar and select the page from the Favorites pane.

> **Exiting Internet Explorer** To close the Internet Explorer window, click the window's Close (X) button. You also need to close your account connection to log off the Internet.

That wraps up our coverage of Internet Explorer. Obviously, there's not enough room to go into great detail; after all, this book is about Quicken. However, if you want to learn more about Internet Explorer, check out *Sams Teach Yourself Internet Explorer 4 in 10 Minutes*.

INDEX

SYMBOLS

A

B

C

E

F

I

J-K-L

M

N

O

P

Q

R

T

U-V

W-Z